PSYCHOANALYSIS
& CINEMA

EDITED BY

E. ANN KAPLAN

ROUTLEDGE
New York • London

Published in 1990 by

Routledge
An imprint of Routledge, Chapman and Hall, Inc.
29 West 35 Street
New York, NY 10001

Published in Great Britain by

Routledge
11 New Fetter Lane
London EC4P 4EE

Copyright © 1990 by the American Film Institute

Printed in the United States of America

Library of Congress Cataloging in Publication Data

Psychoanalysis and cinema / edited by E. Ann Kaplan.
     p.   cm.—(AFI film readers)
   Includes bibliographies and index.
   ISBN 0-415-90028-X.—ISBN 0-415-90029-8 (pbk.)
   1. Psychoanalysis and motion pictures. I. Kaplan, E. Ann.
II. Series.
PN1995.9.P78P79   1989
791.43'01'9—dc20   89-6339

British Library Cataloguing in Publication Data
Psychoanalysis and cinema. - (A F I film readers)
   1. Cinema films. Psychoanalytical perspectives
   I. Kaplan, E. Ann   II. Series
   791.43'01'9

   ISBN 0-415-90028-X
           0-415-90029-8

IN MEMORIAM
CLAIRE JOHNSTON

Contents

Acknowledgments

Let me begin by saying a word in honor of Claire Johnston. I heard about Claire Johnston's tragic suicide just as I was completing work on this project. Her untimely death at the moment when I was involved in a project that already entailed a looking back to the past, indeed, a rethinking of the 1970s British film work to which Claire contributed actively, passionately, made me realize anew her particular influence. It also made me regret the loss to the scholarly community of an energetic and original intellect.

I first met Claire in 1974, when I interviewed her, together with Pam Cook and Laura Mulvey, about theories of women's cinema. I remember Claire as a dynamic, forceful, and articulate speaker. She was enthusiastic about what she was doing, and committed to the May '68 politics that still provided the model for the group. Of all the people involved in film studies that I met that year, Claire seemed to me one of the most committed to combining activist leftist politics with the psychoanalytic, semiotic, Althusserian, and structuralist theories that were newly at the center of British work in film.

Claire's theories of female representation, as evident in her 1973 essay in the booklet, *Notes on Women's Cinema*, that she edited for SEFT, made a great deal of sense to me at the time. In fact, they echoed lines I had been developing in my "Women and Film" courses at Monmouth College, New Jersey, in 1970–73. So from the start I experienced an intellectual sympathy, a similarity in ways of seeing and thinking that was to continue over the years. Doing the interview was important for me in clarifying aspects of the new theories and in helping me to develop a perspective that I was to pursue in later work. I particularly appreciated Claire's work on Dorothy Arzner in 1975; once again, she was at the forefront of theoretical developments in taking on a Hollywood female director, little known beforehand, and in finding ways to illuminate what was going on in the films.

The passion with which Claire engaged theoretical positions did not prevent her from rethinking them later on. Indeed, the very strength of her convictions at any one time perhaps entailed a falling away later on. The extreme point to which she pushed a position enabled her finally to see its problems and the need to develop other intellectual strategies. Her essays in *Edinburgh Magazine*, especially that on *Anne of the Indies* (reprinted here) show her beginning to critique the Lacanian model and to see the urgency of linking psychoanalytic theory to practical politics. Her work on British Independent Cinema in the thirties and that on the Irish Cinema brought her close to important questions about the politics of independent filmmaking and about "nationality" in cinema.

I was safely away from the intellectual and personal battles that were sometimes intense in the heyday of *Screen* and the development of British Film Culture around The British Film Institute. I valued my yearly meetings with Claire in London or over here, and the intense sharing of intellectual ideas that always took place. Claire's contributions to the evolution of feminist film theory go without saying: even where one disagreed with her, or where her ideas later proved incomplete, her brilliance and her foresight were impressive. Her sheer intellectual energy, her ability to articulate her positions, made her an unusual scholar. It was partly her intellectual honesty, her prescience about the disastrous political direction of things in British higher education in the mid-1980s that stymied her work and made her give up hope. We will all miss her energetic mind, even as we honor her contributions to a field in which she was a pioneer.

I would like to thank Paul Willemen, co-editor of *Jacques Tourneur* (Edinburgh: Edinburgh Film Festival, 1985), and Michael Hughes, executor of Claire Johnston's estate, for permission to reprint Claire Johnston's essay "Femininity and the Masquerade: *Anne of the Indies*," originally published in *Jacques Tourneur*, eds. Claire Johnston and Paul Willemen.

I would also like to thank Martha Gever, editor of *The Independent*, for permission to reprint Yvonne Rainer's essay "Some Ruminations around Cinematic Antidotes to the Oedipal Net(tles) while Playing with De Lauraedipus Mulvey, or, He May Be Off Screen, but . . .," originally published in the April 1986 issue of *The Independent*.

In addition, *Discourse* has kindly permitted reprinting Linda Peckham's essay, "Not Speaking with Language/Speaking with No Language: Leslie Thornton's *Adynata*," originally published in *Discourse*, No. 8 (Fall-Winter, 1986–87).

Finally, thanks to Guy Rosolato and Raymond Bellour for permitting us to translate and reprint their interview, "Dialogue se(ce) souvenir d'un film," published in "Analectures," *Hors Cadre*, no. 1 (March 1983), eds. Michèle Lagny and Marie-Claire Ropars (Vincennes: Presses Universitaires), pp. 150–167.

And thanks also to Raymond Bellour for permitting us to reprint his essay on Tourneur, originally in French as "Croire au Cinéma," in *Caméra-Stylu* (Paris), Special Issue on Jacques Tourneur (May 1986), pp. 35–43.

Introduction:
From Plato's Cave to Freud's Screen

E. Ann Kaplan

One of the aims of this book is to make available an anthology of writing about cinema and psychoanalysis comparable to the several anthologies that deal with literature and psychoanalysis.[1] The fact that there are as yet no anthologies dealing specifically with cinema and psychoanalysis, and showing the diversity of methods (as indeed the literature/psychoanalysis volumes do) perhaps accounts for the common misconception that film theory in general (and the feminist approach in particular) relies mainly on Lacan. This book offers representative examples of some diverse ways in which film scholars theorize psychoanalysis and use it in analyzing specific films.[2]

It is unfortunate that, historically, literary and film scholars have not shown more interest in each others' work: it is to be regretted that even very recent literature/psychoanalysis anthologies have not included essays on film[3]: although this is understandable in terms of the disciplinary boundaries around which we continue to construct our scholarly activities (i.e. our journals, our conferences, our departments),[4] it would seem that dialogue could benefit both groups. Indeed, a brief comparison and contrast of the development of psychoanalytic methods in literature and in film raises interesting questions on a series of levels: these have to do with differences between film and literature as aesthetic modes, with differences in the *institutions* of film and literature, including the high/low culture debate, and with historical, cultural, and intellectual issues that influenced when a psychoanalytic method was developed for each mode. A brief review of the main developments in psychoanalytic literary methods will provide a coherent perspective through which to look at film and psychoanalysis; I will then turn to consider what has been going on in film from 1968 to the present.

1

As is well known, psychoanalytic literary methods emerged in Germany in the 1930s and were taken up in the 1940s in America.[5] These early efforts relied heavily on Freud's essays on "Creative Writing and Day Dreaming" and "Family Romances," as well as his various studies of artists from Sophocles and Shakespeare to Leonardo da Vinci and Dostoevsky. Perhaps the genre is best represented in the pioneering book on Poe by Freud's friend and pupil, Marie Bonaparte. In the foreword to the book, Freud wrote that thanks to Bonaparte's study of Poe, "we now realize how many of the characteristics of Poe's works were conditioned by his personality, and can see how that personality derived from intense emotional fixations and painful infantile experiences."[6]

The analyses of authors that followed took these words to heart: written by practicing Freudian psychoanalysts rather than by literary scholars (Edmund Wilson, however, was a rare early exception[7]) the texts show a critic positioned vis-à-vis an author as the psychoanalyst vis-à-vis a patient. The piece of literature stands in the place of the dream or the associational flow on the couch. As in that situation, the analyst/critic infers from the dream/text's themes and manifest content the author's latent content betraying his/her neuroses; usually, as William Phillips points out,[8] these involved the Oedipal complex, anality, and schizoid tendencies. The text was treated like a record of symptoms to the neglect of its specifically literary qualities (its intellectual context, its link to traditions and genres, or its status as an aesthetic object[9]) valued by critics of the period. What we have is a form of literary biography that has come to be known as "psycho-biography."

Brief mention should be made of the work of Abram Kardiner, who was a faculty member in the New York Psychoanalytic Institute and an Associate in Anthropology at Columbia University when he wrote *The Individual and His Society* in 1939. This book in many ways anticipates recent psychoanalytic methods in cultural studies; however, because of his criticism of certain Freudian concepts and his interest in combining psychoanalysis with methods in sociology and anthropology, he does not seem to have influenced psychoanalytic literary methods in the forties. It is Kardiner's interest in the shaping influence on individuals of institutions—including cultural ones like myth and folklore—that distinguishes his work from the psychoanalytic literary work mentioned above.

Kardiner describes the differences between his and other psychoanalytic cultural study clearly: the view that man "is phylogenetically endowed with certain drives or 'instincts' which press for satisfaction through objects in the outer world," leads, according to Kardiner, to a culture being described "in terms of a subjectively felt drive such as 'phallic,' and 'anal sadistic,' etc., in accordance with the phases of development established in the individual."[10] From this point of view, Kardiner points out, the institutions "are adventitious excrescences consequent upon certain drives seeking for expression, and hence quite meaningless as influences on human nature" (p. 16). His own viewpoint in the book rather emphasizes institutions, "and stresses the significant role they play in creating the adaptive systems of the individual" (p. 17). Kardiner remains classically Freudian in regarding the basic biological needs of man (needs for food, sex, procreation, protection, etc.) as determining culture (rather than language, or the history of signifying systems in general); but at the same time he sees the way that institutions (however formed) shape the individual. For instance, representations of Marquesan women in myths and folklore puzzle him because of their discrepancy with observable behavior. He seeks to explain the gap with the theory of representation as *neurotic distortion*, rather than as "autochthonous creations unrelated to the realities in the living social situation" (p. 214). In other words, fantasy is the mediation between mythic conventions and the material pressures of social institutions (family organizations, the systems of laws and taboos) that shape people's psychic lives.

A later generation of critics, now coming from literature, remedied many of the problems with the first wave of psychoanalytic cultural studies that had disturbed academic literary scholars. These authors paid due attention to the special language and status of the work, and its aesthetic nature. Lionel Trilling, for instance, began to analyze some thematic and structural links between psychoanalysis and literature in the early fifties. He stresses Freud's own deep interest in literature (he quotes Freud's "Not I but the poets discovered the unconscious"), but notes that Freud's contribution to literature comes from what he says about the nature of the human mind rather than from what he says about literature.[11] Trilling argues that literature and psychoanalysis share some common themes, i.e. the conception of the self, the opposition between reality and pleasure, and the conflict between love and power; he argues further that they share a structural similarity in terms of the reader's and analyst's willingness to suspend disbelief (in Coleridge's sense) in the selfhood of the other (via identification); both also deal with society's unconscious assumptions (". . . the unconscious of society," Trilling says, "may be said to have been imagined before the unconscious of the individual," p. 104).

Later still, Steven Marcus in his by now classic account of the Dora case history, moved the argument to a different level by claiming that Freud's text fulfilled the demands of modern literature.[12] Literature and the psychoanalytic text are now one and the same, the analyst in fact a novelist—an idea recently explored at some length by Neil Hertz.[13] If the first generation of authors subjugated literature to psychoanalysis, this final move reversed things and subjugated psychoanalysis to literature.

In the late 1970s, a new phase of the literary psychoanalytic approach emerged from Jacques Lacan's writings about literature. (Interestingly enough, this work developed a few years after film theorists had made their own special use of Lacan—described below—beginning in the early seventies). Lacan's essays on *Hamlet* and on Poe, particularly "The Purloined Letter" (dating from 1959 but only recently translated into English[14]), gave rise to numerous debates and opened up a whole new area of work in literary studies, with *Yale French Studies* braving the way.[15]

Interestingly, Lacan's own essays privilege psychoanalysis over literature but in a manner dissimilar from Freud's early followers. Lacan, that is, takes the character rather than the author as a kind of case history, but even here analysis is in the service of uncovering a particular *psychic structure*.[16] A brief look at psychoanalytic readings of *Hamlet* before Lacan will illustrate clearly similarities and differences: First, in his short reading of *Hamlet* in *The Interpretation of Dreams*, Freud asserts (as he would do more formally in "Creative Writing and Day Dreaming") that there is a link between a poet's mind and the psychic state of the characters he creates.[17] In this case, Freud links the producing of the play about the death of a Father to Shakespeare's own loss of a son, Hamlet. He also situates the play in the context of a culture quite different from that in which Sophocles produced *Oedipus Rex* (which Freud had discussed just prior to talking about *Hamlet*). The differences between *Oedipus Rex* and *Hamlet* for Freud are those between a culture that figured forth oedipal desire in a literal way, allowing illicit wishes to be enacted; and one that could not allow itself to know its oedipal desire and thus could only indicate it indirectly, even in works of the imagination. Rejecting earlier interpretations of the play attributing Hamlet's delay either to an excess of intellect or to neuraesthenia, Freud argues that Hamlet's irresolution has to do with Hamlet's unconscious wish to do what Claudius has done, namely kill the Father and marry the mother.

Ernst Jones expands upon this reading in his book, *Hamlet and Oedipus*, but adds a new dimension in an essay on "The Death of Hamlet's Father," namely that the main theme in the play is Shakespeare's homosexuality.[18] The ear, in this reading, stands in for the anus, and the poison for deadly semen. Meanwhile, in an exhaustive study of *Hamlet*, Morris Weitz objected to Jones's reading, not because of any distrust of psychoanalysis as a treatment or cure within the domain of daily life, but because Jones relied on evidence that could not be found within the text itself. For instance, the reader is asked to doubt the textual evidence for Hamlet's unflagging love for his father, and to change this evidence into its opposite, namely hatred for the father. Weitz goes to Wilson Dover for detailing what he sees as the fundamental error of this sort of psychoanalytic criticism, namely treating a character as if he were a living man instead of a figure in a dramatic composition.[19]

Lacan cannot be accused of quite this error, for Lacan sticks to the text in analyzing how *Hamlet* is the drama of a man who has "lost the way of his desire." The reading relies on certain Lacanian theories (such as the dependence of desire on the desire of the Other—in this case Hamlet's mother), but Lacan's concern is to explore the structure of desire evident in the text in order to demonstrate for his students how certain psychic processes *work*.[20] In the case of Poe's "The Purloined Letter," Lacan analyzes the ways in which the letter functions so as to construct/position the characters—to create particular kinds of subjects and intersubjective conditions. Lacan again wants to show something to his students, here "the truth which may be drawn from that moment of Freud's thought under study—namely, that it is the symbolic order which is constitutive for the subject—by demonstrating . . . the decisive orientation which the subject receives from the itinerary of the signifier."[21]

Lacan's psychoanalytic apparatus is different from Freud's in important ways that make his work on a text less of a violation in New Critical terms. First, Lacan does not move back from the text to the author; where the Freudian method is ultimately biographical, Lacan's is textual. In this sense, Lacan may be aligned with structuralist literary and anthropological scholars. Second, the centrality of language, and particularly the devices of metaphor and metonomy, in Lacan's system bring him closer to the specifically "literary" qualities of the texts he handles. Thus, in Lacan literature is not subjugated to psychoanalysis as an institution, as it arguably is in the neo-Freudian readings.

While it is true that Lacan omits other elements traditionally involved in literary analysis—historical context; ideological implications; relation to conventions; genres; the matter of style and other specifically aesthetic issues; or more recent problems of the reader-text relationship—these are matters often omitted by structuralists. If these methods are controversial in literature departments, Lacan's theories are also a problem within the psychoanalytic institution partly because of the centrality of language (the province of literature surely) to his theories.[21]

Lacan's work is part of a larger movement, beginning in France in the sixties, toward breaking down traditional distinctions between literary and other kinds of text that had historically been so central in discussions of the relationship between literature and psychoanalysis. In her pioneering 1977 essay, Shoshana Felman, for instance, put psychoanalysis on a level with literature; she argued for "a real dialogue between literature and psychoanalysis, as between two different bodies of language and between two different modes of knowledge," which has to take place, she says "outside of the master-slave pattern. . . ."[22] She stated that literature and psychoanalysis are linked in the sense that each constitutes the other's "unconscious." In a later essay on the limits and possibilities of psychoana-

lytic approaches, Felman shows how Lacan's *textual*, as against the common *biographical* method, enables him to see that "there is no longer a
clear-cut opposition or well-defined border between literature and psychoanalysis."[23] Using Lacan's seminar on Poe's "The Purloined Letter,"
Felman argues that in Lacan's approach, "The status of the poet is no
longer that of the (sick) patient but, if anything, that of the analyst" (p.
152). For Lacan, "there is no language in which interpretation can itself
escape the effects of the unconscious" (p. 152). For Felman, "Poetry . . .
is precisely the effect of a deadly struggle between consciousness and the
unconscious" (p. 154).

Peter Brooks, meanwhile, seeking like Felman for a *textual* way of
seeing interconnections between literature and psychoanalysis, finds analogies in the concept of transference.[24] Building on work by André Green,[25]
Brooks argues for a structural and rhetorical similarity between transference in psychoanalysis and in the reader-text relationship. One of the few
literary critics to conceptualize a similarity between *processes* in the
psychoanalytic exchange and in the reader-text exchange, Brooks here
approaches an important strand in psychoanalytic film theory, even though
the model he is dealing with is different because of the different aesthetic
modes involved: "In the transferential situation of reading," Brooks argues, "as in the psychoanalytic transference, the reader must grasp not
only what is said but always what the discourse intends, its implications,
how it would work on him. He must, in Lacanian terms, refuse the text's
demands in order to listen to its desire" (p. 12).

Meredith Anne Skura has made an exhaustive study of literary psychoanalytic approaches with the aim of clarifying similarities and differences
between literature and psychoanalysis.[26] Perhaps better than any other
critic, Skura clarifies the difference between unconscious behavior in
literature, in daily life, and in the psychoanalytic session. In Shakespeare's
drama, for instance, "the clusters of traits can only mean what they mean
in the play itself . . ." (p. 41). Further, fictional worlds explain what the
characters do, and the causes of their behavior "work on divine, natural
and social levels, as well as on the level of the individual, divided will"
(p. 40). Meanwhile, in the psychoanalytic session, there is no room for
the cataloging of psychoanalytic theory, "but only for the slow unraveling
of all disowned ideas and experiences, leading from the forgotten past to
present behavior" (p. 40). Skura concludes that the literary critic can
benefit most from simulating the psychoanalytic process *in the critical
process*; the critic should use "all the resources of the psychoanalytic
process—with its attention to the different aspects of the text; its distrust
of literal reference; its lack of tact and its openness to counterintuitive
meanings; and its self-consciousness about the process of interpretation"
(p. 243). (It should be noted that Skura is using "process" in a different

sense than Brooks, who uses the transference process as a model for "talking about the relations of textual past, present and projected future" [p. 6] rather than about any personal past. Brooks is interested in "the rethinkings, reorderings, reinterpretations . . . ," [p. 13] that take place in the reading process.)

Felman, Brooks, and Skura all still implicitly assume a specificity to the literary text that each believes can be honored within a psychoanalytic method. But the very notion of differences between textual modes is called into question by a critical analysis like Barbara Johnson's "The Frame of Reference: Poe, Lacan, Derrida." Johnson is concerned with "the act of analysis which seems to occupy the center of the discursive stage, and the act of analysis of the act of analysis which in some way disrupts that centrality."[27] Johnson reveals in the contrasting readings of Poe's story a debate over psychoanalytic readings of literature like Lacan's: For Derrida, she notes, "the psychoanalytical reading is still blind to the functioning of the signifier *in the narration itself* . . . Lacan, according to Derrida, has made the 'signifier' into the story's truth." For Derrida, the *textual* signifier "resists being thus totalized into meaning, leaving an irreducible residue" (p. 483).

Johnson shows, however, that deconstruction also has a grounding signifier in its claims that nothing is closed, nothing stable. Derrida repeats Lacan's mistake by "filling in what *Lacan* left blank . . . ," thus copying "precisely the gesture of blank-filling for which he is criticizing Lacan" (p. 464).[28] Her own text, however, seeks not to decide which is more true—literature, psychoanalysis—but to unravel the complex problems involved in these very acts of reading. "What is undecidable," she concludes, "is precisely whether a thing is decidable or not" (p. 504).

We see here the movement away from the concept that has hitherto largely set the terms of the debates about psychoanalysis and literature, i.e. that of the literary object as set off against other bodies of knowledge or indeed against a world of other kinds of object. It is no accident that feminist film and literary critics have figured prominently in this move, since feminists have a stake in the critical project different from that of non-feminists: it matters to the feminist critic how "woman" is signified in dominant sign systems including literature and film, since that bears on who she is herself, on *how* she has come to be. The literary object is now seen not as essentially different from other objects but rather as displaying for the reader's contemplation and analysis (as well as enjoyment) linguistic systems that parallel those in life (or, perhaps we should call it, the "life-text"). The literary/film text embodies organizations of codes, signs, ideologies, and structural constraints not that dissimilar from those the reader experiences outside of reading. But the art-text allows these organizations to be seen more clearly than in the rush of the daily round. The

feminist critic, that is, has an investment in explaining female representations on both the level of individual experience (the social) and on the
abstract theoretical level that posits a patriarchal system that works to
position us in oppressive ways.

Given this journey from Freud to Lacan to Derrida—from Freudian to
Lacanian psychoanalysis to deconstruction—in literary studies, what
about film? How do psychoanalytic methods and the issues of reading
intersect with this brief look at some literary moves? I have already noted
that an historical game of tag is at work, whereby the two research areas
leapfrog one another. Since film was slow to gain entrance in academia
as a scholarly subject, there were no psychoanalytic film analyses during
the forties when American psychoanalysts initiated the literary approach.
Indeed, such approaches only appeared in film in the late sixties, and are
in fact gaining more viability as I write.[29] If Raymond Durgnat's 1968
psychoanalytic study of Buñuel's *Un Chien Andalou* (1928) represents
the Freudian analysis of a film text, Donald Spoto's recent study of
Hitchcock provides an example of a Freudian psycho-biography of a
director.[30] (Interestingly enough, this work coincides with the belated
emergence of a similar kind of psycho-biographic criticism within art
history and music. Tied far more closely than literature and film historians
to formalist, iconographic, symbol-motif, and archival historical methods,
art and music historians discovered psychoanalysis only in the seventies
and now seem to be treading a path similar to that in literary psychoanalytic
studies, starting with the 1940s, but moving rapidly through the phases.[31])

However, these Freudian film analyses have not been at the center of
film research, if we judge that by the work represented in the leading
academic film journals, in Ph.D. dissertations, and in papers presented at
the Society for Cinema Studies (the single international academic film
organization). For historical and other reasons—principally the intellectual movements in Britain in the wake of May '68—one dominant strand
in film scholarship between (roughly) 1975 and 1985 developed its own
complex paradigm that included psychoanalysis but that was not limited
to this method. A complicated mixture of various kinds of thought—
semiotics, post-structuralism, Russian Formalism, feminism, a Brechtian
"politics of modernism," Althusserian Marxism, Freudian and Lacanian
psychoanalysis—produced a set of approaches within a circumscribed
frame in the influential British film journal, *Screen*. And, again for historical and cultural reasons too complicated to go into here, this paradigm
became influential in American academic film departments at the same
time that direct influence from French intellectual life was taking place,
particularly through the Paris Film Program to which a number of the best
American graduate students were drawn.

This complex intellectual paradigm is often referred to as "Lacanian

Film Theory," a label which in no way captures the many-sided and complex set of theoretical tools that were in fact involved. The label *does* correctly mark the interest in Lacan that preceded the later interest on the part of Anglo-American literary scholars; but it is an ironic labeling in that many Freudian concepts were central and only limited aspects of Lacanian thought were involved (i.e. the mirror phase, the distinction between the Imaginary and the Symbolic, the notion of the unconscious as "structured like a language," and the constitution of the subject as "split" at the moment of entry into language, which is also entry into lack/desire). What the label erases is the governing *ideological* basis in the paradigm, particularly in the sense of Althusserian Marxism. (Briefly, Althusser argued first that we are always in ideology; and second, that what he called the Ideological State Apparatuses in any culture embody and disseminate a dominant ideology that favors the ruling classes. Important here—despite its problems—is Althusser's attempt to link Lacan's model of subject-formation with the way we come to be subjects in ideology.)[32]

Let me dwell on the original ideological emphasis in the *Screen* paradigm for a moment in that it was precisely the Althusserian British focus that was repressed in development of the paradigm in America. As a result of complex cultural/historical differences, Althusserian Marxism never gained any foothold in American intellectual life; Marxism in general has never had the dominance in the United States that it has had at periods in various European intellectual movements. Thus the original French thinkers, for whom some kind of Marxist-Socialism was often a given, and their British re-interpreters, for whom Althusserian Marxism was central, were further re-interpreted in the U.S. in line with America's governing apolitical intellectual modes. Baudry's apolitical theory of "the apparatus," inspired by Plato's cave-allegory (see below) dominated much USA work in film until Fredric Jameson's crucial interventions in the early 80s (and then film *per se* was not central).

Meanwhile, there was another interesting discrepancy between Britain and the U.S. in relation to psychoanalysis: Freudian psychoanalysis, as is well known, was always more appreciated here than in Britain and France, and in the Post World War II period entered popular discourses (women's magazines, films, and then television and child-care books). Part of the U.S. sixties movement in fact involved a reaction against this fifties popular neo-Freudianism that the sixties generation felt had distorted reality and warped the nuclear family. Sixties American feminism made rejection of Freudian thought a center piece,[33] since Freud was seen as responsible for sex-roles oppressive to women. Leftist movements, meanwhile, were anxious to establish their validity outside of popular Freudian theorizing that reduced all political activities to unresolved Oedipal issues.

It then came as no small surprise to scholars linked with the various sixties movements in America that the British were taking Freud so seriously, and also that they appeared to be newly discovering Freudian thought.[34] For while the Tavistock Institute in London has always been at the forefront of psychoanalytic work (it grew out of Ernst Jones's efforts, the formidable brief London presence of Freud himself, followed by Anna Freud's devotion to her father's name and work in her Hampstead Institute, and the debates with Melanie Klein), psychoanalysis has traditionally been marginalized in British intellectual and cultural life.[35] (Indeed, part of the reason that the British work focused primarily on the child [Klein, Winnicott, Bowlby] and on psychoses [as against neuroses] might have resulted from the resistance to work that would precisely link up with broader humanities interests.)

British popular culture significantly shows a surprising absence of the popularized Freudianisms that by contrast permeated American popular culture from 1945 on. British intellectuals in the mid-1970s thus came to psychoanalysis with a freshness untainted by prior negative associations that marked the American sixties generation. But there are other reasons why Lacanian psychoanalysis in particular seemed immediately relevant to analysis of representation in film: Lacan's theory of the mirror phase, for instance, readily lent itself to analogy with the screen-spectator situation in a way that did not happen in relation to literature. The different signifying systems of film and novel account in part for the different usage of Lacan. The *enoncé/enonciation* axis works differently in literature; it is not so easy for the fiction reader to believe that he/she is creating the text as it is for the cinema-spectator to believe that he/she is producing the images on the screen. For literary texts often insist on the narrational voice, which puts a certain distance between reader and text, or which at least mediates the dyad. In film, the spectator readily loses him or herself in the text as a result of classical cinema's suturing techniques.

Film theorists at this period argued that cinema and psychoanalysis have in common processes of constructing the subject and of the circulation of desire. Baudry's idealist and ahistorical theory of the "apparatus" linked the cinema to the scene of representation in Plato's cave, as well as with Freud and Lacan. The cinema-spectator is positioned by the cinematic apparatus (which involves the condition of the darkened room, the larger than life figures on the screen projected from behind the spectator's head, the methods of classical editing that "suture" the spectator into the filmic narrative, the filmic institution with its methods of exhibition and reception) so that there is a repetition of processes involved in the Lacanian "mirror phase" and the realm of the Imaginary. The structure of the Ideal-Imago, set in play during the mirror phase, is repeated in the process of watching a film whose specular regime permits this.

The seventies U.S. generation crowding into the newly expanded film Ph.D. programs were, by contrast with the sixties generation, quite open to psychoanalytic theories as they had been developed in both France and Britain. The orthodoxy (if one may call it that) of the *Screen* paradigm quickly dissolved once the work was disseminated in America. As always, American scholars were open to everything and held nothing sacrosanct: one could thus at any time find a healthy diversity of critical methods and paradigms being vigorously pursued in the growing number of American academic institutions granting advanced degrees, and in academic film journals.

The original *Screen* paradigm continued to attract scholars, and some of its lines of thought were continued in the important American journal, *Camera Obscura*, which particularly emphasized new feminist film theoretical approaches. But the paradigm was subjected to criticism, its basic assumptions questioned, and at present alternative kinds of criticism are increasingly evident in the journal. Psychoanalysis continues to be central in much film scholarship, but the ways in which the method is used are becoming increasingly diverse, as I hope is clear in the essays collected here.

What surfaces from this brief overview of the use of psychoanalysis in both literature and film scholarship is the issue of method and of disciplinary boundaries. We may well ask (as have many traditional scholars) what the implications are of critics trained to attend to the literary object delving so deeply into intricacies of psychoanalytic theories. Sometimes we sound like lay analysts or philosophers or social theorists rather than like researchers trained to deal with the aesthetic terrain. Sometimes, those of us wanting to use psychoanalysis in criticism, disagree with each other: Peter Brooks, for instance, has charged feminist critics with continuing a version of the long discredited thirties and forties practice (outlined above) of interpreting a text with psychoanalytic tools, "as if," Brooks says, "the identification and labeling of human relations in a psychoanalytic vocabulary were the task of criticism."[36] He goes on to charge feminist critics with performing "situational-thematic studies of Oedipal triangles, of the role of mothers and daughters, situations of nurture and bonding . . . ," and to note how "disquieting" this is.

Before I return to this issue, let me make some general points about new ways of thinking of the aesthetic sphere, and about the psychoanalytic method in film and literature. First, many recent critics (and particularly feminists) no longer subscribe to the notion of the aesthetic as a sphere entirely different from other linguistic or cultural spheres. The concept of the *text* (as an organization of language, codes, and signifying systems generally designed to produce meanings) and its *reader* (or interpreter) constituted both by prior cultural history and in the act of reading, are now common in literary and film analysis. (The analysis of *why* the concept of the aesthetic has waned in the past twenty years or so lies beyond this introduction: but surely it has partly to do with reaction against the extremes of the New Criticism, with the inadequacy of disciplinary boundaries to deal with the pressing questions of our time, and with the failure of modernism to grow into something else.) Second, let me say something about the different usages of the psychoanalytic method in literary and film work both so as to provide a framework for the essays here and so as to discuss some of the implications of the psychoanalytic method raised by Peter Brooks above.

Three separate conceptions of psychoanalysis are already present in Freud's work: namely, psychoanalysis as a science, psychoanalysis as a medical practice (a "talking cure"), and psychoanalysis as a tool for analyzing literature and anthropological texts. For the most part, these three conceptions developed into three separate practices—that of the research scientist in academic psychology, that of the psychoanalyst curing patients, and that of the humanities scholar.

The distinctions I believe need making apply to this latter practice, namely that of the "humanities" scholar (whether s/he be in fact a practicing psychoanalyst or a university professor), in thinking about the relationship between psychoanalysis and literature. For, while psychoanalysis as a science has for obvious reasons not interfered with the humanities method, Freud's second conception—namely that of psychoanalysis as a *cure*—has entered in. There are then six aspects of psychoanalysis that need differentiating:

1) Psychoanalysis as a "talking" cure. This has two parts to it:
   a) the analytic scene (the analysand on the couch, analyst in the chair, the analysand's speech, the analyst's interpretations, the affect in the relationship and other non-verbal bodily or aural signs, the imaginary relations, the transference, etc.);
   b) the theory of human development (if one can call it that) found in Freud's basic concepts (the three phases the child moves through, the Oedipal scenario, the castration complex, defense mechanisms, penis-envy, projection/regression, etc.) and in Lacan's revision of these.
2) Psychoanalysis used to *explain* literary relationships, actions, motives, and the very existence itself of the text. This is the use of the method Freud initiated and that was developed largely by psychoanalysts; it is the method Brooks believes feminists are reviving, as noted above.
3) Psychoanalysis as *structurally* an aesthetic discourse. The main aesthetic category that has been applied to psychoanalytic practice and seen as linking it to the literary mode is narrative. The analyst

and the analysand are seen to construct "fictions" in the course of their interaction that are not that dissimilar from literary use of language. The dream has been one obvious sub-mode of the analytic scene that has links to the realm of fiction.

4) Psychoanalysis *in* a narrative discourse—used as the subject of literary or film texts. Scholars here study psychoanalysis as fictional *theme*, as it provides the narrative content of works about disturbed characters. (e.g. Pabst's *Secrets of the Soul*, Hitchcock's *Spellbound*, Morris West's *The World is Made of Glass*, Judith Rossner's *August*).

5) Psychoanalysis as an historical, ideological, and cultural discourse. Scholars here study how and when psychoanalysis entered into dominant cultural discourses. Feminists may analyze ways in which psychoanalysis as a discourse has been used to oppress women or to position them in specific ways, socially.

6) Finally, there is psychoanalysis as a specific process or set of processes, that the literary or film critic uses as a *discourse* to illuminate textual processes and reader/spectator positions vis-à-vis a text.

Humanities scholars interested in comparing the psychoanalytic exchange (analysand/analyst) with the literary exchange (text/reader) have focused on processes like transference central to the psychoanalytic exchange or on the constitution of the subject at the moment of entry into language in the Lacanian system. Film scholars have stressed the analogy between the spectator-screen situation and the child-mirror situation. In addition, they focus on issues of identification as that relates to the Imaginary/Symbolic axis.

As should be obvious, most of the theories discussed involve one or more of the various aspects of psychoanalysis. The point of detailing the distinct usages is not so much for the purpose of ruling any of them out as to argue for clarity of usage. For instance, some literary critics tend to collapse aspects 1 and 5: that is, they do not distinguish between psychoanalysis as a cure for neurosis (a quasi-medical practice) and psychoanalysis as a discourse used in critical analysis. As Skura aptly notes, "Analyst and poet are dealing with different aspects of human nature and different manifestations of the unconscious."

Let me clarify what I mean by comparing briefly (in humanities research and psychoanalytic practice) the purpose of analysis, transference in the two situations, and the dream/text analogy. First, the narratives that the analysand creates/constructs on the couch and that the analyst helps her to refine, deepen, and clarify may have some structural/linguistic similarities to literary or film narratives, but the aim of their interpretation by both analysand and patient is different from the aim of the critic. The analyst is bent on interpreting what she hears with a view to making the analysand well—the aim of moving through/beyond the pain the analysand feels and the interferences this pain produces in daily life. The analyst and analysand construct the narratives out of characters in the patient's life as an historical subject.

The aims of the analyst are strictly to help the patient—the analysis is in the service of a cure, even if it is also the analyst's livelihood; the critic, meanwhile, has a whole series of possible diverse goals, that range from professional enhancement to a search for "truth" (i.e., intellectual curiosity and debate) to aesthetic pleasure. Understanding herself and her culture may be important for the critic (and this, as we have seen, is certainly a motivation in feminist criticism), but it is an understanding sought under different conditions than those of the psychoanalytic patient.

It is significant that transference has been much discussed by literary critics but not by film scholars. Leaving aside for the moment the reasons for this (they are referred to briefly above), let me note some dis-ease with the easy use of the transference metaphor by literary critics. It is true that structurally there is a similarity between the task of the critic and the analyst: I particularly appreciate Brooks's suggestion that in both cases an exchange takes place within "an 'artificial' space—a symbolic and semiotic medium—. . . ." But I cannot agree with the rest of this sentence that proceeds ". . . that is none the less the place of real investments of desire from both sides of the dialogue" (p. 12–13). At least what needs to be made clear is that the nature of the "investments" is radically different, and also that the "dialogue" is of a dramatically other nature in the two situations. In psychoanalysis, the analysand's ego-identity, the elaborate construction of an illusory "self," is at stake: the speaking and listening has an intensity and immediateness to it quite other than in the reader-text "transference." Desire is elicited and in operation between analysand and analyst—it is being intensely communicated and discussed in the interpersonal interaction. And there is *actual* rather than metaphorical dialogue: words are passed back and forth in a manner that can never happen between text and reader, where the dialogue is internal, carried on by the critic alone.

In psychoanalysis, the transference is difficult to analyze and to move beyond. As Lacan notes, "The omnipotence of which we are always speaking in psychoanalysis is first of all the omnipotence of the subject as subject of the first demand, and this omnipotence must be related back to the Mother."[37] The Mother is, in Lacan's words, "the primordial subject of the first demand," and it is this first demand that enters into the psychoanalytic transference. Regressing to the pre-Oedipal phase, the analysand demands of the analyst the erotic love first experienced at the mother's breast in the oral stage. The painful discovery of this unsatisfied desire, displaced onto the body of the analyst, must be worked through, as must also realizing its impossibility. The analyst, meanwhile, positioned as the "primordial subject of the first demand," must take up this place in order to work with the desire in the analysand's speech. Only in this way may the patient understand the level of the Imaginary within which this is happening.

Finally, let us look at the much-discussed difference between the dreamer vis-à-vis the dream-text and the spectator/reader vis-à-vis the film/literary text. As scholars have noted, the dreamer constructs the dream-text in the analytic situation with a view to understanding her psychic life (regardless of whether or not that can actually happen). Associations flood in from the patient's past, and new stories are created. Much dreaming in analysis involves the figure of the analyst specifically, and in this case extremely fruitful material often emerges that links transference to the analysand's childhood parental experiences.

There is nothing comparable to these sorts of inter-subjective processes in the case of a film or piece of literature. The spectator/reader vis-à-vis a fictional text does not see images of herself and her familial and intimate relations, as Christian Metz has noted.[38] And there is nothing analogous to the analytic relationship as a displaced emotional inter-subjective effect. In the text/reception case, regression to the primal stage is therefore not on the same level as in the "cure" situation; rather than primary identification, it is secondary identification that comes into play in reading or watching texts.

It is interesting that many critics theorizing about the relationship between literature and psychoanalysis or film and psychoanalysis do not go on to apply their theories to the task of criticism itself. One wonders, for instance, how Peter Brooks's theory of the text/reader relationship as one of transference would illuminate a particular text if so applied; one wonders if many of these theories are intended for application in the first place. Often, they appear rather as theories about relationships among the diverse bodies of language or discourses than as *methods* that aim to show what is going on in a text.

Feminist criticism, on the other hand, has focused on interpreting texts, perhaps (as noted above) because the female critic has an investment in understanding how she came to be positioned as she finds herself. Brooks's objection to much feminist criticism as thematic may have some truth to it, but more often feminist criticism looks at themes (such as mother-daughter bonding or Oedipal triangles) in order to understand how *patriarchal signifying systems have represented such relationships*. That is, there is rarely a naive belief that the characters being analyzed have any essentialist core that is being likened to that of people in the world outside the text: it is always clear that the critic is talking about constructions, and using psychoanalytic theory to illuminate them. It is difficult to show how certain patriarchal signs work without resorting to thematic analysis. Psychoanalytic theory is in this case often described as itself a discourse used by patriarchal texts to confine woman to limited representations.

I hope the essays in this book will clarify general methodological debates about using psychoanalysis in criticism, and specifically show what a feminist psychoanalytic method can achieve. Some of the essays, as will be clear shortly, attempt to break through the often-discussed impasse regarding psychoanalysis and history, or psychoanalysis and politics. One of the volume's aims is to move away from analysis within the subject (whether as fictive figure or historical reader/viewer) to the subject's place in history—a place constructed through ideological and institutional constraints which function in psychic as well as other processes.

I set the stage for all the essays by reprinting British work by Laura Mulvey and Claire Johnston that is linked to the *Screen* paradigm. Both essays included here represent a second stage in the critics' development of their theories in that they here re-evaluate prior positions. Together, they contain ideas that have been argued with, developed, applied to specific films, reworked, etc., in the intervening years. (I have omitted work specifically relying on American Freudian theories, such as those of Nancy Chodorow, Judith Kegan-Gardiner, or Carol Gilligan, since they are represented in other anthologies.[39])

Theoretically, the rest of the pieces could be grouped in the following ways: There are essays that represent recent re-evaluations of earlier psychoanalytic film theories (articles by Mary Ann Doane and Anne Friedberg; and, from the different perspective of the woman filmmaker, Yvonne Rainer's critical "ruminations"). There is the Lacanian-based Freudian work that focuses on the links between psychoanalysis as a process of subject formation and the cinematic process (the work would fall into my sixth category) (essays by Ramond Bellour, Deborah Linderman, and Linda Peckham).

Two essays, in different ways, seek explicitly to combine historical and Lacanian/Freudian psychoanalytic approaches (Kaja Silverman and E. Ann Kaplan). Work on psychoanalysis as a historical discourse (category 4) and as narrative content (category 3) is represented by Janet Walker's essay. Janet Bergstrom, meanwhile, argues for the need to consider psychological (as against specifically psychoanalytic) processes at work in a narrative as these relate to the cinematic institution, situated in specific national and historical contexts.

The volume concludes with a discussion between Raymond Bellour (film/video theorist) and Guy Rosolato (a psychoanalyst) that brings us back full circle to some of the issues raised in this introduction about method and about links between film and psychoanalysis.

A brief outline of some points in the essays should make the book's trajectory clear: the reprinting of Mulvey's essay highlights arguments that have dominated feminist film theory of various kinds. Whether interested in the so-called American Freudian revisionist work of Nancy Chodorow or Judith Kegan-Gardiner; or in certain French feminist revisionists (Hélène Cixous, Luce Irigaray, Julia Kristeva), psychoanalytically oriented feminist film work has often taken off from Mulvey's insights. In this essay, Mulvey does not rescind her "Visual Pleasure" arguments but chooses rather to focus on things other than those she dealt with in the earlier essay. Where the "Visual Pleasure" piece worked primarily with a Lacanian formulation of the mirror stage applied to the gaze in film, the present essay returns to Freud's ideas on femininity in order to illuminate fascinations other than the look, mainly those of narrative identification and closure. Mulvey works primarily with Freud's concept of femininity as an oscillation between a passive femininity and a regressive masculinity harking back to the girl's active "phallic phase."

In this essay, Mulvey argues that Hollywood genre films "structured around masculine pleasure, offering an identification with the *active* point of view, allow a woman spectator to rediscover that lost aspect of her sexual identity, the never fully repressed bed-rock of feminine neurosis." Mulvey shows how, when the central figure is a woman, the film becomes a melodrama, overtly about sexuality and about woman's difficulty in finding a stable sexual identity. The relations within the narrative are reworked by the female spectator in the cinema, whose own position mimics that of the heroine. That is, the female spectator discovers in the heroine's conflicting demands her own unstable sexual identity. The processes of the cinematic apparatus that are allied with those of psychoanalysis make this possible.

The next two essays take up different aspects of psychoanalytic film theory for critical re-evaluation. Anne Friedberg's essay builds on Mulvey's work in examining the cinematic processes that explain why classic Hollywood realism is seen as complicit with the status quo. Friedberg first re-evaluates theories of cinematic identification, reviewing and then problematizing the issues. Her overall claim is that "Identification is a process with its own implicit ideology," namely that of the structure of patriarchy itself. Friedberg surveys psychoanalytic accounts of processes of identification preceding cinema viewing, showing how "identification is one long structural repetition of this denial of difference, a construction of identity based on sameness." She then looks at Metzian and other cinema theories involving secondary identifications mainly. Focusing on the gendering of identification, Friedberg details certain problems with each of the theories. Friedberg concludes by looking at "extra-cinematic identification," namely at the consumer economy in which the circulation of the film star is enmeshed. The identificatory relation here exploits the viewing/devouring and buying/owning mechanisms, with the result that one's identity is denied, replaced by the body of the ego ideal (film star). The essay ends with an impasse, namely that cinematic representation cannot avoid the processes of an identification which is always that of patriarchy and the status quo. The best we can do is to continue to critique the "collapse of the subject onto the normative," and the compulsion for sameness.

Mary Ann Doane points out the complicity of feminist film theory with the cinematic construction of the Woman, its participation in the abstraction of women. Doane notes the effort of feminist film theorists to move, through an appeal to history, beyond the impasse that this complicity involves. She proceeds to engage in her own exploration (from within the psychoanalytic sphere) of how history might facilitate a way out of the impasse. Through analysis of cinema apparatus theory, Doane shows that what we have is "another essentializing gesture," a theory of geometral vision (". . . man's desire to represent to himself the working of his own psyche") which is ahistorical and idealist. Doane concludes that it is precisely the links between psychoanalysis and history through the concept of memory that might take us beyond the impasse she describes: "The task must be not that of remembering women, remembering real women, immediately accessible—," she says, "but of producing remembering women. Women with memories and hence histories."

The second part of the volume contains three different applications of psychoanalytic theory to films by Jacques Tourneur: Claire Johnston's now classic essay exemplifies the apparatus theory critiqued by Doane in the phase when theorists were claiming the possibility for "progressive" elements within the hegemonic discourse. Johnston's essay is important in introducing the psychoanalytic function of the masquerade in the Hollywood film. Johnston's main point is that in Tourneur's *Anne of the Indies* (1951), a key aspect of the bourgeois world noted by Roland Barthes, i.e. "the smoothing over of difference and of the value of a radical heterogeneity," is modified since the text exposes the disavowal of sexual difference on which bourgeois culture relies. According to Johnston, Tourneur's film "marks one of the most radical attempts to explore the fact of sexual heterogeneity in the classic Hollywood cinema, foregrounding the repression of the feminine." While Tourneur's other films embody the dominant male myth in classic Hollywood cinema (i.e. the representation of woman as an inexplicable enigma), *Anne of the Indies* "poses the possibility of a genuinely bi-sexual disposition while remaining a male myth."

The conclusion to the essay raises important questions about the limits of the psychoanalytic method, which remain largely undeveloped today.

Influenced by the 1975 Julia Lesage-Ben Brewster/Stephen Heath/Colin MacCabe interchange in *Screen*, Johnston notes the "distinct danger that psychoanalysis can be used to blur any serious engagement with political-cultural issues." Johnston critiques Lacan's theories for the formalism which "ignores the cultural forms and ideological realities by which we live." The problem with asserting a fundamental bi-sexuality as the "solution," is that this formulation erases the basic asymmetry of gender constructs in patriarchy and the ways in which bi-sexuality is one of the contradictions that bourgeois culture represses.

Deborah Linderman's essay on Tourneur's *The Cat People* (1942) demonstrates the incredibly complex dialectic in the film between "the cinema, with its particular phantasmatic forces, and psychoanalysis, with its tactics for palpating and deconstructing the unconscious." Linderman's analysis is important in bringing together the study of psychoanalysis as a narrative discourse within the film, and psychoanalytiç dimensions of cinematic processes (i.e. my categories 4 and 6). Her detailed close-textual reading of the two paradigms (the psychoanalytic, the cinematic) shows how the cinematic triumphs over the psychoanalytic and appropriates its purgative terms.

Using theories of Melanie Klein and Julia Kristeva, Linderman shows how the text constructs the character of Irena as an excluded, phobic object. As in Lacan's studies of literature, the text is seen as displaying psychic structures, here those of "envy as the residue of an archaic oral dialectic between the 'good' (nourishing, gratifying) and the 'bad' (frustrating, withholding) breast. . . ." The film represents for the spectator his/her own phobic propensities in constructing the Irena/cat "with her unlocalized manifestations, her composite indifferentiation and her devouring mouth, as a phobic misrepresentation and hieroglyph. . . ."

However, Linderman shows that having permitted these constructions, the cinema itself becomes what Linderman calls an exorcising and moralizing paradigm. The cinema, in other words, cannot permit the spectator to remain fascinated with the horrors of indifferentiation or fusion with the mother. It must insist on the proper boundaries essential to patriarchal culture, and conclude with the normative couple shoring up the symbolic.

Raymond Bellour's study of Tourneur's *Curse of the Demon* (1957) uses yet another psychoanalytic method, this time that of the spectator's unconscious fascination with the image, which s/he at once desires and fears. While the previous two essays on Tourneur focused on the psychic mechanisms each text displayed and on unconscious gratifications for the spectator through identifying with the psychic states in the text, Bellour's work explores the relationship between the spectator and the cinema image itself, a relationship that derives from the Lacanian theory of the mirror phase. Bellour says he has chosen a film from the last historical moment when cinema still believed in its demonic power, in its own fascination, its power to make us *believe* in it. Bellour argues that Tourneur's film is precisely about cinema's fascination and about the issue of the spectator's belief. The hero, Holden, is ultimately forced to believe in images and to be afraid of them in order to justify the spectator's pleasure. The subject of the film—the debate between belief and non-belief that torments the characters—reproduces the spectator's ability to believe in images. In addition, the whole theme of hypnotism and of hallucination in the film provides an analogy with cinematic fascination. Indeed, Bellour explores the complex interdependence of hypnosis and fascination: the cinema-subject, like the hypnosis-subject engages in regression, idealization. But the cinema-subject has two possible modes to adopt, that of identification or of fascination, the first leading to life, the latter to death.

While essays in Parts I and II critique or re-work the Freud/Lacan/Althusser *Screen* paradigm, those in Part III are linked by their varying attempts to address the problem of history. In this way, they look back to Mary Ann Doane's comments about the feminist film theory "impasse," and the possibility of a way out through history. However, the route chosen in each essay differs. Kaja Silverman adjusts the Lacanian formulation of male subjectivity as founded on castration to accommodate both attention to gender, in thinking about lack, and to "the vicissitudes of history and the particularities of different social formations. . . ." She argues that "the phallus is always the product of dominant signifying and representational activities, activities which are vulnerable to interruption and transformation." Silverman uses theories of Freud, Jameson, and Althusser to examine Hollywood films made between 1944 and 1947 in terms of the rift between the dominant fiction and the larger social formation. These films, according to Silverman, "attest with unusual candor to the castrations through which the male subject is constituted. . . ," but the revelation of male lack is often presented as a symptom of a larger historical crisis, in this case World War II and its aftermath.

Silverman identifies history with trauma: "The social formation," she argues, like Freud's psyche, "develops a 'protective shield' by means of which it guards itself against external stimulation—it develops, that is, a dominant fiction." But history is a force capable of rending the fabric of this dominant fiction, thereby "disrupting its internal economy." Unrepresentable itself, history makes its presence known in the crises it creates and the changes in the dominant fiction it is responsible for. Silverman proceeds to demonstrate the relationship between history and representation in a close examination of William Wyler's *The Best Years Of Our Lives* (1946), which, she shows, is characterized by "a loss of belief in the family, small-town life, and the adequacy of the male subject."

My essay compares *Now Voyager* (1942) with *Marnie* (1964) in order to explore the multiple determinations at work on well-worn Hollywood representations of mother-daughter relations. One of these determinations is history (again used in Jameson's sense), and I deal briefly with the wartime context of *Now Voyager* versus the cold war context of *Marnie*; but others are psychoanalysis as a discourse, child-care discourses, and film *genre*. I am interested in the ideological constraints within which the film narratives function—what mother-daughter representations are repressed, absent, as much as which ones are there—and I account for the repressions via Kristeva's theories of the mother as the culturally necessary "abject" or phobic object.

The changing construction of the mother-daughter relationship from *Now Voyager* to *Marnie*, within an awesome similarity, leads to discussion, in the final section of the paper, of motherhood constructions in our own period. The new appropriation of women's bodies, this time by reproductive technologies, is revolutionizing the concept and practice of mothering. History is once again breaking through the dominant fiction, causing disruptions: extremely complicated adjustments are taking place in the symbolic in response to women's finally declared and irreversible move into the public sphere. I examine some reverberations in recent films and in some postmodern discourses, and conclude with the question as to whether the late 20th century is witnessing the demise of the seemingly eternal 19th-century motherhood-discourse that has structured psychoanalytic discourse, modern myths, and artistic images.

Janet Walker tackles "the question of the legitimacy of psychoanalytic theory for feminist study" by looking at the history of psychoanalysis, as an institution and a method of "cure," as it intersects with discourses about women in the post-war period. Agreeing in part with feminists' condemnation of American psychiatry for abetting women's adjustment to prescribed and oppressive social rules, Walker also shows how American psychiatry opened up profound contradictions in relation to adjustment of deviant women. In a further step, she examines how psychoanalysis as a discourse is represented in two Hollywood films, *The Three Faces of Eve* (1957) and *Tender is the Night* (1962); Walker uses the films to expose the contradictory aspects of American psychiatry established in examining the historical discourses. She discovers "a rhetoric [of resistance] motivated by the wider and quite complicated cultural context of women and psychiatry."

Finally, Janet Bergstrom approaches the relationship between history and representation through focusing on psychological, as against psychoanalytic, processes. Her aim is to compare and contrast ways in which psychological explanation is used in three Weimar films in the 1920s made by G. W. Pabst and Fritz Lang. She is interested in the "actions and motifs that are designated as 'psychological' by the plots of the films themselves, whether or not they are portrayed consistently, whether or not they are intended to convey the structural logic and cultural resonance of psychoanalytic theory."

Bergstrom's detailed textual analysis reveals very different usages of psychological explanation by Pabst and by Lang in terms of aspects Bergstrom identifies, such as plot resolution, symbolic resolution, the weight given to psychological as against other modes of explanation inhering in institutions like the law, the family, etc. Focusing particularly on what is revealed in detail shots, Bergstrom concludes that Pabst is interested in interior states, whereas Lang moves quickly to the abstract level of institutions. While institutions figure in Pabst's narratives, they are usually subordinated to interest in his characters' dilemmas, actions, and reactions. On the other hand, Bergstrom argues that Lang "negotiates between characters and abstract levels of the narrative in a way that resists the traditional conceptualization of character identification." She epitomizes her thesis in the final statement that "Pabst leaves us with unforgettable characters. . .Lang leaves us with the more disquieting, abstract, and unarticulated level of social institutions."

The final section of the book brings together three essays that usefully fill in some gaps: there are first two essays dealing with the avant-garde film, one in which a theorist analyzes a feminist work; another in which a feminist filmmaker critiques feminist film theory. And there is a discussion between a Lacanian film/video theorist, Raymond Bellour, and a Lacanian psychoanalyst, Guy Rosolato. All three pieces take us back to my opening discussion about the relations between psychoanalysis and film, albeit with very different positions.

Linda Peckham's sensitive reading of Leslie Thornton's haunting film, *Adynata*, (1983), argues that the film "interrogates the apparatus of desire that makes the meaning of the spectacle possible." The film also, according to Peckham, presents the problem of "how to approach the dominance of a language which invents femininity, simultaneously territorializing and displacing women." While the film (and the theoretical discourse about it) start out from the Lacanian concept of woman positioned in the symbolic as lack, both discourses search for a way to use woman's powerlessness as a means to open up space in representation. The film is seen to deny identification and to destabilize representation, perhaps challenging Anne Friedberg's earlier pessimism about the possibility of any cinematic practice avoiding an identification oppressive to women. According to Peckham, the film functions through " 'a stringing together of impossibilities' as a means of speaking."

Yvonne Rainer's witty "cinematic antidotes" allows us to see the intersection of feminist film theory with feminist film practice. In the essay, Rainer meditates on her responses to recent feminist film theory, and on what implications it has for her practice. At once very much influenced by the theories but also healthily skeptical and ironic about them, Rainer in fact reveals their importance to one of her recent films, namely *The Man Who Envied Women*, (1985), which in some ways is a film *about* feminist film theory, or one that positions and explores some of its ideas.

Finally, the interaction between Raymond Bellour and Guy Rosolato returns us to a discussion of how to conceive the relationship between psychoanalysis and cinema with which the book started. The discussion moves from exploring the paradoxical desire for the illusory life of the cinema and its immediate effacement from memory, to analysis of how cinema itself (and particularly Hitchcock's films) prepares the spectator for its status as "a vanishing object" (as Bellour puts it at one point). Rosolato develops this idea in talking about what he calls the "object of perspective" that replays that "reality-unreality expressed in the child's history through his/her phantasms of castration. . . ." Bellour points out that the Oedipal scenario "supports the entire dynamic of the narrative, puts the identifications into play and activates sexual difference," and the discussion moves into comparisons with Freud's dream theory. Bellour contrasts the use of psychoanalysis "as an instrument of knowledge" in analyzing films (i.e. the desire for a system, for intellectual hypotheses), and the incredible impact/fascination of a single image on the researcher as he/she works with a film on the VCR.

After this, the speakers take up the issue of cinema's semiotics and they debate the nature of the cinematic apparatus. This in turn leads to analysis of the pleasure in the cinema, and of how cinema enters into Rosolato's clinical practice. The phenomenon of projective identification in film viewing comes up, he says, as well as the way a film scene can function as a "memory-screen," opening up a path to a patient's traumatic childhood experience.

Towards the end of the interview, the speakers return to the opening exploration regarding cinema as an illusion, as an escape from life, as well as a form whose impact on the memory is intense if fleeting. Cinematic enunciation (the Hitchcockian "auteur" who inserts himself in the text in a special manner), the star system, and projective identification, are topics that bring the interview to its close.

1

Afterthoughts on "Visual Pleasure and Narrative Cinema" inspired by *Duel in the Sun*

Laura Mulvey

So many times over the years since my article, "Visual Pleasure and Narrative Cinema," was published in *Screen,* I have been asked why I only used the *male* third person singular to stand in for the spectator. At the time, I was interested in the relationship between the image of woman on the screen and the "masculinization" of the spectator position, regardless of the actual sex (or possible deviance) of any real live movie-goer. In-built patterns of pleasure and identification impose masculinity as "point of view," a point of view which is also manifest in the general use of the masculine third person. However, the persistent question "what about the women in the audience?" and my own love of Hollywood melodrama (equally shelved as an issue in "Visual Pleasure") combined to convince me that, however ironically it had been intended originally, the male third person closed off avenues of inquiry that should be followed up. Finally, *Duel in the Sun* and its heroine's crisis of sexual identity brought both areas together.

I still stand by my "Visual Pleasure" argument, but would now like to pursue the other two lines of thought. First (the "women in the audience" issue), whether the female spectator is carried along, as it were by the scruff of the text, or whether her pleasure can be more deep-rooted and complex. Second (the "melodrama" issue), how the text and its attendant identifications are affected by a *female* character occupying the center of the narrative arena. So far as the first issue is concerned, it is always possible that the female spectator may find herself so out of key with the pleasure on offer, with its "masculinization," that the spell of fascination is broken. On the other hand, she may not. She may find herself secretly, unconsciously almost, enjoying the freedom of action and control over the diegetic world that identification with a hero provides. It is *this* female spectator that I want to consider here. So far as the second issue is concerned, I want to limit the area under consideration in a similar manner. Rather than discussing melodrama in general, I am concentrating on films in which a woman central protagonist is shown to be unable to achieve a stable sexual identity, torn between the deep blue sea of passive femininity and the devil of regressive masculinity.

There is an overlap between the two areas, between the unacknowledged dilemma faced in the auditorium and the dramatic double-bind up there on the screen. Generally it is dangerous to elide these two separate worlds. In this case, the emotions of those women accepting "masculinization" while watching action movies with a male hero are illuminated by the emotions of a heroine of a melodrama whose resistance to a "correct" feminine position is the crucial issue at stake. Her oscillation, her inability to achieve stable sexual identity, is echoed by the woman spectator's masculine "point of view." Both create a sense of the difficulty of sexual difference in cinema that is missing in the undifferentiated spectator of "Visual Pleasure." The unstable, oscillating difference is thrown into relief by Freud's theory of femininity.

The female spectator's pleasure
Freud and femininity

For Freud, femininity is complicated by the fact that it emerges out of a crucial period of parallel development between the sexes; a period he sees as masculine, or phallic, for both boys and girls. The terms he uses to conceive of femininity are the same as those he has mapped out for the male, causing certain problems of language and boundaries to expression. These problems reflect, very accurately, the actual position of women in patriarchal society (suppressed, for instance, under the generalized male third person singular). One term gives rise to a second as its complementary opposite, the male to the female, in that order. Some quotations:

> In females, too, the striving to be masculine is ego—syntonic at a certain period—namely in the phallic phase, before the development of femininity sets in. But it then succumbs to the momentous process of repression, as so often has been shown, that determines the fortunes of a woman's femininity.[1]

> I will only emphasize here that the development of femininity remains exposed to disturbances by the residual phenomena of the early masculine period. Regressions to the pre-Oedipus phase very frequently occur; in the course of some women's lives there is a repeated alternation between periods in which femininity and masculinity gain the upper hand.[2]

"Femininity":
We have called the motive force of sexual life "the libido." Sexual life
is dominated by the polarity of masculine–feminine; thus the notion
suggests itself of considering the relation of the libido to this antithesis.
It would not be surprising if it were to turn out that each sexuality had
its own special libido appropriated to it, so that one sort of libido would
pursue the aims of a masculine sexual life and another sort those of a
feminine one. But nothing of the kind is true. There is only one libido,
which serves both the masculine and the feminine functions. To it itself
we cannot assign any sex; if, following the conventional equation of
activity and masculinity, we are inclined to describe it as masculine,
we must not forget that it also covers trends with a passive aim.
Nevertheless, the juxtaposition "feminine libido" is without any justification. Furthermore, it is our impression that more constraint has been
applied to the libido when it is pressed into the service of the feminine
function, and that—to speak teleologically—nature takes less careful
account of its [that function's] demands than in the case of masculinity.
And the reason for this may lie—thinking once again teleologically—
in the fact that the accomplishment of the aim of biology has been
entrusted to the aggressiveness of men and has been made to some
extent independent of women's consent.[3]

One particular point of interest in this passage is Freud's shift from the
use of active/masculine as *metaphor* for the function of libido to an
invocation of Nature and biology that appears to leave the metaphoric
usage behind. There are two problems here: Freud introduces the use of
the word *masculine* as "conventional," apparently simply following an
established social–linguistic practice (but which, once again, confirms the
masculine "point of view"); however, secondly, and constituting a greater
intellectual stumbling block, the feminine cannot be conceptualized as
different, but rather only as *opposition* (passivity) in an antinomic sense,
or as *similarity* (the phallic phase). This is not to suggest that a hidden,
as yet undiscovered femininity exists (as perhaps implied by Freud's use
of the word "Nature") but that its structural relationship to masculinity
under patriarchy cannot be defined or determined within the terms offered.
This shifting process, this definition in terms of opposition or similarity,
leaves women also shifting between the metaphoric opposition "active"
and "passive." The correct road, *femininity*, leads to increasing repression
of "the active" (the "phallic phase" in Freud's terms). In this sense Hollywood genre films structured around masculine pleasure, offering an identification with the *active* point of view, allow a woman spectator to rediscover that lost aspect of her sexual identity, the never fully repressed bed-
rock of feminine neurosis.

Narrative grammar and trans-sex identification

The "convention" cited by Freud (active/masculine) structures most popular narratives, whether film, folk-tale or myth (as I argued in "Visual Pleasure"), where his metaphoric usage is acted out literally in the story. Andromeda stays tied to the rock, a victim, in danger, until Perseus slays the monster and saves her. It it not my aim, here, to debate on the rights and wrongs of this narrative division of labor or to demand positive heroines, but rather to point out that the "grammar" of the story places the reader, listener, or spectator *with* the hero. The woman spectator in the cinema can make use of an age-old cultural tradition adapting her to this convention, which eases a transition out of her own sex into another. In "Visual Pleasure" my argument was axed around a desire to identify a pleasure that was specific to cinema, that is the eroticism and cultural conventions surrounding the look. Now, on the contrary, I would rather emphasize the way that popular cinema inherited traditions of story-telling that are common to other forms of folk and mass culture, with attendant fascinations other than those of the look.

Freud points out that "masculinity" is, at one stage, ego-syntonic for a woman. Leaving aside, for the moment, problems posed by his use of words, his general remarks on stories and day-dreams provide another angle of approach, this time giving a cultural rather than psychoanalytic insight into the dilemma. He emphasizes the relationship between the ego and the narrative concept of the hero:

> It is the true heroic feeling, which one of our best writers has expressed in the inimitable phrase, "Nothing can happen to me!" It seems, however, that through this revealing characteristic of invulnerability we can immediately recognize His Majesty the Ego, the hero of every day-dream and every story.[4]

Although a boy might know quite well that it is most *unlikely* that he will go out into the world, make his fortune through prowess or the assistance of helpers, and marry a princess, the stories describe the male phantasy of ambition, reflecting something of an experience and expectation of dominance (the active). For a girl, on the other hand, the cultural and social overlap is more confusing. Freud's argument that a young girl's day-dreams concentrate on the erotic ignores his own position on her early masculinity and the active day-dreams necessarily associated with this phase. In fact, all too often, the erotic function of the woman is represented by the passive, the waiting (Andromeda again), acting above all as a formal closure to the narrative structure. Three elements can thus be drawn together: Freud's concept of "masculinity" in women; the identification triggered by the logic of a narrative grammar; and the ego's desire to phantasize itself in a certain, active, manner. All three suggest that, as desire is given cultural materiality in a test, for women (from childhood onwards) trans-sex identification is a *habit* that very easily becomes *second Nature*. However, this Nature does not sit easily and shifts restlessly in its borrowed transvestite clothes.

A heroine causes a generic shift
The Western and Oedipal personifications

Using a concept of character function based on V. Propp's *Morphology of the Folk-tale,* I want to argue for a chain of links and shifts in narrative pattern, showing up the changing function of "woman." The Western (allowing, of course, for as many deviances as one cares to enumerate) bears a residual imprint of the primitive narrative structure analyzed by Vladimir Propp in folk-tales. Also, in the hero's traditional invulnerability, the Western ties in closely with Freud's remarks on day-dreaming. (As I am interested primarily in character function and narrative pattern, not in genre definition, many issues about the Western as such are being summarily side-stepped.) For present purposes, the Western genre provides a crucial node in a series of transformations that comment on the function of "woman" (as opposed to "man") as a narrative signifier and sexual difference as personification of "active" or "passive" elements in a story.

In the Proppian tale, an important aspect of narrative closure is "marriage," a function characterized by "princess" or equivalent. This is the only function that is sex-specific, and thus essentially relates to the sex of the hero and his marriageability. This function is very commonly reproduced in the Western, where, once again "marriage" makes a crucial contribution to narrative closure. However, in the Western the function's presence has also come to allow a complication in the form of its opposite, "not marriage." Thus, while the social integration represented by marriage is an essential aspect of the folk-tale, in the Western it can be accepted . . . or not. A hero can gain in stature by refusing the princess and remaining alone (Randolph Scott in the Budd Boetticher "Ranown" series of movies). As the resolution of the Proppian tale can be seen to represent the resolution of the Oedipus complex (integration into the symbolic), the rejection of marriage personifies a nostalgic celebration of phallic, narcissistic omnipotence. Just as Freud's comments on the "phallic" phase in girls seemed to belong in limbo, without a place in the chronology of sexual development, so, too, does this male phenomenon seem to belong to a phase of play and phantasy difficult to integrate exactly into the Oedipal trajectory.

The tension between two points of attraction, the symbolic (social integration and marriage) and nostalgic narcissism, generates a common splitting of the Western hero into two, something unknown in the Proppian tale. Here two functions emerge, one celebrating integration into society through marriage, the *other* celebrating resistance to social demands and responsibilities, above all those of marriage and the family, the sphere represented by woman. A story such as John Ford's *The Man Who Shot Liberty Valance* (1962) juxtaposes these two points of attraction, and spectator phantasy can have its cake and eat it too. This particular tension between the doubled hero also brings out the underlying significance of the drama, its relation to the symbolic, with unusual clarity. A folk-tale story revolves around conflict between hero and villain. The flashback narration in *Liberty Valance* seems to follow these lines at first. The narrative is generated by an act of villainy (Liberty rampages, dragon-like, around the countryside). However, the development of the story acquires a complication. The issue at stake is no longer how the villain will be defeated, but how the villain's defeat will be inscribed into history, whether the *upholder* of law as symbolic system (Ranse/Jimmy Stewart) will be seen to be victorious or the *personification* of law in a more primitive manifestation (Tom/John Wayne), closer to the good or the right. *Liberty Valance* as it uses flashback structure, also brings out the poignancy of this tension. The "present-tense" story is precipitated by a funeral, so that the story is shot through with nostalgia and sense of loss. Ranse Stoddart mourns Tom Doniphon.

This narrative structure is based on an opposition between two irreconcilables. The two paths cannot cross. On one side there is an encapsulation of power, and phallic attributes, in an individual who has to bow himself out of the way of history. On the other, an individual impotence rewarded by political and financial power, which, *in the long run,* in fact becomes history. Here the function "marriage" is as crucial as it is in the folk-tale. It plays the same part in creating narrative resolution, but it is even more important in that "marriage" is an integral attribute of the upholder of the law. In this sense Hallie's (Vera Miles) choice between the two men is pre-determined. Hallie equals princess equals Oedipal resolution rewarded, equals repression of narcissistic sexuality in marriage.

Woman as signifier of sexuality

In a Western working within these conventions, the function "marriage" sublimates the erotic into a final, closing, social ritual. This ritual is, of course, sex-specific, and the main rationale for any female presence in this strand of the genre. This neat *narrative* function restates the propensity for "woman" to signify "the erotic" already familiar from *visual* represen-

The Man Who Shot Liberty Valance (John Ford, 1962)

tation (as, for instance, argued in "Visual Pleasure"). Now I want to
discuss the way in which introducing a woman as central to a story shifts
its meanings, producing another kind of narrative discourse. King Vidor's
Duel in the Sun (1946) provides the opportunity for this. While the
film remains visibly a "Western," the generic space seems to shift. The
landscape of action, although present, is not the dramatic core of the film's

Duel in the Sun (King Vidor, 1947)

story, rather it is the interior drama of a girl caught between two conflicting desires. The conflicting desires, first of all, correspond closely with Freud's argument about female sexuality quoted above, that is: an oscillation between "passive" femininity and regressive "masculinity." Thus, the symbolic equation, woman equals sexuality, still persists, but now rather than being an image or a narrative function, the equation opens out a narrative area previously suppressed or repressed. She is no longer the signifier of sexuality (function "marriage") in the "Western" type of story. Now the female presence as center allows the story to be actually, *overtly,* about sexuality: it becomes a melodrama. It is as though the narrational lens had zoomed in and opened up the neat function "marriage" ("and they lived happily . . .") to ask "what next?" and to focus on the figure of the princess, waiting in the wings for her one moment of importance, to ask "what does *she* want?" Here we find the generic terrain for melodrama, in its woman-oriented strand. The second question ("what does *she* want?") takes on greater significance when the hero function is split, as described above in the case of *Liberty Valance,* where the heroine's choice puts the seal of married grace on the upholder of the Law. *Duel in the Sun* opens up this question.

In *Duel in the Sun* the iconographical attributes of the two male (oppositional) characters, Lewt (Gregory Peck), and Jesse (Joseph Cotten), conform very closely to those of Ranse and Tom in *Liberty Valance.* But now the opposition between Ranse and Tom (which represents an abstract and allegorical conflict over Law and history) is given a completely different twist of meaning. As Pearl (Jennifer Jones) is at the center of the story, caught between the two men, their alternative attributes acquire meaning *from* her, and represent different sides of her desire and aspiration. They personify the split in *Pearl,* not a split in the concept of *hero,* as argued previously for *Liberty Valance.*

However, from a psychoanalytic point of view, a strikingly similar pattern emerges, Jesse (attributes: book, dark suit, legal skills, love of learning and culture, destined to be Governor of the State, money, and so on) signposts the "correct" path for Pearl, towards learning a passive sexuality, learning to "be a lady," above all sublimation into a concept of the feminine that is socially viable. Lewt (attributes: guns, horses, skill with horses, Western get-up, contempt for culture, destined to die an outlaw, personal strength and personal power) offers sexual passion, not based on maturity but on a regressive, boy/girl mixture of rivalry and play. With Lewt, Pearl can be a tomboy (riding, swimming, shooting). Thus the Oedipal dimension persists, but now illuminates the sexual ambivalence it represents for femininity.

In the last resort, there is no more room for Pearl in Lewt's world of misogynist machismo than there is room for her desires as Jesse's potential fiancée. The film consists of a series of oscillations in her sexual identity, between alternative paths of development, between different desperations. Whereas the regressive phallic male hero (Tom in *Liberty Valance)* had a place (albeit a doomed one) that was stable and meaningful, Pearl is unable to settle or find a "femininity" in which she and the male world can meet. In this sense, although the male characters personify Pearl's dilemma, it is their terms that make and finally break her. Once again, however, the narrative drama dooms the phallic, regressive resistance to the symbolic. Lewt, Pearl's masculine side, drops out of the social order. Pearl's masculinity gives her the "wherewithal" to achieve heroism and kill the villain. The lovers shoot each other and die in each other's arms. Perhaps, in *Duel,* the erotic relationship between Pearl and Lewt also exposes a dyadic interdependence between hero and villain in the primitive tale, now threatened by the splitting of the hero with the coming of the Law.

In *Duel in the Sun,* Pearl's inability to become a "lady" is highlighted by the fact that the perfect lady appears, like a phantasmagoria of Pearl's failed aspiration, as Jesse's perfect future wife. Pearl recognizes her and her rights over Jesse, and sees that she represents the "correct" road. In an earlier film by King Vidor, *Stella Dallas* (1937), narrative and iconographic structures similar to those outlined above make the dramatic meaning of the film *although it is not a Western.* Stella (Barbara Stanwyck), as central character, is flanked on each side by a male personification of her instability, her inability to accept correct, married "femininity" on the one hand, or find a place in a macho world on the other. Her husband, Stephen, demonstrates all the attributes associated with Jesse, with no problems of generic shift. Ed Munn, representing Stella's regressive "masculine" side, is considerably emasculated by the loss of Western accoutrements and its terrain of violence. (The fact that Stella is a mother, and that her relationship to her child constitutes the central drama, undermines a possible sexual relationship with Ed.) He does retain residual traces of Western iconography. His attributes are mapped through associations with horses and betting, the racing scene. However, more importantly, his relationship with Stella is regressive, based on "having fun," most explicitly in the episode in which they spread itching powder among the respectable occupants of a train carriage. In *Stella Dallas,* too, a perfect wife appears for Stephen, representing the "correct" femininity that Stella rejects (very similar to Helen, Jesse's fiancée in *Duel in the Sun*).

I have been trying to suggest a series of transformations in narrative pattern that illuminate, but also show shifts in, Oedipal nostalgia. The "personifications" and their iconographical attributes do not relate to parental figures or reactivate an actual Oepidal moment. On the contrary, they represent an internal oscillation of desire, which lies dormant, waiting to be "pleasured" in stories of this kind. Perhaps the fascination of the classic Western, in particular, lies in its rather raw touching on this nerve. However, for the female spectator the situation is more complicated and goes beyond simple mourning for a lost phantasy of omnipotence. The masculine identification, in its phallic aspect, reactivates for her a phantasy

Stella Dallas (King Vidor, 1937)

of "action" that correct femininity demands should be repressed. The phantasy "action" finds expression through a metaphor of masculinity. Both in the language used by Freud and in the male personifications of desire flanking the female protagonist in the melodrama, this metaphor acts as a straitjacket, becoming itself an indicator, a litmus paper, of the problem inevitably activated by any attempt to represent the feminine in patriarchal society. The memory of the "masculine" phase has its own romantic attraction, a last-ditch resistance, in which the power of masculinity can be used as postponement against the power of patriarchy. Thus Freud's comments illuminate both the position of the female spectator and the image of oscillation represented by Pearl and Stella.

> In the course of some women's lives there is a repeated alternation between periods in which femininity and masculinity gain the upper hand.

> The phallic phase . . . but it then succumbs to the momentous process

of repression as has so often been shown, that determines the fortunes
of women's femininity.

I have argued that Pearl's position in *Duel in the Sun* is similar to that
of the female spectator as she temporarily accepts "masculinization" in
memory of her "active" phase. Rather than dramatizing the success of
masculine identification, Pearl brings out its sadness. Her "tomboy" pleasures, her sexuality, are not accepted by Lewt, except in death. So, too,
is the female spectator's phantasy of masculinization at cross-purposes
with itself, restless in its transvestite clothes.

2

A Denial of Difference: Theories of Cinematic Identification

Anne Friedberg

When you look in the mirror
do you see yourself
do you see yourself
on the T.V. screen
do you see yourself
in the magazine
when you see yourself
does it make you scream
"Identity," Poly-Styrene of X-RAY SPEX

Identification is NOT a process unique to the cinema. It pervades all object relations, is inscribed in every interaction between subject and object. While psychoanalytic accounts describe identification as the central mechanism in the construction of identity, they do not offer a critique of its strategies or effects. Identification has been treated as both innocent and assumed. This paper intends to offer a review of psychoanalytic accounts of identification and its placement in the construction of subjectivity, while at the same time suggesting a critique of its basic operation in the form of this monumental claim: identification is a process which commands the subject to be displaced by an *other;* it is a procedure which refuses and recuperates the separation between self and other, and in this way replicates the very structure of patriarchy. Identification demands sameness, necessitates similarity, disallows difference. Identification is a process with its own implicit ideology.

Identification with a film star does not entail a cognitive choice, but draws upon a repertoire of unconscious processes.[1] The film star is not a random object, but is rather a particular commoditized human, routed through a system of signs with exchange value. To formulate a full critique of what it means to identify with this particular object, it seems necessary to begin with the following review and problematization of cinematic identification itself.

Most accounts of identification and the cinematic begin with a description of what is basically *pre*-cinematic identification. The dossier of descriptions provided by Freud and his elaborators (Otto Fenichel, Melanie Klein, and others), the retheorizations by Jacques Lacan in his description of the mirror phase, are formulations which bear summary whenever

36

homologies are drawn between the set of object-relations which play in the construction of identity and the replication of this process in cinema viewing. Yet to refine this analogy, a taxonomy of identificatory processes can be made by separating the following three levels of identification: *pre-cinematic, cinematic, extra-cinematic*.

Pre-Cinematic Identification

In order to consider the set of unconscious identificatory processes which *pre*cede cinematic viewing, it is worth conducting a brief survey of psychoanalytic accounts of the assimilative relations between subject and object, the series of interactions which construct identity.

Pre-Freudian accounts of hysterical identification, based on the models of imitation, mimicry, and mental contagion, described the process in behavioral not intra-psychic terms. While Freud made no mention of identification and its role in hysterical symptom formation in *Studies in Hysteria* (written between 1893–1895), the theorization of hysteria depicted it as a process of displacement; the *absences* of the hysteric were a mimicry of a psychic elsewhere. In fact, Freud's attempt to map the various pathways of displacement (*Verschiebung*), which deposit their psychic conversions in processes other than identification, became a central task for charting a psychic economy. In *Interpretation of Dreams* (1900), Freud asserted the unconscious components of identification and insisted that identification was not "mere imitation, but an assimilation," that "expresses a 'just like' and refers to some *common* condition (*Gemeinsames*) which has remained in the unsconscious"[2] (emphasis mine).

Freud also specified the bisexual components of the *multiple* identifications found in hysterics. In an example he frequently returns to, Freud recalls a patient who tore at her dress with one hand (identifying with a man) and pressed it to her body with the other (identifying with a woman).[3] Despite Freud's limitations in realizing his own counter-transferential identification with Dora's case, he narrated her situation as a multiple cross-gendered identification with her mother, Frau K. *and* Herr K.[4]

Yet, the gender components of identification are not mentioned in one of Freud's rare attempts at applying these theories of identification. In "Psychopathic Stage Characters" (1906), Freud considers of the identificatory effects on the spectator at the *Schauspiel:*

> The spectator is a person who experiences too little, who feels that *he* [sic] is a "poor wretch to whom nothing of importance can happen," who has long been obliged to damp down, or rather displace, his ambition to stand in his own person at the hub of world affairs; he longs to feel and to act and to arrange things according to his desires . . .

> And the playwright and actor enable him to do this by allowing him to
> *identify* himself with a hero . . . His enjoyment is based on an illusion.[5]

Displacement recurs here, but not as in hysteria. In this account the
spectator-effect provides an identification with a compensatory other.
Displacing oneself, identifying with a stage character also offers, as Freud
suggests, the satisfaction of giving vent—"blowing off steam"—an outlet
for unfulfilled desires.

As Freud began his work on narcissism and ego development, he
moved away from the model of hysterical identification and toward a
conceptualization of identification as a mechanism that occurs in *all* object
relations. Sandor Ferenczi's introduction of the term *introjection* was
coincident with this conceptual broadening in Freud's work.[6] By the time
that Freud wrote "Instincts and Their Vicissitudes" in 1915, the terms
incorporation, introjection, and identification were used as terms referring,
not to a neurotic process, but to a structural phase of development. The
pathological connotation of identification was gone. Identification was
described as a functional mechanism in development, related to the oral
phase of libidinal organization in which the subject desires to incorporate,
in a bodily way, or to introject, in a non-bodily way, pleasurable external
objects.

In *Group Psychology* (1921),[7] one of Freud's most succinct summations
of the ordinal registers of identification, he defines primary identification
as "the original emotional tie (*Gefühlsbindung*) with an object." Secondary
identification is defined as "the regressive way it becomes a substitute for
a libidinal object-tie" which replaces an abandoned or lost object by means
of introjection. Tertiary or partial identification is based on the perception
of a *common* quality *(Gemeinsamkeit):*

> . . . it may arise with any new perception of a common quality shared
> with some other person who is not an object of the sexual instinct. The
> more important this *common quality* is, the more successful may this
> partial identification become, and it may thus represent the beginning
> of a new tie.[8]

This form of partial identification is an important mechanism in the formation of groups, and as Freud describes it, the basis for the "herd instinct."

Partial identification is the one form of identification which Freud
explicitly predicates on *perception.* There seems an implicit assumption,
however imprecise, of the relation between perception and identification.
While the visual is not the only mode of perception, it seems the overdeter-
mining one in Freud's work. (There are, of course, scattered examples of
identification through other channels—invocatory identification seems

evident in Freud's reading of Dora's cough as a symptom of her identification with Frau K.[9]) Lacan's reformulation of (Freudian and post-Freudian)
object-relations insisted on the primacy of the visual and deemphasized
other channels of introjection. The *stade du miroir* describes a transformation in identity which is scopic-dependent.[10] Lacan describes a subject
whose identity is constituted through the specular misrecognition of an
other. Prior to Lacan, the work of Otto Fenichel also addressed the
specular role in identification. Fenichel defines identification as: "characteristics which were previously *perceived* in an object are acquired by the
perceiver of them"[11] (emphasis mine). These notions are refined in an
essay written in 1935, "The Scoptophilic Instinct and Identification," in
which Fenichel considers the process of ocular introjection, incorporation
through the eye:

> In the unconscious, to look at an object may mean various things, the
> most noteworthy of which are as follows: to devour the object looked
> at, to grow like it (be forced to imitate it) or, conversely, to force it to
> grow like oneself.[12]

Ocular introjection takes its place, in Fenichel's formulation, alongside
of oral, anal, epidermal, and respiratory introjection as "I wish what I see
to enter me."[13]

Jean Laplanche and J.-B. Pontalis describe these directions of identificatory relations as *heteropathic/centripetal* (the subject identifies self with
other) and *idiopathic/centrifugal* (subject identifies other with self). Cen-
tripetal identification is introjective, incorporating the other, as an external
ego ideal; whereas centrifugal identification is projective, projecting narcissistic self onto an external object.[14] As we will see, the cinema plays
upon introjective identification while at the same time providing the illusion of projective identification.

Although the relation might not be immediately apparent, fetishism, a
term which is most commonly called upon in its metaphoric capacity, has
certain structural similarities to the process of identification. In psychoanalytic terminology the two terms have paradoxical counter-purposes. Fetishism is an object-relation (an object-cathexis) that is used to *disavow*
the site of sexual difference, of castration. To Freud, the discovery of
difference was a matter of sight; castration anxiety, a scenario of the
visible.[15] Yet the Freudian model of fetishism allows only one possibility:
that the woman is object in such an object-relation; that the male is
the subject. The fetishist object-choice has a value dependent upon its
disavowal (i.e., how well it denies or distracts from the anxiety-provoking
scene of difference.) The fetishist object-relation is that of acknowledgment and disavowal in constant oscillation. Identification is an object-

relation in which the subject disavows—not the scene of castration, the "seen" of sexual difference—but disavows the "seen" of difference nevertheless; the difference between subject and object, between self and other. Identification is that which conceals and defers the recognition of dissimilitude. *If fetishism is a relation incurred by the anxiety of sexual difference, identification is a relation incurred by the anxiety of pure difference.*

If we accept psychoanalysis as a descriptive tool provided by patriarchy to describe its own oppressive structures, or, as many feminists have done, appropriate its use as a "political weapon," it still remains that the description of fetishism, pivoted on the *have/have not* conceptualization of sexual difference, makes evident the difficulty of acknowledging difference other than as a binary comparison, the measurement of an absence, a *lack*.[16] Yet even if we attempt a counter-theory, reconceptualizing outside of existing psychoanalytic parameters, by exploring pre-Oedipal formations, alternative accounts of mothering, etc.,[17] we still must avow that the process of identification is one of denying the difference between self and other. It is a drive that engages the pleasures of sameness. If the subject is constituted in a series of identifications which force similarity, identification is one long structural repetition of this denial of difference, a construction of identity based on sameness.

Cinematic Identification

Once one has separated the range of identificatory processes which precede cinema viewing, it becomes apparent that secondary and partial identification are the registers of identification which are called upon in identifications beyond the earliest ties with the "parenting other." Yet all three registers of identification, as described in psychoanalytic terminology, incur some confusion when one begins to adopt the terms for cinematic identification introduced by Christian Metz. Since "The Imaginary Signifier"[18] remains a key text for its outline of the registers of cinematic identification, some distinction between Metz's use of primary and secondary identification and the common psychoanalytic usages must be made.

Primary cinematic identification, as Metz describes it (distinct from Freud's use of "original emotional tie"[19]), is identification with the "look" of the camera and the projector. Like the child positioned in front of the mirror, the cinema spectator, positioned in front of the cinema screen, constructs an imaginary notion of wholeness, of a unified body. Yet unlike the mirror, the cinema screen does not offer an image of oneself. Metz's account subsumes all other registers of identification under the primary—an all-perceiving subject, absent from the screen, who is transformed into a transcendental *not* empirical subject. Metz also assumed that Lacan meant an empirical mirror rather than a parent (mother or father) who is seen as a more perfect, more complete object.

For Metz, *secondary* identification is with an actor, character, or star. It is at this level of identification that one contends with the gendering of identification. In the Metzian system, primary identification is apparently gender-neutral. While Jean-Louis Baudry's theorization of the apparatus maintains the ideological basis of the apparatus itself—as a machine of domination, an instrument of control—he does not go as far as maintaining the entire apparatus is gendered as male.[20]

All cinematic representation of the body has a complex function in this regard. The screen is not a mirror. (As even Metz points out, there is one thing that is never reflected in it—the spectator's body.) Yet identification requires recognition before it functions as misrecognition. Here, there are at least three limitations to Metzian-inspired theories of cinematic identification. **First,** the conventions of cinematic representation enforce a metonymy of the body; a face, a hand, a leg, all cut up. A star, like most human forms in cinema, is not presented as a unified body. In fact, it is often precisely this metonymy which is transformed into part-object commodities. Garbo's face is transformed into the most highly commoditized part of her, as are Grable's legs, Bacall's voice etc. The star becomes recognizable and familiar (hence the compulsion to return to it) yet it is never fully unified as a body. The cinema provides part-object identifications, creates part-object fetishes. Wholeness is not offered here; the ego-ideal represented is not unified or whole, but a synecdochal signifier.

Second, the most overriding difficulties with the structure of identificatory relations begin when one considers the variables of gendered body identification. Laura Mulvey's landmark essay, "Visual Pleasure and Narrative Cinema,"[21] opened this Pandora's box. (The gendering of identification has remained the locus of most debates in feminist film theory.) In Mulvey's account, the codification of pre-existing "patterns of fascination" in narrative cinema structure the "look" in a split between male-as-bearer-of-the-look and female-as-object-of-the-look. In order to accept her account—which details the dual pleasures of voyeuristic scoptophilia and narcissistic identification—the question remains: is the female spectator forced to identify with the male protagonist?

If film stars are possible ego ideals, what are the gender implications of identification with stars of both genders? As the range of stars in classical cinema attests, few strong female ego ideals exist. In cases where they do, their strength is often mitigated or recuperated by their placement in a narrative whose closure disallows such strength. If one follows the implications of Mulvey's account, the female spectator is placed in a masochistic position of identifying either, on the one hand, with the woman who is punished by the narrative or treated as a scoptophilic fetish

OR, on the other hand, identifying with the man who is controller of events. This is not unlike the gender confusion of the hysteric who simultaneously clutches and pulls at her dress. In the cinema, in both cases, her *difference* from the screen star is vanquished, she is neither the female-as-represented nor is she the male-as-represented. For men the problem is less complex. Either way, their power is endorsed; they are allowed the bisexual play of misrecognition (with the male body/with the female body) without losing their sameness to the male.

Thirdly, secondary identifications seem to be predicated on the recognition of a human form, bodies like our own. Yet identification may not be just a gendered interaction, but a process which offers more fluid, cross-special displacements. There are a range of examples of anthropomorphic but un-human stars—from Lassie and Benji to Flicka and Flipper to Yoda and R2D2. The "star quality" of these creatures indicates that the human form is not required for identification. In the cinema, the spectator does not identify with his or her own image anyway. The pleasures offered are precisely this denial: the star's body is *not* the subject's body, not his, or hers. This might explain the fascination with the non-human in cinema, a projection into the NOT self, a bestial other. As countless films (with monsters, robots, animals) attest, *any* body offers an opportunity for identificatory investment, a possible suit for the substitution/misrecognition of self.

Extra-cinematic Identification

There is a category of identificatory investments that are related to and dependent on cinematic viewing yet extra-specular, their effects maintained outside of viewing. I've chosen to refer to them as *extra-*cinematic to avoid the temporal construction of *post*-cinematic. Certainly primary and secondary identifications have extra-cinematic effects, most easily observed in the auxiliary systems of commodification, marketing the cinematic "experience."

Identification with a film star is a process which extends beyond secondary cinematic identification, an engagement that occurs for the duration of spectation, into extra-cinematic identification, an engagement which is prolonged and amplified by the auxiliary systems of codification that extend beyond the specificity of a single film's signification. And it is precisely outside of the viewing experience, in the economic and social context, that identification has become one of the most pivotal figures of the institution. The fascination with a film star is not a fascination with a single signified person (Norma Jean Baker, Marion Morrison, Greta Gustafson) or with a single signifier (Monroe in *Niagara,* Wayne in *She Wore a Yellow Ribbon,* Garbo in *Mata Hari)* but with an entire system of signifiers and a code—the commercialized erotic system that fits, what Jean Baudrillard has called the "metaphor of fetishism."[22]

When used in pure homology to cinema viewing, the metaphor of fetishism does not suggest a literal reference to castration. The structure of oscillation between acknowledgment and disavowal occurs in the cinema spectator who simultaneously disavows (not castration but) absence or the *not there* of the cinematic scene while at the same time acknowledging its presence, however illusory.

Yet fetishism has another metaphoric function, unlike its nonmaterialist operation in the unconscious. For Marx, the term was used to describe the value of an object, in economic not psychosexual terms. To Marx, the commodity was a fetish, its value transformed from a product of labor with a use value to an object in a system of capital with an exchange value. The commodity fetish is an object which has value beyond its use, in the "social hieroglyph" of exchange.[23]

The film star fits both these models exactly. As an object in an identificatory relation, the film star is simultaneously recognized (acknowledged) as other and misrecognized (disavowed) as self. As an object transformed in a commodity system, the film star is marketed not for pure use, but for his/her exchange value. The film star is an institutionally sanctioned fetish.

Most accounts of the star-audience relation draw upon economic and sociological explanations precisely because of the indeterminant relation between star and star system, between sign and intertextual system of signification. The borders of the star sign are not clearly drawn. Economic accounts offer explanations of how stars are used in a market of entertainment products,[24] how stars were developed as a strategy of product differentiation in the U.S. film industry's battle between the Patent's Trust and the "independent" producers and distributors (between 1912–1918),[25] how stars are continually used for their exchange value as commodities. Stars, as we know, were not an intrinsic part of the cinema institution in its first formulations, but were only marketed a full fifteen years after the cinema was introduced as a publicly projected entertainment form. Economic determinist arguments explain how economic considerations determine film form, but do not explain *why* certain marketing strategies work. In these accounts, which construct an almost behaviorist model of the masses, the audience is conceived of as a group of voluntarist respondents to publicists and studio heads. Economic descriptions emphasize *fabrication* not *effect*.

Sociological accounts seek some empirical or impressionistic account of how stars function in a social system. While, the quasi-religious, cultic nature of much of the discourse which surrounds the film star—interviews, biographies, gossip sheets, fan clubs, autographs, *papparazzi*—demands some account of the social valence of film stars, most sociological accounts do not offer a full explanation of *why* stars sell, *why* they fascinate the viewer or *why* in cinematic representation, they are placed in the center of the narrative.[26]

The relation between viewing and devouring is exploited in the star system in a more complicated manner than the metaphoric language of the consumption of commodities might suggest. The variety of product tie-ins which suggest either literal bodily incorporation (Jimmy Dean Whole Hog Pork Sausage, Roy Rogers hamburgers, Paul Newman salad dressing and spaghetti sauce, the "Shirley Temple" cocktail, etc.) or epidermal incorporation (Farrah Fawcett shampoo, Elvis "Love Me Tender" Body Lotion) draw upon the close relation between VIEWING and DEVOURING and VIEWING and BECOMING.

This model of introjective identification is consistent with the acquisitive forms of incorporation commanded by a consumer economy. VIEWING/ DEVOURING and BUYING/OWNING are exploited in the identificatory relation and turned into VIEWING/BECOMING and BUYING/BECOM-ING. The process of identification is designed to encourage a denial of one's identity, or to have one construct identity based on the model of the other, mimetically repeating, maintaining the illusion that one is actually inhabiting the body of the ego ideal.

What cinematic devices enhance identification and what devices fore-stall it? At question here is the power of a specific text to contest the operations of the apparatus. All demands for film censorship stem from the position that the cinema encourages imitation/ mimetic incorporation of the harmful, illegal, or immoral actions of a character, actor, or star. In short, a fear of identification. The imitation of activity seen in the fictive world is a measure of the power (and hence) the threat of the cinema. Yet those who fear the ideological effect of "wrong values" most frequently counter-argue for the portrayal of "right values." Arguments for alternative cinema practices which pose "positive" identification with "improved" ego ideals, refuse to realize the basic operation of identification itself. To create more "realistic" less-stereotyped ordinary people, to move away from gods and goddesses, still demands the same processes of identifica-tion. Realist cinema, just like non-realist cinema, effaces its own construc-tion. The basic identificatory structure, denying difference, is still in effect.

Yet the limitations of such a monumental critique should be immediately avowed. First, as with all claims which attempt to describe basic operations of the cinema apparatus, the apparatus is hyperbolically described as if it is outside of history, as if a "constructed subject" in 1937 is the same as one in 1987. Secondly, apparatical claims also refuse the specificity of single texts, disallow strategies that might counter the code. One of the boons of textual analysis has been the discovery of the complexity of each film text.[27] Thirdly, while apparatical descriptions attempt to describe essential properties, they also make alternative practice seem almost impossible. At its most extreme, if the cinema is an apparatus which has developed as a specular regime of power which replays the construction of the subject in patriarchy and, if the "nature" of cinema viewing is to designate passive subjects, subjected to instruments of control, there are few alternative possibilities for cinematic practice. The binds of cinematic representation seem impossible to avoid, short of devising new systems of representation based on the relatively underdetermined channels of perception—taste, touch, smell. (Even the imagined formulations of such apparati make one wonder about the alternative—palatographs, sensoramas, perfume-o-coasters . . .) Is the most thorough solution for combating the unavoidable overdetermination of vision by patriarchal and ideological conventions to demand blindings (gouge squads performing radical ocular occlusions) as an alternative to the specular past?

This leaves us, as viewing subjects, caught in the bind between specular cannibalism and scopic bulimia, between the introjection of an imposed other and the rejection of what the eye has taken in. Yet, visual bulimia is only a construction of metaphor. The eye is an organ which will devour but not disgorge.

Bearing the limitations of such a critique in mind, it still follows that identification has the following problematic functions: identification can only be made through recognition, and all recognition is itself an implicit confirmation of the ideology of *status quo*. The institutional sanction of stars as ego ideals establishes normative figures, authenticates gender norms. Here we are left with a question that is unerringly political. Identification enforces a collapse of the subject onto the normative, a compulsion for sameness, which, under patriarchy, demands critique.

3

Remembering Women: Psychical and Historical Constructions in Film Theory

Mary Ann Doane

Max Ophuls's 1934 film, *La Signora di tutti,* makes uncannily explicit many of the most crucial themes of contemporary feminist film theory.[1] Its protagonist, Gaby Doriot (Isa Miranda), as the star of the film within the film, also entitled *La Signora di tutti,* is indeed "Everybody's Lady"— she is the signifier of a generalized desire. The film demonstrates the intimate relation between the woman and the specifically cinematic and delineates the role of the cinema as a machine for the generation of desire. Gaby's final words—a response to the claim of her inaccessible lover that he will see her soon, when her current film comes to Italy—are "On film, on film, on film . . . ," musingly trailing off into nothing. They indicate the tautological nature of her relation to the medium.

In *La Signora di tutti,* the woman is explicitly represented as a construction, as the sum total of a disembodied voice and an image (the two sensory registers of the cinema). Furthermore, it is, precisely, a technological construct which is at issue here—the mechanization of her voice and image is stressed. The woman becomes the exemplary work of art in the age of mechanical reproduction. The first indication of her presence within the diegesis is in the form of a recorded voice emerging from a spinning record, revolving in close-up. Here, as represented by her voice, she becomes the object of a financial transaction, a contractual dispute— signified metonymically by the hands gesturing over the record. The spectator's first glimpse of Gaby is in the image of her poster, rolling repeatedly off a printing press. Later in the film, her death is represented as the bent or warped image produced as a result of the abrupt shutting down of the printing press. From the combination of a disembodied voice and a mechanical image emerges the figure of a generalized Woman— "Everybody's Lady." Here, the woman is indeed the product of the apparatus.

46

But the woman is also *like* the cinematic apparatus insofar as she constitutes a lure for the male subject—more dangerous even than the cinema since she frequently leads him to his doom. Yet, without knowledge of her effect, she has no access to subjectivity. The narrative of *La Signora di tutti* is grounded in Gaby's lack of conscious agency. She is the pure object of the desires of men, subject of nothing. As her father points out early in the film, "The girl is dangerous and she doesn't realize it." She unwittingly or unknowingly causes death or disaster. This is accomplished without the category of deception precisely because all subjectivity is lacking. As the unconscious cause of desire, Gaby's operation is that of the detached image or the detached voice—both of which become the fetish objects of the film. Gaby is the Signora di tutti—everybody's lady. Possessed by all men and therefore by none in particular, she becomes the axiom of femininity. But this necessitates a process whereby she is clearly differentiated from other women. A character tells her at one point, "You're not like the other girls. I wish I had met you before." Gaby represents the woman in general, but is like none of them in particular.

There is a disorienting contradiction at work here. Gaby becomes the image of Woman because no other—ordinary—woman is like her. The image is characterized by a lack of resemblance. Nevertheless, she somehow represents all women through her incarnation as a generalized femininity, an abstraction or ideal of femininity. The monolithic category of Woman here is not even an alleged average or distillate of concrete women but their abstraction, their *subtraction* (in its etymological sense, abstraction is a "drawing away from"). Not like other women, Gaby becomes Woman. *La Signora di tutti* chronicles the expropriation of the woman's look and voice and the consequent transformation of the woman into Woman—a position inaccessible to women.[2] This is not only the process of the narrative trajectory of *La Signora di tutti* but of the cinematic institution as well—in its narratives, its star system, its spectacle. But further, it specifies something of the process of feminist film theory which, in a way, mimics the cinematic construction of the Woman, reinscribing her abstraction. It is not only the apparatus which produces Woman but apparatus theory, in strange complicity with its object.

This attachment to the figure of a generalizable Woman as the product of the apparatus indicates why, for many, feminist film theory seems to have reached an impasse, a certain blockage in its theorization.[3] For the often totalizing nature of its analysis of patriarchy leaves little room for resistance or for the elaboration of an alternative filmmaking practice which would not be defined only negatively, as a counter-cinema. In focusing upon the task of delineating in great detail the attributes of the woman as effect of the apparatus, feminist film theory participates in the abstraction of women. The concept "Woman" effaces the differences between women in specific socio-historical contexts, between women defined precisely as historical subjects rather than as *a* psychical subject (or non-subject). Hence, Teresa de Lauretis' attempt to specify the task of feminist film theory leads, through a series of hyper-generalizations of femininity, to the historical as the privileged term.

> This is where the specificity of a feminist theory may be sought: not in femininity as a privileged nearness to nature, the body, or the unconscious, an essence which inheres in women but to which males too now lay a claim; not in a female tradition simply understood as private, marginal and yet intact, outside of history but fully there to be discovered or recovered; not, finally, in the chinks and cracks of masculinity, the fissures of male identity or the repressed of phallic discourse; but rather in that political, theoretical, self-analyzing practice by which the relations of the subject in social reality can be rearticulated from the historical experience of women.[4]

The appeal to history made here is shared by other feminist theorists (including E. Ann Kaplan, Annette Kuhn)[5] who, in different contexts, also call for a dismantling of the hegemony of *the* theorization of *the* woman through an attention to the concrete specificities of history. This is not a naive appeal to history (all agree that history must be theorized) but it is an invocation of history designed to counter certain excesses of theory (especially psychoanalytic theory) and the impasse resulting from those excesses. History is envisaged as a "way out."

Psychoanalysis has been activated in feminist film theory primarily in order to dissect and analyze the spectator's psychical investment in the film. But to accomplish this, theory had to posit a vast synchrony of the cinema—the cinema happens all at once (as, precisely, an apparatus) and its image of woman is always subservient to voyeuristic and fetishistic impulses. In this context, woman - lack - the cinematic image. Within such a problematic, resistance can only be conceptualized through the idea of "reading against the grain," as leakage or excess—something which emerges between the cracks as the by-product of another process. Such a definition of resistance is merely another acknowledgment of the totalizing aspect of the apparatus.

The desire to add the dimension of diachrony, to historicize, is one way of dismantling the pessimism of apparatus theory. For it opens up the possibility of an escape from its alleged determinism and hence the possibility of change or transformation through attention to the concreteness and specificity of the socio-historical situation. The ever-present danger here is in the temptation to use the gesture of historicizing as a covert means of dismissing theory which is then opposed to the "real" of the

particular historical conjunction where we can somehow unproblemati-
cally observe, once again—free from the restrictions of a theoretical
framework—what women actually did or even how their representations
reflected something of the "real" of their situation. Perhaps we need to
look more closely at what "theory" is or might be and what "history"
denotes in opposition to that term—for it is "history" which promises to
find a way around the theoretical impassse. For that reason, what I would
like to do here is to isolate and examine two moments in the archaeology
of that impasse: 1.) the elaboration of apparatus theory as a specific reading
and reduction of the object of psychoanalytic theory and the aim of a
metapsychology 2.) the appeal to history as an "outside" of psychoanalysis, a realm beyond memory and subjectivity which nevertheless seems
to guarantee the dispersal of a monolithic, theorized subjectivity. My
reading of these two moments will be situated within the purview of
psychoanalysis. For psychoanalysis has its own theory or speculation
(linking it to paranoia and delirium) and its own pursuit of history (acted
out primarily in the case histories and in the theory of transference).

The apparent exhaustion of psychoanalytic film theory, its impasse, is
closely linked to its activation of the metaphor of the apparatus or *dispositif*. In two essays, "Ideological Effects of the Basic Cinematographic
Apparatus" and "The Apparatus: Metapsychological Approaches to the
Impression of Reality in the Cinema," Jean-Louis Baudry outlined the
problematic whereby the cinema becomes a machine with a certain arrangement, a disposition.[6] His theses concerning the positioning of the
spectator as the transcendental gaze of the camera and the screen's operation as the Lacanian mirror were taken up and expanded by theorists such
as Christian Metz and Stephen Heath. Feminist film theory inherits many
of the assumptions of this mode of theorizing—its transference onto
psychoanalysis is mediated by apparatus theory.

Freud uses the term "psychical apparatus" to emphasize certain attributes of the psyche—"its capacity to transmit and transform a specific
energy and its subdivision into systems or agencies."[7] The apparatus
specifies a series of relations: relations between spaces, operations, temporalities. The psyche is not a monolithic block but must, instead, be
conceptualized as a dynamism of parts, a differential machine. This is
why Freud tends to choose as metaphors for the psychical apparatus objects
which constitute combinatories of specific elements—the microscope, the
camera, the telescope, the early model of a network of neurons and their
facilitations, the mystic writing pad. Although Freud activates the analogy
of the apparatus in order to conceptualize a certain chronology and its
effects as well as the notion of psychical locality, optical instruments such
as the microscope and the telescope lend themselves more readily to the
description of a spatial arrangement. In response to G. T. Fechner's idea

that "the scene of action of dreams is different from that of waking ideational life," Freud states,

> What is presented to us in these words is the idea of *psychical locality* . . . I propose simply to follow the suggestion that we should picture the instrument which carries out our mental functions as resembling a compound microscope or a photographic apparatus, or something of the kind. On that basis, psychical locality will correspond to a point inside the apparatus at which one of the preliminary stages of an image comes into being. In the microscope and telescope, as we know, these occur in part at ideal points, regions in which no tangible component of the apparatus is situated. . . . Accordingly, we will picture the mental apparatus as a compound instrument, to the components of which we will give the name of "agencies," or (for the sake of greater clarity) "systems." It is to be anticipated, in the next place, that these systems may perhaps stand in a regular spatial relation to one another, in the same kind of way in which the various systems of lenses in a telescope are arranged behind one another.[8]

Baudry is, of course, attracted to the analogies of the telescope and photographic apparatus precisely because they are *optical* metaphors comparable to the cinematic apparatus. To the spatial arrangement of lenses in the telescope corresponds the spatial disposition of projector, spectator/camera, and screen.

The decisive rupture effected by the concept of the apparatus with respect to previous film theories lies in its engagement with the issue of realism. In Baudry's analysis, the impression of reality is a subject-effect and has nothing to do with the possibility of a comparison between representation and the real. In the scenario of Plato's cave, invoked by Baudry to buttress his claim that the cinema is the machine of idealism, the prisoners are chained since birth, habituated to their cinema, and have nothing with which to compare the shadows cast on the wall of the cave. As in Freud's theory of hallucination, reality is given all at once or not at all—it is not attained by degrees or gradual approximations as in theories of adaptation. Jean Laplanche points out, "*The hallucination is or is not,* and when it is, it is absolutely useless to imagine a procedure allowing one to demonstrate to the hallucinator that he is wrong."[9] Yet, there is an illusion at work here, both in Plato's scenario of the cave and in Baudry's scenario of the cinema. For Plato, whether the prisoners are aware of it or not, the shadows are merely copies of copies of the Idea, which is the only Real. For Baudry, the illusion is located in the deception of the apparatus which conceals its own idealist operation. Hence, when Baudry defines the apparatus it is as a unique spatial arrangement which explains the production of "truth," giving the analyst knowledge of a differentiation between real and illusion.

> For we are dealing here with an apparatus, with a metaphorical relation-
> ship between places or a relationship between metaphorical places, with
> a topography, the knowledge of which defines for both philosopher and
> analyst the degree of relationship to truth or to description, or to illusion,
> and the need for an ethical point of view.[10]

And what Baudry produces by means of the analogy of the apparatus is precisely an ethical point of view—the cinema, the toy of idealism and of a 2000 year old desire on the part of man (sic) to represent his own psyche to himself, dupes its spectator. In psychoanalytic film theory, the cinema seems inevitably to become the perfect machine for the incarnation or institutionalization of the wrong idea—here it is Platonic idealism; in Metz and Comolli, it is a Bazinian phenomenology.[11]

It is not surprising, given the definition of the apparatus as a topography, that the duping of the spectator should be coincident with the conceptual-ization of that spectator as a point in space, a site. Through its reinscription of Renaissance perspective, the apparatus positions the spectator, on this side of the screen, as the mirror of the vanishing point on the other side. Both points stabilize the representational logic, producing its readability, which is coincident with the notions of unity, coherency, and mastery. The cinema, according to Baudry, "constitutes the 'subject' by the illusory delimitation of a central location. . . ."[12] From the point of view of psychoanalytic theory this is, of course, an ideologically complicit fiction of the "self"—the result of a denial of the actual division, instability, and precarious nature of subjectivity. The cinema as an institution would thus insure that the Freudian/Lacanian theory of subjectivity be repressed, excluded from its operation. (Ideology here would truly be a kind of "false unconsciousness.")

This insistently spatial logic of apparatus theory has rigidly restricted the way in which vision has been understood as a psychical process within film theory. The gaze, enamanting from a given point in this configuration, is the possession of the camera, and through identification with that camera, the spectating subject. Hence, it is not at all surprising that this gaze should be further characterized, in the work of Metz, Mulvey, and others, as precisely controlled in the service of voyeurism and fetishism—its subject male, its object female. Joan Copjec strongly criticizes this particular implementation of the theory of the apparatus and its correspond-ing description of the gaze:

> My question is not whether or not the gaze is male, for I know that it
> certainly is. While it is clearly important to remark on a certain social

ordering which rakishly tilts the axis of seeing so that privilege piles up on the side of the male, it is a slip, and enormously problematic to posit something like a gaze, an idealized point from which the film can be looked at. Defined in this way, at this moment, such a gaze can only be male. My question is prior to this other; I would ask, instead, if there is a gaze . . . It is legitimate to ask whether it is the cinerama [Copjec's term to denote the combination of panoptic and cinematic] or the cinematic *argument* which positions the subject through an identification with an anonymous gaze. What does it mean to say that the subject so identifies himself? It means the abolition of the alterity of the Other—the discursive apparatus—the elimination of difference. It means the construction of a coherent subject and of an all-male prison. This is an argument offered by obsession; it covers over the desire in the Other with the Other's demand, averts attention from the gaze and focuses on the eye.[13]

The obsessiveness of the argument is linked to its espousal of the idea of a perfect machine. The problem with the theory of the cinematic apparatus is that the apparatus always works. It never breaks down, is never subject to failure. This is what Copjec refers to as the "delirium of clinical perfection." The infallibility of the apparatus in this account is a function of the limitation of subjectivity to a single locale—the gaze of the spectator/camera. Since there is no otherness, no difference, no subjectivity associated with the discourse, its readability is always insured in advance. That readability becomes its most important psychical effect.

I would agree with Copjec that apparatus theory here operates a specific reduction of Lacan's theory of the gaze, particularly insofar as it is always articulated with the concept of desire. Furthermore, the gaze is in no way the possession of a subject. Rather, Lacan effects a separation between the gaze and the subject—the gaze is outside: ". . . in the scopic field, the gaze is outside, I am looked at, that is to say, I am a picture . . . the gaze is the instrument through which . . . I am *photo-graphed*."[14] The term "gaze" always signals in Lacan's text the excess of desire over geometral vision or vision as the representation of space through perspective. And the subject's desire is the desire of the Other—it is characterized by its alterity. In film theory, the gaze has become substantialized, directed—we speak of the gaze of the camera, the gaze of the spectator. By associating the gaze with lack, with the small object "a", with, in effect, nothing, Lacan de-essentializes it. The gaze is beyond appearance but beyond appearance, "there is nothing in itself."[15]

Baudry's apparatus theory, critical as it may be of idealism's dichotomy between surface and depth, appearance and reality, reinscribes the dichotomy through a recourse to Plato's allegory of the cave. Idealism is the only guide to the spectator's apprehension of the image. Lacan, on the other hand, constructs an anti-idealist discourse on the gaze. The gaze indicates the necessity of a gesture pointing beyond the veil (the inescapability, in other words, of desire)—but beyond the veil there is nothing. He produces a sustained critique of the reduction of vision to geometral perspective. Because geometral perspective involves the mapping of space not sight, it is an understanding of vision which is accessible to a blind man, as Diderot demonstrates. What is specific to vision escapes this delineation. While in the geometral relation, vision is calculated as an effect of light deployed in a straight line, the gaze indicates the dispersal of light—its irradiation, refraction, diffusion, scintillation. In the geometral mapping of vision, the subject is centered as the master of representation; through the gaze the "I" is grasped by the depth of field, by the "beyond" which endlessly solicits desire. Perspective guarantees the maintenance of the subject and its place. Alternatively, in perspective's own aberration— anamorphosis—one gets a glimpse of the fascination of the gaze as the annihilation of the subject. In Holbein's painting, "The Ambassadors," what lures the subject is the distorted image of its own death—the skull whose readability is a function of the subject's decentering.

The gaze is always in excess—it is that which cannot be mapped, diagrammed, only, perhaps, suggested in the impossible topological figures Lacan appeals to in his later work. For it is that which escapes the vision of a consciousness allegedly in control:

> In our relation to things, in so far as this relation is constituted by the way of vision, and ordered in the figures of representation, something slips, passes, is transmitted, from stage to stage, and is always to some degree eluded in it—that is what we call the gaze.[16]

The apparatus, as the exemplary model of cinematic representation, is incapable of theorizing this slippage, bound as it is to the construct of geometral perspective. It cannot accommodate the notion of desire as a disorganizing force in the field of perception. What is specific to Lacan's gaze is not the maintenance of the subject but its dispersal, its loss of stable boundaries. The gaze situated outside, the subject necessarily becomes a part of the picture, assimilated by its own surroundings. Differentiation is lost and, with it, subjectivity as a category. Here, Lacan is drawn to Roger Caillois's surrealist theory of mimicry in insects and its implications for human psychical processes. Certain insects do not come to resemble their surroundings through any defensive or adaptive procedure. Rather, becoming *like* one's environment involves succumbing to a "real *temptation by space.*"[17] The lure is that of depersonalization, a lack of differentiation manifested in the form of a kind of death drive. The subject is, above all, *displaced* with respect to the usual coordinates of consciousness: ". . . the organism is no longer the origin of the coordinates, but one point among others; it is dispossessed of its privilege and literally *no longer knows where to place itself.*"[18]

The spectator of apparatus theory would seem to be diametrically opposed to this displaced subject who gives in to an overwhelming desire to become a picture, and hence to lose any mastery to which it might have laid claim. For the spectator of the apparatus is quite clearly and unambiguously placed as a controlling gaze, whether the control is illusory or not—it knows precisely where to place itself. And such an illusion requires a geometrical configuration, a mapping and, above all, a distance between subject and picture. However, Baudry has not entirely neglected the annihilation of subjectivity attendant upon processes of looking. In fact, the second essay on the apparatus could be said to revolve around the fascination and corresponding regression of a spectator who loses himself. This is the pre-Oedipal spectator of the cinema whose relation to the image is that of the dreamer or the hallucinator, who persistently confuses representation and perception, giving in to the temptation of space. Across the two essays by Baudry, there are, in effect, two subjects of the apparatus which would seem to be in conflict.

On the one hand, the first article, "Ideological Effects," theorizes the impression of reality in the cinema from the point of view of the image and its construction. The Renaissance perspective of that image insures the positioning of the subject as point of control. This spectator, prey to the illusions of the ego, is a post-Oedipal subject. In this way, the cinema acts as an ideological instrument for the perpetuation of a subject situated as a stable, transcendental gaze. The second essay—"The Apparatus," on the other hand, in its attempt to explicate the power and fascination of the cinema, posits a pre-Oedipal subject, a subject who regresses to the point where differentiation and distance are no longer feasible. This is the effect of the "more-than-real" which Baudry allies with both the cinema and the dream. The subject is not the unified origin of its own dream—or even an onlooker. Rather, the dream envelopes the subject just as the child is enveloped by its world. This description of the cinematic effect as dream is quite close to Lacan's delineation of the dream and its relation to the gaze. In the dream "it shows"—which is to say, the unconscious exhibits itself—and to that extent, "some form of 'sliding away' of the subject is apparent." The subject is not fully present or fully in control of the field of the visible: ". . . in the final resort, our position in the dream is profoundly that of someone who does not see. The subject does not see where it is leading, he follows."[19]

From the point of view of apparatus theory, then, the subject is both there and not there, maintained and annihilated. There is a certain tension between the positioning of the subject as point, control, unity (which requires distance) and the temptation of space, of losing oneself in a process of de-individualization and the corresponding annihilation of sub-jectivity. One might object that there is no contradiction here at all—that the constitution of the subject is always accompanied by its dismantling, that the subject must always undergo a process of placing and displace-ment. But what I am interested in isolating here is the apparent necessity of specifying the second subject—the one who ceaselessly witnesses its own annihilation—as a non-ideological subject. That which escapes geometral vision would also seem to escape both ideology and history in order to designate the "real" of the psychical. In this respect, Baudry's re-writing of Plato's allegory of the cave is particularly symptomatic. He can activate a 2000 year old scenario in the analysis of the cinema precisely because the psychical force he examines is characterized as ahistorical. Desire in the cinema becomes, specifically, *Man's* desire—his desire to represent to himself the working of his own psyche. What we are faced with is another theory of Man, another essentializing gesture.

Hence, apparatus theory seems to be caught in something of a bind. It can activate an ideological analysis of the cinema at the cost of reducing vision to geometric perspective and theorizing history as a trap. The spectator is stuck at that ideal point of illusory mastery. Conversely, it can take into account other aspects of the gaze—its excess, its annihilation of subjectivity—only by, paradoxically, rigidifying that gaze, situating it outside of time as psychical essence. It is an alternative which is particu-larly alarming from the point of view of feminist theory. For the first reading of the ideological implications of the cinematic ordering of vision reproduces the totalizing tendency discussed earlier and hence reinforces the theoretical impasse. The second, while certainly more "faithful" to Lacanian theory, works only by assuming the autonomy of the realm of the psychical—its freedom from both historical and ideological determina-tions. Lacan's gaze cannot be used to analyze sexual difference because it allows no differential analysis of mastery and subjection—everyone is subjected to a gaze which is outside.

Yet, before fully accepting the notion of a theoretical impasse, it might be helpful to interrogate the idea of theory itself. What is it that theory hopes to accomplish? What is its function? And, more specifically, what is the role of theory and its relation to its object in psychoanalysis? Apparatus theory rests on the assumption that what psychoanalysis lends to film theory is a kind of map, or even a cognitive machine. Psychoanaly-sis is the science of the unconscious; the cinema clearly appeals to the unconscious; therefore, psychoanalysis must be able to give us the laws of its discursive formulation. The map can simply be laid over the new terrain. The desire of the analyst, which would require the replacement of the notion of the cognitive machine by that of the encounter, is rarely taken into account. Yet, psychoanalysis itself proposes the fragility of any theoretical construct, its affinity with paranoia and delirium, and hence the problematic status of knowledge and of he who purports to know. In other words, psychoanalysis must be contaminated by its own theorized and simultaneously untheorizable object—the unconscious. For the unconscious is by definition resistant to the coherence and rationality of conscious meaning, of the systematicity associated with theory. The unconscious is characterized by its alterity. As Freud pointed out with respect to the dream, "To explain a thing means to trace it back to something already known, and there is at the present time no established psychological knowledge under which we could subsume what the psychological explanation of dreams enables us to infer as a basis for their explanation."[20] This destabilization of theory with respect to its object has frequently been noted. Samuel Weber describes psychoanalytic theory as "the struggle to wrest meaning from a process that entails the deliberate dislocation of meaning."[21] In its striving after unity and totality, theory (i.e. systematic thinking) is comparable to an animistic form of thinking which dictates that everything is meaningful, explicable—nothing can remain outside the limits of the system. In this sense, theory is narcissistic, organizing reality as the image of the ego's own psychical organization:

> The pursuit of meaning; the activity of construction, synthesis; unification; the incapacity to admit anything irreducibly alien, to leave any residue unexplained—all this indicates the struggle of the ego to establish and to maintain an identity that is all the more precarious and vulnerable to the extent that it depends on what it must exclude. In short, speculative, systematic thinking draws its force from the effort of the ego to appropriate an exteriority of which, as Freud will later put it, it is only the "organized part."[22]

The theorist is not dissociable from the other which he hopes to define and theory betrays its links with speculation and its etymological affiliations—specular, speculum—as a mirror image.

This is why François Roustang argues that psychoanalysis is not a science insofar as a science generally presupposes the foreclosure of the subject. Theory organizes the fantasies, dreams, and desires of the theorist and to deny this is to remain perpetually in a transferential relation with a "subject supposed to know." Hence it is also to deny one's own fantasies and desires and their potential activation within theory. From this point of view, theory is a process of continual revision which always bears the traces of its historical moment. The contradictions in Freud's text, the constant changes in his conceptual framework, are not accidental but an acknowledgment of theory's inevitable failure in the face of the alterity of the unconscious. Hence, the apparatus cannot be a cognitive machine or the concept which fits its object as in film theory. According to Roustang, "the hypothetical and conjectural character of the apparatus is an integral part of the discourse"[23] and, with reference to Freud's style in *The Interpretation of Dreams,* "The psychical apparatus that Freud constructs in the course of chapter 7 is chapter 7 itself."[24] The object is indissociable from the theoretical style.

Consequently, Roustang finds the whole question of the transmissibility of psychoanalytic theory, its institutionalization, and its tendencies toward dogma and orthodoxy extremely problematic. The work of theory is the practice of analysis, the encounter between analyst and analysand which inevitably produces the surprise, the destabilization of the given theories—the constant shock of otherness we associate with the unconscious. It is a process of reading and encounter. Psychoanalytic theory has its own peculiar temporalization: ". . . there is no analytic theory *in advance* on which one can lean, but rather a possibility of theorization in *deferred action,* which, although necessary, is never guaranteed."[25] Psychoanalysis is, above all, a form of listening in the intersubjective relation:

> If analytic practice is to be effective, it is only insofar as the peculiarity of the theory is abandoned in favor of a peculiarity that cannot at first be theorized. What counts in such cases is not the desire for the father, but the relationship to him which is revealed by some tiny unbearable memory. When something like this emerges through an association, what is important is not the verification of the theory, but the intensity of an incomprehensible particularity.[26]

The issue in analysis becomes how to grasp the history indicated by the resistance associated with "some tiny unbearable memory"—how to understand that history without reducing it. There is certainly no immediacy presupposed in this form of historical understanding—theory is crucial even if it makes its appearance only through deferred action. Psychoanalysis is a mode of writing history which fully acknowledges—and attempts to theorize—the resistance of its own material. The validity of psychoanalysis would hence be linked to the style of its confrontation with history. Instead of atemporalizing psychical operations, as Baudry's analysis does, it is crucial to *saturate* them with temporality—to demonstrate that the psyche is constructed in, through, and as a history.

Thus, psychoanalysis would seem inevitably to propose the articulation of theory and history rather than their polarization. In film theory this aspect of psychoanalysis is too frequently ignored in favor of a static, inflexible theorization of an apparatus which is always in place, always functioning. Here, Baudry's comparison of the cinema with the psychical mechanism of hallucination is symptomatic. For hallucination, in Freud's work, signals a retreat from an intersubjective relation which is inevitably marked by failure. Freud's persistent attempts to theorize resistance, transference, the terminability or interminability of analysis, on the other hand, indicate the crucial importance of coming to grips with that failure of intersubjectivity. The construction in analysis, its force as a fiction, is the evidence of the subjectivity of the historian, her desire—which will inevitably miss its mark. Film history is, precisely, a problem of memory—an institutionalized memory of what would otherwise remain an incomprehensible particularity.

And Freud appealed to the apparatus primarily as a support for his attempts to theorize memory. In an early letter to Wilhelm Fliess concerning the psychical apparatus, Freud wrote:

> I am working on the assumption that our psychical mechanism has come about by a process of stratification: the material present in the shape of memory-traces is from time to time subjected to a rearrangement in accordance with fresh circumstances—is, as it were, transcribed. Thus what is essentially new in my theory is the thesis that memory is present not once but several times over, that it is registered in various species of "signs."[27]

Memory is a palimpsest—the sum total of its various rewritings through time. The "event" which is remembered is never really accessible as such.[28] Indeed, it would be more accurate to point out that there is no single event which could be isolated as a psychical determinant. Things "happen" in the history of the individual but memory resides in the reverberations between events. Trauma has no real existence as such but is a function of representation. What Freud refers to as "deferred action" (*Nachträglichkeit*) is a working over, through time, of the implications of one event as its reading feels the impact of other events. Thus, memory does not *grasp* an event, accurately or inaccurately, but subjects it to a process of inscription and reinscription.

The insistence upon the metaphor of inscription requires that Freud abandon the optical tropes he had used earlier—the microscope, the telescope, the camera. And it is not accidental that they were replaced by the "Mystic Writing Pad," the only apparatus in which unlimited receptive capacity and the retention of permanent traces—i.e. memory—are not mutually exclusive. Film retains permanent traces but can continue to receive fresh impressions (in the same space of celluloid) only at the cost of an absolute unreadability. In fact, film annihilates memory in the measure to which it adheres to presence—everything takes place in the present tense. Freud's fantasy about the Mystic Writing Pad, on the other hand, was that by virtue of its discontinuous method of functioning (mirroring that of the system Perception-Consciousness), it could indicate that which "lies at the bottom of the origin of the concept of time."[29] Freud's dream of a representative apparatus which would explain our subjective experience of temporality and demonstrate how memory is the transcription and retranscription of an event would seem to be particularly *inappropriate* for the cinema. Perhaps this apparatus is more suggestive of how we might think, not about film, but about film history as a continual process of retranscription of our memory of the cinema—a memory which is "present not once but several times over, that . . . is registered in various species of 'signs.' "

There are, of course, crucial differences between the terms of "memory" and "history"—differences which are frequently invoked in order to distinguish between the disciplines of psychoanalysis and history as well. While "history" generally refers to the social complexity of a past which transcends the individual, "memory" is always resolutely linked to the "I"—these are "my" memories, they belong to no one else; they form the basis of my particular psychical history. The historian's account does include memories but it also brings into play other types of evidence as well and aims at the construction of a collective, social text.[30] Nevertheless, Freud's excursions into the realm of what might be termed a "collective memory" (the most influential of which is, perhaps, *Totem and Taboo*) are symptomatic of the constant desire to articulate the notions of individual memory and individual psychical history with a symbolic order of representations. The theory of subjectivity, particularly as it is linked to language, is not reducible to a theory of individuality, despite the fact that its formulation is dependent upon the encounter with individual discourses. Furthermore, to deny any link between memory and history is to totally desubjectivize history, to presume that its account has the status of a purely objective science. While it might seem paradoxical to say that I remember someone else's past, there is a sense in which, when I read or construct a history, I do precisely that. And although I certainly do want to acknowledge the limits of psychoanalysis, its specificity and divergence from history as an enterprise, this essay is predicated on the belief that a great deal can be gained by noting their similarities and points of coincidences. Psychoanalysis is, in some sense, the construction of a history, and history, in its turn, an act of remembering.

Freud's role as historian is perhaps most visible in the essay, "Constructions in Analysis," in which he claims that the task of the analyst is "to make out what has been forgotten from the traces which it has left behind or, more correctly, to *construct* it."[31] In this sense the analyst's work is like that of the archaeologist who reconstructs, from the vestiges or surviving remains, the shape of a building or even a city. But there is one major difference: the archaeologist is often confronted with the loss or destruction of crucial pieces while nothing in the unconscious is ever destroyed. Yet, it is precisely this divergence and the guarantee that psychical truth is there, somewhere, that leads Freud at times to collapse the opposition between construction and historical truth and thereby to bypass the subject's own discourse. It all depends on the conviction of the patient—his or her belief in the knowledge of the analyst: "Quite often we do not succeed in bringing the patient to recollect what has been repressed. Instead of that, if the analysis is carried out correctly, we produce in him an assured conviction of the truth of the construction which achieves the same therapeutic result as a recaptured memory."[32] There is a relation of transference at work here whereby the fictional and provisional status of the construction is elided. Instead, the construction comes to match perfectly, in a one-to-one correspondence, the historical truth. At these moments, Freud forgets his own insight linking the construction of analysis to the delirium of the patient. As Roustang points out,

> Construction (which is always a part of the theory) is in an unstable position and can readily turn into madness if one takes it too seriously, if one forgets that, like an hysteric, it suffers from memories, that is, it cannot be separated from the particular discourse of a particular analyst. . . . Historical truth exists no more than do the origins of revolutions or of the Indo-European languages. What exist are delusions founded upon the supposition of its existence . . . truth has always had a strength which comes from the fact that it has none, that is, that it draws all its force from its nonexistence and that this nonexistence is precisely what provokes, through a horror of the void, the feverish and indefinite production of cultural substitutes.[33]

But if construction is acknowledged to be a fiction, a particularly potent myth or delirium which is open to rewriting, it is more easily aligned with the work of memory as transcription.

In analysis, transference provides the mirror image of the psychoanalyst's adherence to the historical truth of his own constructions. The patient, mimicking this presumption, believes that the analyst is the subject supposed to know. Feminist film theory can easily maintain such a transferential relation to psychoanalytic authority if it takes its constructions—its apparatuses—too seriously. It is at this point that they become totalizing, allowing of no resistance which is not foreseen, assimilated. What is productive for feminist film theory would then be that which stops—astonishes—the machine of analysis with its own incomprehensible particularity. In psychoanalysis, by Freud's admission, there are (at least) two unanalyzable phenomena. One would be psychosis in its refusal of a language directed toward the other. The second would be a certain type of woman whom Freud, in the course of a discussion concerning how the analyst can tame and exploit the transference-love of the female patient, describes in the following way:

> There is, it is true, one class of women with whom this attempt to preserve the erotic transference for the purposes of analytic work without satisfying it will not succeed. These are women of elemental passionateness who tolerate no surrogates. They are children of nature who refuse to accept the psychical in place of the material, who, in the poet's words, are accessible only to "the logic of soup, with dumplings for arguments." With such people one has the choice between returning their love or else bringing down upon oneself the full enmity of a woman scorned. In neither case can one safeguard the interests of the treatment. One has to withdraw, unsuccessful; and all one can do is to turn the problem over in one's mind of how it is that a capacity for neurosis is joined with such an intractable need for love.[34]

Freud's failure here is not due entirely to the excess of female sexuality exhibited by this woman but to her literal-mindedness. She will accept no surrogates, no substitutes—no rhetorical blockades to her desire. The sheer force of her presence cannot be fended off through recourse to the trope. She cannot be abstracted; she is not "Everybody's Lady." Still, Freud tries. Symptomatic of his failure to make her love sublime is his recourse to the poet's words, subjecting her to the "logic of soup, with dumplings for arguments." She may be literal-minded but he is not—he can find her trope.

It is this process of troping which feminist theory must resist. "Everybody's Lady" is no one. The refusal of the apparatus as fully adequate to its object is a refusal of its totalizing force and the concept of Woman which it produces. The task must be not that of remembering women, remembering real women, immediately accessible—but of producing remembering women. Women with memories and hence histories. The abstracting work of *La Signora di tutti* is the annihilation of the woman's memory through its appropriation and naturalization. Gaby remembers—the bulk of the narrative is in the form of her flashback—but it is a forced memory induced by the administration of anaesthesia, a blockage of consciousness. The poster, fixing her image as star, is produced at the cost of a subjective history, for her public cinematic life excludes her private melodrama.

There is a sense in which Sally Potter's explicitly feminist film, *The Gold Diggers* (1984) is a work of remembering or retranscription of *La Signora di tutti* and its embodiment of the cinematic Woman. In the course of its sustained meditation on the relations between the circulation of women and the circulation of money in a patriarchal and capitalist society, *The Gold Diggers* also produces a discourse about film history, the history of a representation of Woman. Julie Christie (and the use of Julie Christie, of course, triggers certain cinematic memories of the spectator) is that cinematic image and one of her distinctive attributes is amnesia—a total amnesia for she lacks memory altogether. When Colette Lafonte, the representative spectator in the film, interrogates her about her past, Julie Christie can only reply, "I remember very little. I've been kept in the dark." *The Gold Diggers* is a resolutely literal reading of the woman as image, of the only discourse she can produce. In the beginning of the film, Julie Christie's voice-over proclaims, "I'm born in a beam of light. I move continuously yet I'm still. I'm larger than life, but yet do not breathe. Only in darkness am I visible. You can see me but never touch me. I can speak to you but never hear you. You know me intimately and I know you not at all. We are strangers and yet you take me inside of you. What am I?" Julie Christie's only memory is a cinematic one of various images and scenarios—"I was first seen tied to tracks and hanging from cliffs," she tells Colette Lafonte. To the extent that the cinema is represented here as the space of an enclosure, a prison, *The Gold Diggers* explicitly reveals the impact of apparatus theory on feminist reasoning about the cinema. The apparatus obliterates memory and confines its figures. Like *La Signora di tutti, The Gold Diggers* traces the apparatus's production of the woman. With one difference of course: Julie Christie is saved from the cinematic scene, saved from the confines of the apparatus by another woman—Colette Lafonte—riding in on a white charger. The film uses the cinema's own iconography to dislodge it—resistance is also a cinematic scene—this time retranscribed, remembered. *The Gold Diggers* is symptomatic of the influence of apparatus theory and of the consequent need to violently tear the woman from the screen.

From *La Signora di tutti* to *The Gold Diggers* what is returned to the woman is her memory through construction. The process of abstraction of Woman is undone through a laborious construction of a memory and hence a history. *The Gold Diggers'* analysis of the circulation of women and money as defined by a certain social symbolics is supplemented by the elaboration of a subjective history. The scenarios of the wooden cabin in a snowy landscape all concern this effort to recapture or construct a memory—and ultimately it is recaptured through representation, in the theater, where the woman, constituted through division, simultaneously plays the role of herself and is the spectator of her own drama. What is crucial here is the elaboration of a new process of seeing and remembering. The final words of Colette Lafonte's character in the film are: "I know that even as I look and even as I see I am changing what is there." Feminism must refuse empiricism. But at the same time it must avoid the enclosure of rigid theoretical constructions misrecognized as historical truth (in other words, the problem of apparatus theory). In *The Gold Diggers,* the compulsion to repeat is resisted through an active process of remembering. The compulsion to repeat, based on forgetting, is a loss of temporal differentiation, the collapse of the past onto the present. The term "history" can figure most prominently in feminist theory not as an appeal to the "real" of women's lives, but as precisely this refusal of the compulsion to repeat in its own theoretical formulations the abstraction of the woman.

4

Femininity and the Masquerade:
Anne of the Indies

Claire Johnston

In the last few years the underlying assumptions of the classic text have become the subject of scrutiny by critics, and more recently this critical approach has been directed towards the classic Hollywood film (cf. Paul Willemen's analysis of Raoul Walsh's *Pursued* in *Raoul Walsh*, E.F.F. 1974 and Stephen Heath's analysis of Orson Welles's *Touch of Evil* in *Screen,* Spring and Summer, 1975). In his book *Le Plaisir du Texte* (Paris 1973), the French semiologist Roland Barthes described how the very process of story-telling itself, the construction of the narrative, is rooted in the myth of Oedipus. The classic text is a heavily closed discourse, characterized by its linearity, transparency, the necessity for coherence of action and character and the drive towards closure and resolution in terms of a final, full truth augmented and affirmed by a process of identification between reader/viewer and character. It is in this sense that the classic text has been described as the custodian of human nature, as the manner in which society speaks itself, providing a much-needed confirmation of the unproblematic nature of social "reality." Barthes describes how the mechanisms of story-telling parallel those of the child perceiving the fact of sexual difference in the mother's lack of a penis. The child acknowledges this new and bewildering fact, at the same time disavowing it: "I know, but nevertheless." The child's refusal to recognize the reality of such a traumatic perception (the absence of the woman's penis) can be likened to that of the reader/viewer, who knows these are just words/images, and yet derives his/her pleasure and security from following the narrative through to the end: "I know, and yet I don't know." Barthes cites a key aspect of the bourgeois world to be precisely this mechanism of disavowal, the smoothing over of difference and of the value of a radical heterogeneity; the reality of contradiction itself. It is this mechanism of disavowal of sexual difference which is at the heart of the dominant forms of understanding in our culture, the very system of intelligibility by which we live. It is in this sense that Barthes stipulates that to construct a narrative is indeed to search for one's cultural origins, to confront the Law of the Father. Within such a closed, over-determined discourse the reader/viewer is held in a fixed position which denies the possibility of a radical heterogeneity and imposes a false homogeneity; it is in this sense that Stephen Heath talks about the aim of narrative as being one of the framing of the subject (cf. *Screen,* Summer 1975). It must be pointed out, however, that within these terms, Barthes admits that the classic text can accommodate a limited plurality (cf. his study *S/Z).* It is precisely the trouble brought about by such a plurality in the classic text which will be the subject of this essay, a trouble which derives from Jacques Tourneur's choice of subject-matter itself: the masquerade.

There can be no doubt of the massive importance of Barthes's work for feminism, and feminist readings of classic Hollywood films have in fact developed along these lines in recent years (cf. the reading of *Morocco* in *Cahiers du Cinéma* Nov./Dec. 1970, Pascal Kané's article on *Sylvia Scarlett* in *Cahiers du Cinéma* May/June, 1972, and *The Place of Women in the Cinema of Raoul Walsh* by Pam Cook/Claire Johnston in *Raoul Walsh,* E.F.F. 1974) where the classic text's disavowal of sexual difference is shown to deny the opposition man/woman altogether. Whether or not the central protagonist is a hero or a heroine, the central opposition posed by the classic text is invariably that of male/non-male. In his analysis of Cukor's *Sylvia Scarlett,* Pascal Kané shows how Sylvia must cut off her pigtails in order to become the "hero" of Cukor's movie, suspending the desire of the character and excluding herself from the social order altogether. Woman as a social/sexual being is repressed in the classic text, and if the male does not, as is usually the case, dominate the film at the narrative level, the woman can only become the pseudo-center of the filmic discourse. In terms of the Patriarchal Order and the working through of the Law of the Father in the film text, there can be a validation of one only of the terms of the opposition male/female. Seen in this light, films which center around the question of female masquerade in the classic Hollywood cinema could not only be seen to offer new insights into the nature of classic Hollywood cinema and the reduction of difference into the ideological dichotomy male/non-male, but also serve as a paradigm for the trouble of the feminine for the classic Hollywood text, a trouble which must finally be eliminated.

Tourneur's *Anne of the Indies* (1951) is a key film in his *oeuvre* in that the problem of sexual difference forms the central articulation point of the film, and as Paul Willemen demonstrates in his essay, difference and absence are the pivotal questions raised by Tourneur's texts. It is hardly surprising that he should have chosen a pirate film aimed at children's audiences to represent such an extraordinary masquerade, for children's literature is rich in bi-sexual phantasy (cf. Barrie's *Peter Pan*). Indeed, it is doubtful whether such a radical depiction of the masquerade would have been acceptable outside this context. It is therefore interesting to compare the film with Cukor's *Sylvia Scarlett* (1935). In Cukor's film Sylvia relinquishes her femininity on the death of her mother to become the "hero" of the classic narrative and to follow his normal itinerary: she becomes Sylvester. But unlike the hero of the classic narrative who, in order to gain access to desire must assume his castration, Sylvester/Sylvia can only mimic a castration, and is forced to suspend her desires in order to operate as the film's central protagonist. In this way, Sylvia's masquerade effectively excludes her from the social order, and Cukor's use of the notion of masquerade itself is very much bound up with the central preoccupation with acting and performance throughout his work. Tourneur's approach to the question of the masquerade is rather different and somewhat more radical. He stresses that Captain Providence/Jean Peters is fatherless, that she is named after Providence Island, usurping the Name of the Father (Providence as in "Divine Providence") and attempting to function as the signifier of the Symbolic Order: the Phallus. This means that she is not just acting out a "masculinity" as is the case in Cukor's movie, but that she constitutes an utter and irrevocable refusal of "femininity." Protegé of Blackbeard, she avenges her brother's death at the hands of the English by assuming the persona of a pirate captain, fighting the English on the high seas. While Cukor presents a static signifier within his masquerade, in that Sylvia consistently mimics a "masculinity," the Phallus thus remaining the signifier, Tourneur does not. Captain Providence/Jean Peters oscillates between two radically different orders, the male and the female, throughout the narrative until its resolution, and there is no way in which we can know which sexual position is to be taken up. This refusal of the reality of castration, however, is delimited by one boundary in the film. In the first images of the film we are shown the entries in the register of Lloyd's of London, one official name after another being crossed out as a result of her appropriation of these names through the fraudulent means of piracy. It is precisely in this same official register that the resolution of the trouble constituted by Captain Providence/Jean Peters will be shown in the final crossing out of her name. In this way, Tourneur both establishes and exposes her usurpation of the Name of the Father in relation to the official register of names.

   The distinct sexual ambiguity of the first sequence of the film in relation to Captain Providence/Jean Peters derives from her image as erotic paradigm, in which Tourneur appears to be presenting a conventional, fetishized image of her masquerade, the female star Jean Peters appearing in male attire. Though present in person, the masquerade itself indicates the absence of the male, the image of Jean Peters serving as no more than the trace of the exclusion and repression of the feminine: the refusal to recognize the contradiction masculine/feminine altogether. This highly fetishized image of the star enveloped in male attire serves as a phallic substitute, a projection of male phantasy, in which the woman uses her body to disguise herself. But Tourneur goes one step further, and as the film progresses it becomes evident that a distinct foregrounding of this process of fetishization is taking place, the consistent play and oscillation between the person Jean Peters and the character Captain Providence attaining a particular emphasis and meaning within the text of the film.

In the first place, these initial images of Captain Providence/Jean Peters situate the masquerade in relation to the question of castration quite explicitly. She is wounded ("scars from the English"), and in locating the problem of castration, the mechanism of the fetish itself is foregrounded— the denial of the Otherness of woman in favor of her as phallic substitute, symbolizing the fear of castration and man's narcissistic wound. The fetish both marks and masks the oscillation between the two poles of sexual difference. The woman as fetish is foregrounded, and serves as an articulation point, a pivot, between the two radically different orders of the masculine and the feminine which Captain Providence/Jean Peters embodies, signifier of absence, of castration. Nevertheless it would appear that Captain Providence at one and the same time represents and conjures away the problem of radical sexual heterogeneity, constituting a problem, a trouble within the text; both a threat (i.e. the threat of castration) and a spectacle (i.e. the masquerade designed to disavow the fact of absence, of the lack). Having captured the English and seized their bounty, she discovers Pierre François Le Rochelle/Louis Jourdan, who refuses to ignore her femininity as the other men have been instructed to do, for which she slaps his face, the blood on his lips suggesting for a moment the possibility of a grotesque inverted masquerade: the mirror of her own masquerade, with the castrated male in the position traditionally occupied by the female. In the scene of the division of the bounty which follows, "shown to contain the signs of both sexual terms," Tourneur follows up this suggestion when La Rochelle chooses a dress while she chooses a sword, after which he can receive his papers as master of the ship. However, if the narrative were to become fixed in the interplay between these two images, the film would be destined to develop into crazy comedy, and Tourneur does not appear to be interested in such a possibility. For Tourneur it is the play and dramatization of the circulation of the problematic term, the phallus, which is at stake in the text. Therefore the state of balance between Providence and La Rochelle must be broken, the image shattered, although its possibility always remains as a continuous threat or temptation in the background. To maintain the closed economy of the classic narrative, Captain Providence/Jean Peters's masculine stance must be challenged. She meets with Blackbeard, possessor of the Law and father-figure, and in the sword fight which follows she is forced to acknowledge that he could "cut her down at his pleasure." In this scene, a new representative of the Symbolic Order is introduced, who re-locates the problematic term and starts it once more in circulation in relation to the various protagonists. The recurring process of oscillation generates a new image of Captain Providence/Jean Peters. Through the introduction of Blackbeard she is now able to present her other face (i.e. her feminine appearance). But what has been relinquished resurfaces elsewhere in terms of a new desired object, represented by Captain Morgan's Treasure. This imaginary presence (only a fragment of the map exists) once more underlines the nature of the trouble in the narrative. Providence and La Rochelle form a pact to find the treasure, she tries on his dress, asks him how men and women make love, inquires into the mystery of female passivity, plans a trip to Paris with him and contemplates becoming the object of desire for him. But the signifier oscillates once more and she declares "all wenches mad," tears off the dress, at the same time refusing Blackbeard's advice, quarreling with him, and ending up with the declaration of war between them. Meanwhile La Rochelle grows a beard and becomes a new "Blackbeard," the Law which possesses the knowledge of the treasure. But having been duped and betrayed by him, she relinquishes the feminine position and kidnaps his wife, whom she dresses in her husband's dress, planning to sell her as a slave to wreak her revenge on him. This last oscillation is imbued with a certain ambiguity due to the remarkable resemblance between the two women, which makes Captain Providence's sales-talk in the slave market all the more telling, the impression being of her selling her own body. The final revenge of her femininity follows, in which, having captured La Rochelle once more, she leaves him with his wife to die on a barren stretch of land in the middle of the ocean, Dead Man's Cay, where their love can "scald in the sun." But believing she has betrayed herself, she relents and sends the doctor to save them before engaging in her last battle with Blackbeard and the Law, in which she and her men fight to the bitter end, raising the skull and crossbones in defiance, in a final suicide. La Rochelle comments "she is home at last," death being the location of all impossible signs. The last images of the film delineate the boundary to the masquerade—she is struck off the register. The radical heterogeneity which her masquerade dramatized has finally been played out and frozen in the ultimate place of radical absence—death itself.

The masquerade in *Anne of the Indies* is described by the child analyst Joan Rivière as the central phantasy of one of her patients in an important essay on the nature of femininity under patriarchy, *Womanliness as a Masquerade* (in *Psychoanalysis and Female Sexuality,* edited by Henrick M. Ruitenbeek, New Haven, USA, 1966). In this essay Joan Rivière examines how homosexuality/heterosexuality in the subject results from the interplay of conflicts rather than a fundamental tendency. In this case study she discusses a woman whose desires are "masculine" in terms of the definitions imposed by patriarchal culture (her wish is for her place not to be the feminine one) and who fulfills such a desire not through homosexual object choice, but by assuming the mask of "femininity" in order to avert her own anxiety and imagined retribution from the Patriarchal Law in working through these desires. In this way, "femininity" is assumed as a mask to hide the possession of "masculinity" in the female subject; it becomes a masquerade. Thus a homosexual woman asserts her masculine characteristics as a game, while retaining the heterosexual love object, the mask of femininity, and all the visible attributes of "normal" womanhood. The central phantasy of the patient involves an infantile megalomania reminiscent in every important respect to that depicted in *Anne of the Indies*. In this phantasy the female child seeks supremacy over her parents and the Law by working out a sadistic fury upon them in which all women are rejected and scorned and the father is finally overcome. The aim of the phantasy is to achieve a position where no harm can be done her, to gain supremacy over the Law of the Father. Seeking to avoid the reality of castration and the impoverished human heritage of "femininity" in our culture, she can thus pursue her "masculine" desires without being "found out."

From Rivière's study we can see that *Anne of the Indies* is concerned essentially with the problematic nature of the fundamental fact of bi-sexuality, the working through at the Symbolic level involving a flight from the full implications of a bi-sexuality, despite the masquerade. As both men and women in our culture are condemned to live out in their mental life the great difficulty posed by sexual difference (resolving the dilemma only in their wildest dreams), so the central phantasy of the film and its refusal of the reality of castration (through suicide and the final striking off of the name in the register) must be eliminated. Nevertheless, Tourneur's depiction of the masquerade itself constitutes a radical attempt to situate this dilemma afresh for us, to open our eyes to the mechanism of the fetish, to explore new venues of desire and phantasy. The film perhaps marks one of the most radical attempts to explore the fact of sexual heterogeneity in the classic Hollywood cinema, foregrounding the repression of the feminine. The masquerade, trace of the exclusion and repression of the feminine, becomes the pivot upon which Tourneur plays out the trouble of a radical heterogeneity. Though finally eliminated, this very foregrounding of its impossible presence opens up, in phantasy, the possibility of sexual difference itself, of a bi-sexuality beyond the determinations imposed by culture and the classic text. In the film the trouble is constituted by a woman, and it is interesting to note in this connection Freud's observation that women are more inherently bi-sexual than men.

It would appear that *Anne of the Indies* is a unique film both in terms of Tourneur's *oeuvre* as a whole, and in terms of the classic Hollywood cinema. The central phantasy of the film can be seen as the polar opposite of the dominant male myth in classic Hollywood cinema, celebrated most fully in the "film noir" and the "horror" genre and exemplified by many of Tourneur's other films—which is the representation of woman as an inexplicable enigma,[1] a mask behind which man suspects some hidden danger. Kathy in *Out of the Past*, Jessica in *I Walked With a Zombie*, Alida in *Experiment Perilous*, and Irena in *Cat People* are in all essential respects enigmas, traumatic presences which must ultimately be negated. Behind the mask of the engima lies nothing but man's dread of the Otherness of woman, his disavowal of sexual difference itself. For in the enigma rests the possibility of "lack," the fear of castration. It is this misogyny which is internalized in the persona of Captain Providence/Jean Peters in *Anne of the Indies*. Her scorn and loathing for femininity however, involves a refusal to accept the human heritage of femininity, the secondary feminine identity opened up by the Oedipus Complex under Patriarchy. It therefore poses the possibility of a genuinely bi-sexual disposition while remaining a male myth.

Conclusion

The increasing use of psychoanalytic concepts in film studies has not gone unchallenged, particularly by feminists (cf. Julia Lesage's article *The Human Subject—You, He, or Me?* in *Jump Cut* Nov/Dec 1974 and re-printed with a reply in *Screen,* Summer 1975). This is not the place to enter into a detailed discussion of the question, but one or two points suggest themselves in relation to this essay. It seems to me that it would be a fairly fruitless exercise to attempt a serious study of the masquerade in the classic Hollywood cinema without making use of psychoanalytical concepts, for the universal human phenomenon of bi-sexuality would appear to be its driving force. However, the use of psychoanalysis, it has to be acknowledged, poses serious political problems. There is a very distinct danger that psychoanalysis can be used to blur any serious engage-ment with political-cultural issues. There are elements of such a tendency in the statement made by Ben Brewster, Stephen Heath, and Colin Mac-Cabe in *Screen,* Summer 1975, in their reply to Julia Lesage's attack on psychoanlysis. In this article in which the authors put the case for the psychoanalytical analysis of classic film texts and its relation to symbolic castration, the authors lay particular emphasis on Freud's theory of bi-sexuality as a fundamental human phenomenon, not restricted, as is often supposed, to homosexuality alone, and use the theory to refute one of the central assumptions of feminist readings of films "that there is a definitely defined male sexuality which can simply find expression and an also already existent female sexuality which simply lacks expression." Their view of the feminist reading involves seeing the fetishistic structure into which the spectator is fixed as essentially a masculine structure with the aim of reducing the "difference in each individual into the straight opposition—masculine/feminine." This essay suggests a different emphasis, where the reduction of difference into the dichotomy male/non-male involves the repression of femininity within the text, and this emphasis derives from Juliet Mitchell's feminist reading of Freud (*Psychoanalysis and Feminism,* Allan Lane, 1974). While accepting that all our psychologies contain both masculine and feminine characteristics, Freud shows that the Oedipus Complex and the acceptance of symbolic castration of necessity forces a meaning to this distinction. What feminist readings of Freud seek to do is precisely to indicate in what way symbolic castration bears the transmission of culture: for it is with the dissolution of the Oedipus Complex and through the child's acquisition of a super-ego that our cultural heritage is acquired and the patriarchal order is reproduced. What is completely lacking in the Brewster/Heath/MacCabe formulation is a sense of the asymmetry of patriarchal culture: Freud himself demonstrated clearly that there is no symmetry in the cultural formation of men and women. The point is not simply to assert a fundamental bi-sexuality, blurring the effects in culture of sexual difference, because under patriarchy we are condemned to live by our sexed identities, the ideological definitions of the "masculine" and the "feminine." Juliet Mitchell makes a strong case for seeing femininity in patriarchal culture as to some extent a repressed condition, which can only be acquired partially and in a distorted form. Perhaps it can only be fully understood in its symptoms, as in the case of hysteria ("a disorder with feminine characteristics"—Freud) which embodies both the representation of desire and its prohibition. It would seem to me that within patriarchal culture there is a "definitely defined male sexuality" which can find expression (the fetishization of woman as spectacle is one example) while female sexuality is indeed repressed, its real nature only fully knowable with the overthrow of patriarchal culture itself. It seems that in this respect Freud had a profounder understanding of femininity than the French analyst Jacques Lacan, from whom the Brewster/Heath/MacCabe formulation derives, which in its formalism ignores the cultural forms and ideological realities by which we live.

It is fascinating to learn in Tourneur's interview that one of his dreams has been to make a film about the nineteenth-century neurologist and precursor of Freud, J. M. Charcot, whose work on the aetiology of hysteria marked a revolutionary step forward for the development of psychoanalysis as a science. The mechanisms of hysteria which so interested Charcot represent a dramatization of the very problems of representation itself, and with them the problem of the "feminine" for Patriarchal culture. In his paper "Hysterical Phantasies and Their Relation to Bi-Sexuality" (cf. Standard Ed. vol IX) Freud observed that the hysterical symptom represented two sexual phantasies, a masculine and a feminine one. It is in this symptom, embodying in inherent bi-sexuality repressed by culture, that the asymmetry of Patriarchal culture finds its most striking representation. The film on Charcot would have been a logical companion piece to *Anne of the Indies*.

5

Cinematic Abreaction: Tourneur's
Cat People

Deborah Linderman

A good deal has been said about the auspicious connection between psychoanalysis and the cinema, their joint emergence around the turn of the century, their commensurate involvement in phantasmatic production, their mutual address to the unconscious, etc. Accordingly, considerable attention has been given to the way in which the cinema has represented the procedures and protocols of psychoanalysis. *The Cat People* (directed by Jacques Tourneur, 1942)[1] is a particularly interesting film in this regard, because it structures itself as a dialectic between the cinema, with its particular phantasmatic forces, and psychoanalysis, with its tactics for palpating and deconstructing the unconscious. In fact, this dialectic is organized by the filmic narration in such clearly drawn terms that it is even possible to speak of two strictly oppositional paradigms that regulate the play of the text; one such paradigm, which we shall refer to as Paradigm A and which is represented by the figures 1 and 3–7 is a paradigm of psychoanalysis insofar as it establishes a matched set of exorcising male figures which function to probe the central hermeneutic of the narrative, the mystery of the cat woman, and to demystify that hermeneutic. The other, the B paradigm which is represented by the constellation of images (figures 2 and 8–12) has to do with the construction of the cat fantasy itself, linked in ways that will be specified below to cinematic production and representing a teratology of the feminine and of evil; it is this cinematic paradigm with its imaging of feminine mystery that the psychoanalytic paradigm struggles to control and purge.

There is, in other words, a discourse of psychoanalysis which is commanded by a succession of "good" male figures who act to exorcise the "other" discourse, that of the "bad," demonic, monstrous term, the cat, which is attached to the feminine. And if this schema seems too neat, it should be acknowledged that Paul Willemin in an essay in *Edinburgh '75*[2] warned against overstructuring the Tourneur-text in terms of a simple dualism, so one stresses that these two paradigms are heterogeneously inflected. But for another thing, the cinematic discourse ultimately abandons its phantasmatic production and becomes itself an exorcising and indeed a moralizing discourse in order to achieve the film's closure. In the dialectic between them, then, the cinematic discourse supervenes over that of psychoanalysis and appropriates its purgative terms, containing the cat fantasy in order to proffer it for collective and ritual abreaction. Despite the heterogeneous inflection, however, and despite this crossing over of the cinematic function, the text sustains such a rigorous bipolarization of "good" and "bad" that it might be said to base itself on an essential phantasy of *splitting,* one side of the representation functioning to deny precisely the viability of what can only be called its "other side."

In terms of this split sustained by the text, the cinematic function is expressly posited as carrying on the good work of the abreaction of the bad phantasm. The film begins with one quotation and ends with another, and this crossing-over of the cinematic function into the exorcising paradigm is marked in the fact of the off-match between the two quotations. For in the first shot of the film (Figure 1, Paradigm A), the quotation, which reads "Even as fog continues to lie in the valleys, so does ancient sin cling to the low places, the depressions in the world consciousness," is superimposed on an image of an equestrian spearing a cat, an image which is refigured in variants throughout the paradigm. But the final shot of the film (Figure 2) heads up the B paradigm, which one can locate in relation to Figures 8 and 9 of the producer and director credits, as part of a specifically cinematic function. The concluding quotation reads "But black sin hath betrayed to endless night/ My worlds both parts, and both parts must die." The off-match between the bracketing quotations is a sign that, through the complex processes of textual unfolding, the psychoanalytic work of exorcism has been appropriated by the film work.

Because the textual transformations are of course fluid, the paradigms established here cohere only in abstraction from the actual processes of the film work; one ought to try to read them nevertheless within the meshes of the text. The markers of cinematic production (Figures 8 and 9) appear over the image of a pouncing panther, an image borrowed from inside the diegesis proper where it appears on a room-divider or screen in Irena's (Simone Simon) apartment (Figure 10). Now the screen is ever familiar as a support for the unconscious, a kind of membrane through which hallucinatory images appear. In front of this screen, in a sublimate project, Irena, who is a fashion designer, seems to reconstruct the image on yet another screen, the canvas. Against the screen, Irena-the-cat will fatally attack the psychoanalyst, the scene of this attack being rendered in shadows projected onto the screen: barred by it, Irena stands separated from Oliver (Kent Smith); alienated on this "other side," other scene, etc. (Figure 11), Irena is thus located as the male's disavowed half. Switching now to the other, male, paradigm, we go back to the quote from the psychoanalyst, Dr. Louis Judd, superimposed on another object from the inside of both the diegesis and Irena's apartment, a statuette of an equestrian spearing a cat (Figure 4). Irena explains this figurine to Oliver in a little narrative of good and evil; the cat represents

> the evil ways into which my village has fallen. At first the people were good and worshiped god in a true Christian way. Little by little, the people changed. When King John drove out the Marmadukes and came to our village, he found dreadful things: people bowed down to Satan and said their masses to him. They had become witches and were evil. King John put some of them to the sword, but some escaped into the mountains. Those who escaped, the wicked ones, their legend haunts the village where I was born . . .

The image of scourge and phallic projectile is recoded in the shadow of the cross cast on the wall by the T-square which Oliver shoulders (Figure 6), grabbed from the wall of the rational, geometric world of his office in order to fend off Irena ("Leave us," he breathes, and she is instantly evacuated from the space), and in the blade which Dr. Louis Judd conceals in his walking cane which he will unsheathe to protect himself from Irena's fatal attack (Figure 7). Irena's dream, which is also the text's dream, its mode of replaying its images displaced both backward and forward along the linearity of the syntagm, sums up this paradigm and exorcism quite handily (Figures 5.1–5.3) in an explicit reference to the syntagmatically consequent figure of Dr. Judd (Figure 7). The quotation, then, drawn from a text by Dr. Judd never again alluded to in the diegesis, puts this paradigm under the sign of psychoanalysis.

The insuccess of the paradigm to contain Irena with its purgative methods is measured by a shift in the order of citation from the first shot to the last. For whereas the first is a "made-up" quotation, fabrication, *The Anatomy of Atavism* being a completely hypothetical work, the last comes from one of the Holy Sonnets of John Donne, and is "real," a sign that the cinema has abandoned its represented or interior frame with its inadequated methods of containment in order to effect recontainment at a metatextual level, that of the cinematic phantasy itself. In other words, the Judd quote governs the represented intradiegetic means of exorcising the cat, while the Donne quotation, imported from without and appended to the text in an *ad hoc* procedure of closure, governs the abreactive means of the cinematic function. Superimposed on the image of an empty cage, which recodes a number of shots within the diegesis of caged leopards and panthers, the quotation moralizes the matter of "letting the cat out of the bag," or as we might want to put it, of returning the repressed to consciousness. The image of the key that closes Irena's dream (Figure 5.3) circulates in the text as the enfiguration of this process of disinterment, and it acts, as the dream suggests by its fade-in from the image of King John unsheathing his sword, as a variant on the penetrative expulsion of the cat: to unlock the cat, to release it, to free the phobic (caged, repressed) object. In a parapraxis that is most telling, therefore, the zookeeper forgets his key in the lock of the cage. When Irena returns it to him, he rejects with all the forces of scriptures—the zookeeper is a priest *manqué* and therefore a term in the psychoanalytic paradigm—the possibility of the cat's escape, or more exactly purloining:

> Ain't nobody want to steal one of them creatures . . . he's an evil critter ma'am. Read your Bible . . . *Revelations,* where the book's talkin' about the worst beast of them all. It says, "and the beast which I saw was like unto a leopard." Like a leopard, but not a leopard . . .

Dr. Judd himself, apprehending Irena in one of her habitual visits to the cages, accuses her of wishing to purloin the key: key as the letter, mark of the difference of the repressed. He moralizes the cat too, like the zookeeper, denying it with equal vehemence:

> You resist temptation admirably . . . The key. There is in some cases a psychic need to loose *evil* upon the world, and while all of us feel a desire for death, you fear the panther, yet you're drawn to him, as an instrument of death.

Dr. Judd will himself gain access to the phobic object, terrible and fascinating, in an act that recodes the wish of the purloined key; springing the lock on the door to Irena's apartment, he will trespass on forbidden territory and be eaten for it. Following which act of cannibalism, Irena, who has finally acceded to the phantasies of the countertransference and indeed purloined the zookeeper's key, will go back to the cages to undo the lock, an undoing which is at last her own. For she dies because the released and springing panther "crosses her path" and knocks her down (Figure 12). The quotation inscribed on the evacuated cage refers to an alchemical rule governing the miscibility of elements, but also of matter and spirit[3]; Irena dies because the splitting is not maintained, because her base part contaminates the angelic part, because—to import another line from the Donne corpus—she "is not mixed equally." As the alterity of the freed panther seems to signify, she is admixed, heterogeneous, a composite body called up by the cinema from a barred place, an elsewhere. In this sense, the two framing quotations do match, despite the shift in their order of citation, for they are both at pains to bracket the space of the film's phantasy as an "otherness" and to moralize that "otherness" in terms of "sin." The atavism referred to in the first quote, with its gothic evocation of mist, valleys and an animistic world, is intradiegetically actualized as the "old world" of Serbia, scene of the obscure history of the cat people, of which a trace appears in the New World in the form of the cat woman who visits Irena's table during the latter's wedding party in the restaurant pointedly named "Belgrade." But the atavism is also self-designating, for "anatomies" are themselves a throwback to a literary genre of the fifteenth through seventeenth centuries, despite Dr. Louis Judd's status in the "present." Under the twin markers of atavism and anatomy, then, the film purports to recover the repressed, unfolding as what Oliver calls a "fairy tale"—quaint, antique, other, alien to the space of spectatorship. The textual disinterment of the cat, its imaging, is thus redoubled by Irena's own final gesture, and the concluding citation, again from the seventeenth century, repeats in a different—moral—register the imperative of what one might call a politics of the "inmixing" of parts: that collective and social repression of atavism and otherness which constitutes the main ideological project of the New World (a project intensified historically by the wartime campaign to end evil that defines the film's moment of production).

Irena's wish to "be good," or to put it otherwise, to assimilate, locates the textual split between good and evil intrapsychically. The good Irena situates herself in the masculine paradigm as one of its collaborators. Thus, for instance, she evacuates her "sister," the look-alike avatar of the cat people who appears in the Belgrade and alleges sorority, by crossing herself without a word (Figures 13–16). Similarly, the sketch that she has been preparing in the first sequence of the film records a phantasy of exorcism; tossed away by her as waste but recovered from a drift of leaves by the camera in a nonsubjective close-up, it functions as a kind of establishing shot for the masculine A paradigm (Figures 3.1–3.2). Actually in its status as waste, this shot is a pivot between the two paradigms, for it also functions as a sign of Irena's despoilations. It marks her predilection for littering as a preliminary to her ensuing oral carnage; as she rips the sketch from her pad, crumples and aims it toward a trash container, which it misses, Oliver relays her gaze to a sign in the park that unmistakably designates her as a despoiler (Figures 17–19). She accedes to his correction, but it is this sign that mediates the terms of her first meeting with Oliver, whom she expressly calls her "first friend" in this country, and the sketch, a bit of trash retrieved by the camera to be contained after all, is a metonymy for Irena herself: both trash and exorcist, excluded object and would-be excluder.

The text constructs her much more insistently, however, as excluded and indeed phobic object. Her exclusion manifests itself in her avowed envy, envy in general—

> I envy every woman I see on the street . . .
> I envy them. They're happy, they make
> their husbands happy, they lead normal,
> happy lives. They're free.

—and envy at Alice. It is envy of Alice in particular that brings out the "bad" Irena and provokes the first transfiguration, and although one effect of her negative animus is that she terrifies domestic animals (the flight of the kittens, the uproar in the pet store, the death of the canary), its chief mark is one of oral aggressivity or incorporation, a tear in the flesh. Thus, by displacement, it is not the panther but Irena who "swallows the canary,"

> when I went past the panther's cage, I had to open the box, I had to throw the bird to him . . . Do you understand, I had to, I had to do it . . .

which has been described by the pet-store owner as "a ducky little angel . . . peaceful as my dream of heaven"; and by displacement likewise it is Alice's flesh that is represented in the torn-up beach coat (Figure 20) and the mutilated bodies of sheep, in a sequence to be considered below. And again, it is the body-in-pieces of the psychoanalyst that is rendered in the broken phallic blade still grasped in his hand (Figure 21). The "bad" paradigm is thus articulated upon the "good" in traces of oral despoilation that actualize a phantasmatic of the empty and devouring (envious) mouth. Both the splitting and the orality here lead "naturally" to Melanie Klein's theorizations of envy as the residue of an archaic oral dialectic between the "good" (nourishing, gratifying) and the "bad" (frustrating, witholding) breast in which the latter, to which are attached murderous impulses of rage and hate, has been introjected as the "primal object" and then reprojected. Envy is then the name of a primitive oral-sadistic phantasy of despoiling the good object by "completely scooping out, sucking dry, and devouring" it,[4] and splitting is the disavowal of this envious aggressivity by its exclusion from consciousness. We may thus see in the bad Irena, constructed as the shunned and phobic object, the structuring absence of the "good" paradigm, that exclusion which is the condition of its coherence.

It is nothing else than murderous oral envy that provides the narrative motivation for the scene of Irena's first transformation. The sequence proceeds with an extreme metaphoric reticence (contrasting in this with the vulgarization of the 1982 remake in which the composite body is shown literally as a human inside a cat skin). The sequence begins with Oliver walking Alice part way home after they have worked late together at the office. Irena follows unseen. Oliver offers to walk Alice to her door, she refuses and they wave good-night. As Alice walks on alone, Irena turns the corner and continues to trail her. A series of binary alternations is punctuated by the sound of their stiletto heels clacking on the sidewalk, during which Alice looks over her shoulder a few times at the stalking Irena. As Alice begins to hurry, the clacking sound accelerates, documented by inserts of their racing feet (Figures 22–23). The transfiguration is represented by the space of a frame, held empty of both Alice and Irena (Figure 26), synchronized with the abrupt cessation of the sound of the heels. The impact of the interruption of binary alternation produced by this empty frame and this silence is registered in reaction shots of Alice (Figures 27–33), stopping short and looking puzzled, glancing over her shoulder at the space of the sidewalk behind her now void of any figure, then breaking into a run. The brief low sound of an animal roar merges into the racing sound of a bus motor as that vehicle pulls into frame alongside Alice; the subsegment concludes as she mounts the bus, her backward glance producing a shot of some rustling bushes above the wall flanking the sidewalk she has just left. As the length of the bus slides through the frame toward screen left, the sound track registers the bleeting of sheep, a sound which bleeds over the first two shots of the ensuing subsegmental montage, one of a prowling caged leopard (Figure 34), one of a panther (Figure 35), and synchronizes with the third shot (Figure 36) of a stampeding flock of sheep. In the next shot, a zookeeper[5] (Figure 37) enters in the distance at frame right and walks forward to frame left, carrying a lantern which, when he lifts it, lights the torn bodies of dead sheep; in the subsequent shot (Figure 38), a slight rightward pan of that lantern is held, to illuminate in the mud the large paw-tracks of a cat. In the following shot (Figure 39), the zookeeper blows a whistle as a sound of alarm; the whistle bleeds slightly over the next shot (Figures 40–41), in which the camera itself repeats the pan to the right, traversing first the cat prints this time on a sidewalk and then, in a continuous motion, a different print which clearly shows the mark of a stiletto heel. The whistle sound is interrupted and replaced during this pan by the slow tap of clacking heels, which produces the next shot (Figure 42) of Irena walking in synch into the frame at the left, looking dazed; as she enters the frame, the tap of heels is in turn replaced by the blasting whistle. The sequence concludes as a cab pulls into frame from the left alongside her, and the whistle stops as the driver says "taxi, lady?"

Thus with immense clarity of formal means, the sequence manages to scotomize the moment of transfiguration, evoking it very actively, nonetheless, very richly in absences. The Christian allusion plainly lent by the sheep reinflects the good/bad binarism that structures the text, pushing it in the direction of sacral allegory; the oral marks on the sheep bodies localize the imprint of a satanic force. These marks are then recoded as the paw and shoeprints which themselves re-render the empty, silent frame that had provoked Alice's flight, and which, in their discontinuity, designate the space of demonic transfiguration as that of the interval between them: the violence of the composite body as agrammatical and unnameable, an empty slot without a name. These literal absences, however, are a sign of the structuring absence of the cat-cinema paradigm in the text. They give presence to the cat's shunned, phobic aspect, registered almost as a withdrawal of the camera, displaced from the object which is scanned only in its heterogeneity of traces. Except for various shots of the panther cages, and one gratuitous shot of the panther in the shipbuilder's offices insisted upon by the front offices of RKO,[6] the demonic body is always enfigured heterogeneously in its effects: Alice's scream, the intermittent sound of low growling, shadows (Figure 43), the silent evacuated space of a still frame or the indexical motion of the camera across an empty space (Figure 44), the imprint of Irena's fingernails on the velour upholstery of a sofa (Figure 45), the cat-foot of the tub in which she cleanses herself after the first transformation (Figure 46). This heterogeneity of marks is consolidated and condensed, however, in a single nonsubjective shot of Irena standing posed for the camera/spectator eye beside the hieroglyph of a sphinx-like statue (Figure 47). (The narrative motivation for the shot, interestingly, is that Oliver and Alice have just excused her against her wishes from their presence, on grounds that she would be bored by the architecture of ship-models which interests them; she has left the museum room, accordingly, and descended a staircase to another level of the museum.)

Irena as phobic object as hieroglyph: in a rather dazzling formulation in *Powers of Horror,* Julia Kristeva describes the phobic object as a visual condensation, a cathexis of looking, and a "drive presentation" (as opposed to a word or thing presentation).[7] As a drive presentation, the phobic object registers an inability to signify in words a turbulence of the drive economy connected to the earliest experiences of orality. The phobic subject is one in whom, as a result of primitive experiences of frustration and "want"—which is not the same as desire—the subject/object boundaries are not well-constituted; an intolerable confrontation with originary want, lack (*béance*), produces in the phobic a fear and an aggressivity intended to protect him from unlocalizable terrors. A consequent fantasy of incorporation of the mother's breast, holding on to her, counteracting the gap of separation, is projected onto and condensed in an unlikely object. Through operations of transformation and passivization, the wish to devour becomes a terror of engulfment by the maternal term: "I am not the one that devours, I am being devoured . . . a third person therefore . . . is devouring me" (p. 39). The phobic object is thus a misrepresentation, a kind of non-object, or abject, which interprets the relationship to the *mother* (p. 67), the dread of being swamped by the dual relationship, of one's own identity being incorporated into the maternal term. And the phobic subject is a subject "in want of metaphoricalness" (p. 37), one who produces metaphors not by signs alone but by the projection of oral drives in *images*. The phobic mirage is thus a hieroglyph of archaic oral pulsions tied to the mother and, tracing the anguish of originary want, of the terrors of indifferentiation. It should by now be clear that the film constructs the Irena/cat, with her unlocalized manifestations, her composite indifferentiation and her devouring mouth, as a phobic misrepresentation and hieroglyph, a projection of the spectator's own phobic virtualities.

We are now in position to consider the termination of the analyst. He is called into play in the narrative by Oliver and Alice, but also by Irena, as the way of "curing" her of her supposed "symptoms." In the initial consultation, Dr. Louis Judd hypnotizes her. In so doing, he expressly competes with the cinema: he darkens his consulting room and trains on her a beam of light that illumines only her face, seating himself in the shadows behind this illumination apparatus (Figures 48–52). He projects her, in other words, as an image for his gaze, a classifying, taxonomizing gaze which is a metaphor for the hermeneutic work of analysis itself. Since the state induced by hypnosis—what is called a hypnoid state when it occurs in conscious, waking life—is one in which split-off associations and affects kept strenuously separate from consciousness are liberated, Dr. Judd evidently takes Irena for an hysteric and creates a little cinema, a theater in which she is to "act out" the buried ideations that provoke her ostensible "conversions," liberating the distorted affect, etc.[8] He takes Irena's fascination with the zoo cats, her surrounding herself with cat objects, etc., as a projection into external objects of the pathogenic experiences of which she knows nothing. The problem is, of course, that Irena is completely conscious of her split, and moreover that she is a signifier in a textual system that exceeds her subjectivity. The system accordingly invalidates the apparatus of hypnosis, the psychiatric theater—what Gilles Deleuze and Felix Guattari in *Anti-Oedipus* refer to as a "bourgeois theatre" and a bourgeois scenarization of "Daddy, Mommy, me." For Dr. Judd "reterritorializes" the couch in the name of the family; his "interpretation" at the end of the session proposes for Irena an encounter with the constituents of her Oedipal scene:

> These things are very simple to psychiatrists. You told me about your childhood. Perhaps we'll find this trouble comes from some early

experience. You said you didn't know your father, that he died in some
mysterious accident in the forest before your birth, and because of that,
the children teased you and called your mother a witch, a cat woman.
These childhood *tragedies* (my emphasis) are inclined to corrode the
soul, to leave a canker in the mind. We'll try to repair the damage.

But of course the confrontation with origins, against which is to be
measured the cinematic production of effects, would only turn up not
a "tragedy" but a "Mommy" who was a cat woman and a "Daddy"
who had been torn to pieces by her. In other words, the childhood
sources of Irena's supposed symptomatology contribute nothing to its
explanation, for the explanation of the cat mother herself is dependent
on the effects of the composite body of the daughter: the genesis can
only be defined in terms of the present formation. The film inadequates
the psychoanalyst, then, with his endoscopic eye. The camera's trope,
on the other hand, of averting the literality of the composite body is
actually a scanning of the textual surface for the phantasmatic effects
which articulate that composite.

This phantasmatic structure manifests itself with decisive violence at
the moment of the kiss. Having transgressed a barrier and admitted himself
into the forbidden territory of Irena's apartment, Dr. Judd might imagine
that he is in place to liberate desire, his and Irena's, into the textual system.
But it is desire precisely that the text shuns, having constructed Irena
repeatedly not as the object "a" of the desiring quest but as a phobic
misrepresentation, a non-object, a metaphor for the engulfing mother,
total and oceanic, before objects. In his project of seducing Irena, Judd
presumably imagines that his ardor would be curative, would prove to her
that her fears are unfounded, her imaginations vain, and so he sets himself
in place to receive the benefits of her positive transference. But of course
he has failed to counteract the countertransference, and he violates his
prescriptively neutral role as "dummy." His mistake in positing Irena as
an object of desire is fatal, of course, for Irena is a non-object or, to return
again to Kristeva, an "abject."

This neologism is the name Kristeva gives in *Powers of Horror* to
negated objects or pseudo-objects, such as bodily waste and defilement,
anything indeed outside the circulation of desire which is metonymically
or symbolically assimilable to the archaic dialectic over borders and
boundaries negotiated with the maternal term. The abject is marked by
subjective intensities and preverbal, "semiotic"[9] codings which define it
as a universal carrier of the archaic indifferentiate (and Kristeva does
stress the universality of abjection, akin to that of the incest taboo, p. 68).
Manifesting as it does an uncertainty over difference, hence a crisis in
boundaries and exclusions, the abject is a subjective and/or cultural locus

where the fragility of symbolicity and the weakness of paternal repression are tried. To abject (verbal) the abject (nominal) is to enforce, whether subjectively or in a socially elaborated form, the exclusions that found the symbolic order. The phobic object, with its writing of a crisis in demarcation, is a species of the abject. When the analyst kisses Irena, therefore, he violates a textual imperative of exclusion. The moment of consummation occurring as it does between two inviable paradigms, becomes a moment of consumption, for as we have seen, the articulation point is ever-already a site of despoilation. The effects of the kiss are registered by Irena's slight withdrawal from the point of the close-up, complemented by a backward motion of the psychiatrist, but the camera moves forward toward her *to elide his recoil.* Two pronounced points of light in Irena's eyes announce the transfiguration, a convulsion in the text this time screened, as we have noted above, against the image on the room-divider. The moment of contact is deadly, fatal: lest the point be missed, the analyst is terminated by the film text as a sign of the fact that Irena's analysis would otherwise be of the interminable sort.

Dr. Judd's exorcising blade, however, which is left stuck in her shoulder, remains as a sign of the specifically closural work of termination yet to be done. In the dialectic mentioned above, between psychoanalysis and the cinema, therefore, the cinema performs an *Aufhebung* on its own representation of psychoanalysis, negating it as impossibly domestic, Oedipal, and symptom-based, contravening it by the insistence of the cat transfiguration not as symptomatic but "real."[10] The cinema itself, accordingly, carries on Judd's purgative work and appropriates Irena, but only in order to abject her, i.e., to affirm via the peculiar demise of the composite body (Figure 12, a shot in which the leaping panther collides with Irena and fells her, articulates a virtual condensation of bodies) the necessity to the symbolic order of differentiation. Hence the cinema is an institution which has ritual efficacy; for collective fascination, it calls up the horrors of the indifferentiate, of fusion and engulfment, of the old maternal imago, only to reject (abject) them with all possible force. The cinematic ritual, in other words, operates to shore up the symbolic by applying to that frail order the greatest pressure. "She never lied to us," the normative couple Oliver and Alice admit as they gaze down upon the fallen Irena. The cinema is finally homeopathic, the politics of the institution are abreactive, for it affirms, as fiercely as those other exorcists it has supervened against, the cultural imperatives of exclusions.

Paradigm A

1

3.1

3.2

4

Paradigm A (continued)

5.1

5.2

5.3

6

7

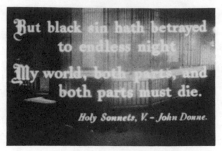

2

8

9

10

11

12

13

14

15

16

17

18

19

20

21

22

23

24

25

26

27

28

29

30

31

32

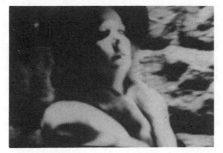

33

34

35

36

37

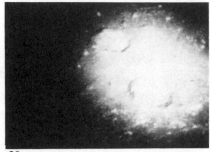

38

39

40

41

42

43

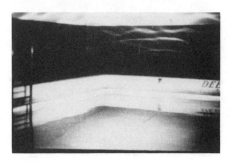

44

45

46

47

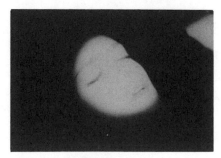

48

49

50

51

52

6

Believing in the Cinema

Raymond Bellour

That Jacques Tourneur is par excellence one of the directors of fascination (that is, of belief and its manifestations)—this is something that is visible to the naked eye: frames, gazes; camera distances; lighting; the calculated play of the actors seized up as if they were sorts of figures; ellipses and durations. That Tourneur "theorized" this in the most fictive of his tales (*Curse of the Demon,* 1957, a.k.a. *Night of the Demon*) allows us to measure how a director can reflect upon the power of cinema. For a director inclined as he was toward abstraction, the fantastic is a privileged terrain since the spectacular elements of the story serve all the better to represent this other spectacle of the fantastic that is the cinema itself. The overall setting of the film is interesting in this respect. The hero arrives in London from the United States. By means of a film whose situation is localized, but also that has itself been directed and produced in England by a French director who has become a cog in the Hollywood machine, the American cinema can observe itself more clearly, through an inner-directed, extralucid look. The power of which it speaks to us can seem today to be outmoded; in the case of this film it culminates in what may well be one of the last nights wherein the cinema really pretended to believe in its demons. In (briefly) recounting the film, I simply want to show how this belief is built up, how fascination is constructed. Nothing more, nothing less.

From the first moment, belief is at stake. A man (Harrington, a doctor, a psychologist) comes to meet another man (Karswell, a "magician," the leader of a sect). In the grip of an extreme panic, he says to him: "I didn't believe you, and I was wrong; I've heard it. I know it's real. I'll admit

Translated by Dana Polan

publicly that I was totally wrong and that you were totally right. Call it off." The other replies to him: "Some things are more easily started than stopped. You said: do your worst, and that's precisely what I did. You've still got that parchment I gave you?" "The runic symbols? They burned up," says Harrington, "I couldn't stop it." "I will do what I can," Karswell ends by saying, "but I of course cannot guarantee anything."

We know already that he won't be able to do anything: this is the price of the contract that has been signed between the film and its spectator. Harrington is this spectator, one who didn't believe in the power of spectacle and dies as a result. As soon as he gets back home, he sees and hears an unbearable image and an unbearable sound. The sound is a vibration which detaches itself from the musical background after being blurred with it for a moment; the image, a floating ball of light, advances from the depths of the nocturnal horizon, hurls itself on him and destroys him.,

At the end of its trajectory, this ball of fire takes on the form of a monster: an extreme and even absurd monster, as is the case with the majority of movie monsters (its sole advantage is to provide representation of a gigantic devil which the film will later make further use of). Tourneur didn't want this monster, preferring to confront his character with a pure force of light (and this is what Harrington will in fact be killed by): when Karswell tries to flee, his car hits an electric pole and this starts another fire, whose flames light up the night between the claws of the improbable demon.[1]

Harrington is that sort of spectator who did not believe in the truth of the image. The spectator of this misguided spectator—the true one—has been warned. Over the credit image of the stones of Stonehenge, the spectator could hear that since the beginning of time man has used the magical power of the ancient runic symbols to call forth demons out of the world of darkness and that this is still going on. Credulous and incredulous, the spectator knows that he/she has been taken to the cinema. The following shot (the first real shot of the film) seizes up the spectator as spectator: a light appears from far off, to the left, in the night, drawing the beam of a projector; the light advances, blinding the eye, and then blinks weakly. It is nothing more, one quickly realizes, than the headlights of a car on a road bordered by trees. In the car, a horror-struck man: Harrington is going to Karswell. Before any development of the story, the force of this shot suggests what is at stake: this intermittent light has the effect of life and death on the spectator. It is the spectator's "truth." Without light, there is no image; and a naked light produces only a blinding. Between the two, there is a blinking: the cinema.[2] The capacity that spectators have to believe in images that they are modeling is translated in the story by the debate between belief and disbelief that torments the characters. This equivalence is also, clearly, a matter of shots and framings. The trajectory of the ball of fire that menaces Harrington will double (by the axis of the gaze, by the boundary between black and white, by the relation between far and near) the trajectory of the headlight-projector of the car by means of which the spectator, recognizing the cinema-apparatus, enters into the fiction.

For the spectator to believe not so much in the story as in the film that tells it, and through this film in the cinema that enables it, it is necessary that the presence of the supernatural become manifest. The best motif for this involves an attempt to persuade someone—the hero, for example— someone whose incredulity will be the motor-force of a debate that will last almost as long as the film. This debate puts the spectator in a double position: on the one hand, the spectator takes the side of all of those who believe in the fantastic and produce it, since, like them, the spectator sees the fantastic invade the story and the image; but the spectator also sympathizes with the hero who, in spite of all the proofs that he is confronted with, will deny them until almost the end of the film, since his role is to render evident the split [*clivage*] that is provoked in the spectator by the simple fact of being at the cinema. Holden (a second psychologist) thus takes up the relay for Harrington. He picks up the question where death left it; but he goes back to its sources since, like Harrington in the past of the diegesis, he does not believe in Karswell's powers. The advantage of the prologue is that it enables us now to watch Holden be caught up in a disbelief analogous to our own, the only difference being that his problem is trying not to believe in the devil, while ours is trying to accept belief in the cinema. The film will thus have as its subject the conversion of the hero. He will finish by reaching the point that the spectator was in from the start: Holden will be obliged to believe in images and to be afraid of them so that we might be justified in finding pleasure in them [*d'en jouir*] and having enjoyed them while never believing in them more than half way.

This question of belief can be expressed thus: the scene of shadow and light, the scene of death that the spectator, along with the victim, was the sole witness to, was this scene "true"? Or, to put it otherwise, did this scene really take place? Or yet again: can it be repeated, but in front of witnesses this time and thereby become more true or at least appear to be more true? The film will thus serve as the trajectory that enables this repetition, in such a way that the spectator can really know what are the obligations of choosing to go to the cinema.

This is the perspective in which the arrival of Holden finds us. Holden is renowned for his research on hypnotism; he is the author of a book that sets out to prove that demonology has vanished since the Middle Ages. He has come to England to participate in a conference on paranormal psychology. One of his goals is to oppose the truth of reason to the fanatic theses of Karswell's followers. Like Harrington, whose colleague and friend he was, Holden is a scientist, he believes only in facts, visible and tangible ones. When he hears of Harrington's death, he decides all the more to continue Harrington's work. Dana Andrews gives Holden that square-shoulderedness, that distant allure, that barely expressive look, that manner of keeping his thoughts to himself and of believing without believing (just like a spectator) that make him into one of the strongest actors of a certain type of American cinema. The belief that the script refuses him adheres in fact to the figure that his character becomes. One might say that, in posing an obstacle to the image that he refuses, Andrews becomes all the more a screen onto which that image projects itself (thus, he excels in the last American films by Fritz Lang, the most abstract ones).

The film will thus try to recreate for the hero the conditions for the reality of a scene that he becomes an actor and witness of so that the spectator can continue to believe in that which he/she has already seen. Tourneur's art consists in developing his story (around Holden whom the narrative almost never leaves) in such a way that each strong moment of the plot contributes either to imposing the rememoration of the initial scene or to preparing its reiteration. The characters around Holden have as their only function to enable this process. One can see them, as in a dream, as so many figures revolving closely around the character of the dreamer, even representing this character and to such a degree that that character comes to be defined more by their pressure than by the resistances of his/her own evanescent being. Each in their own manner, the protagonists thus contribute to the formation of an apparatus [*dispositif*] in which the hero will end by recognizing (as does the spectator) the desire, built out of fear, that one has of the image.

1. Holden speaks with two participants of the conference. The first is a Hindu; he quite simply believes in the truth of the supernatural. The second, Mark O'Brien, Harrington's assistant, shows Holden the crude sketch of a devil; its creator is Hobart, a fanatic accused of murder. Under hypnosis, he drew this figure quite similar to those woodcuts from Late Medieval and Renaissance traditions that represent the devil. Thus, it is perhaps not Hobart who killed, but the devil; he may have also killed Harrington, on whose body strange marks were found, marks that cannot be attributed to his death by electrocution. The initial scene is thus immediately replayed two times over for Holden, who takes amusement in it, and for the spectator, who remembers it.

2. Karswell approaches Holden at the British Museum. Holden is there looking for an ancient book, *The True Discoveries of Witches and Demons,* which curiously is missing from the collection. Karswell invites Holden to come to his place to look at the only other copy which is in his possession. After a fruitless debate on their goals and their respective

ideals which Holden puts an abrupt end to ("I'm not open to persuasion"), Karswell departs and leaves Holden his calling card. Around the printed name, Holden reads the following handwritten words: "In memoriam Henry Harrington, allowed two weeks." He rubs his eyes; the text has disappeared. He calls one of the staff members; there is no longer anything on the card. Later, a lab test confirms this. Holden is the only one (along with the spectator) to have read what he read.

3. Joanna Harrington (the niece of the dead man) advises Holden to give up his investigation. She has found her uncle's diary. It tells how Karswell surreptitiously gave him a sort of parchment, covered with runic symbols—a frightening bit of paper, gifted with an autonomous life force. Joanna doesn't believe in the accidental death of her uncle. Holden suggests that she is engaging in auto-suggestion. Here again, we relive the initial scene. Joanna (who is a kindergarten teacher) invokes the belief of children in things in the dark. She no longer wants to be treated as a child. Like her, the spectator, no longer a child, is an adult who still believes in ghosts.

4. Joanna and Holden go together on Halloween to Karswell's. Karswell, dressed up as a clown, is doing a magic show for a crowd of children. The debate between the two men starts up again. Karswell reaffirms his belief in a blurring of reality and imaginary which shows up in the powers of darkness as in the powers of the mind. To prove his argument, he causes a storm. When Holden says to him, "I didn't know that you had cyclones in England," he replies, "We don't." He predicts the day and hour of Holden's death: ten in the evening on the 28th of the month. Thus, Holden has only three more days to live. This has been decided since the meeting in the Museum. Karswell dismisses Holden who hasn't had a chance to look at the famous book (and this, the magician says to Joanna who is interested in it, would be useless anyway: Holden wouldn't be able to decode it).

Karswell thus really becomes the representative of the *mise-en-scène*. But this power has its limits. Karswell is the first to fall under the sway of the very powers that he seemed the master of: the storm has gone beyond his plans. And he is anxious to know if his mother really believes in the magic (of cinema); he confides in her, as he had formerly with Harrington, that he cannot stop what he has started. And he clarifies the stake of this: it is a question of his life or of someone else's.

5. A second debate between Mark O'Brien and the Hindu about Hobart and the devil (same setting as before: Holden's hotel room). Mark suggests that they are all giving in to auto-suggestion and mass hysteria (in other words, that they are too good as spectators.) Marks asks for permission to look in his appointment book at the notes for the lecture he is going to give at the conference: the pages after the 28th of the month are torn out.

6. A second evening with Joanna (same setting as before: in her apartment). She has found that pages are torn out of her uncle's diary: after the 22nd, the date of his death. "Nobody is free from fear. I have an imagination like anyone else. It's easy to see a demon in every dark corner. But I refuse to let this thing take possession of my good senses." "Fine," answers Joanna, "But are you sure that Karswell didn't pass you anything?" Holden checks the folders he had at the British Museum: the piece of parchment, a long sliver of paper, slips out, flies across the room, and flattens up against the screen of the fireplace where there's a fire burning. Holden picks up the paper and slips it into his case. His scepticism is beginning to be called into question (an unexpressed question) without it yet coming to coincide with that belief that has more or less taken over the other characters.[3]

7. Holden goes to see Hobart's family. He asks the mother for permission to treat her son by hypnosis so that he might be able to say what he did and saw on the day of the murder. Everyone considers Hobart to be damned, chosen by the devil. Holden opens his case, giving a glimpse of the parchment which trembles. "He was chosen."

Holden wanders among the stones of Stonehenge: the hero has come to take up his full place in the credit-image.

8. Mrs. Karswell has organized a seance with a medium. The circle of spectators forms: around the medium, we find Mrs. Karswell, one of her friends, Joanna, Holden (brought by the young woman). In a trance, the medium successively "plays" several people. A child, an Indian, a Scotsman, and finally Harrington. Once again, the initial scene is replayed but this time it is mimed, dramatized. Holden interrupts the seance: he breaks the circle of spectators so that the scene can begin again elsewhere, since he must end up being the object of this scene.

9. In the night, Joanna and Holden go to Karswell's. Holden breaks into the library (he goes in instead of Joanna who first had the idea). A cat is on the table. The book is on a night table. He looks through it. The light goes off. The cat becomes a leopard that attacks Holden. The light goes on. Karswell comes in. The cat is curled up in an armchair. Karswell says to Holden, who accuses him once again of madness: "It's you who seems to be mildly unhinged. Is breaking into my house at night an indication of sanity? You will die tomorrow night. If you're thinking of going through the woods, you might find it unpleasant." Fiction loves these contradictory propositions that make it move forward.

In the woods, Holden is pursued by the ball of fire which forms on the horizon, glides among the trees, fills up the image. The scene is played out again with an insistent precision: it becomes real even for Holden who sees and gives in to the beginnings of fear. But it stops: the ball of fire disappears when Holden trips while running. All that was necessary was that Holden believe in the power of hallucination and that the spectator participate in this.

Holden goes with Joanna to the police station and recounts what he saw. For a short moment, the policeman takes over Holden's earlier role: that of a skepticism which leads to belief. But Holden quickly retreats to his earlier position in spite of the mounting proofs. He reproaches Joanna for passing her hysteria on to him: "I am not a superstitious sucker like about 90 percent of humanity" (in other words, the world of spectators given over to phantasms). This works all the better to set up the final reversal.

10. An auditorium. A scene. Spectators. Hobart is brought out on stage. He is injected with Pentothal. He wakes up and screams. He is put under restraint. Holden hypnotizes him. Hobart goes to sleep and answers questions from Mark O'Brien who takes up the relay for Holden. The dialogue takes as its subject the sect of "true believers," adepts of the demon, and their leader, Julian Karswell. Mark forces Hobart to relive the initial scene. "It is the night of the demon." Hobart recreates it exactly as Holden has just lived it. "It's there, I see it in the trees, a smoke . . . and a fire, my time allowed is almost over." Holden intervenes: he wants to know more about this:

> "What do you mean by 'your time allowed'?"
> "To prepare for my death."
> "Why must you die?"
> "I've been chosen."
> "How will you die?"
> "The parchment was passed to me. I took it without knowing."
> "Hobart, open your eyes." (Holden takes the parchment out of his case and shows it to him.)
> "No . . . I passed it back to the brother who gave it to me. That's the only way. I had to return it to him. I didn't want to, but it was the only way I could save myself."
> "To save yourself, you had to give it back to the one who gave it to you."
> "Yes, I had it, and the demon took him, not me. Not me. You're trying to pass it to me again. I won't take it, I won't, no . . ."

Hobart gets up, struggles with Holden, takes flight, goes out into the hall, runs to the window and leaps out. Holden gets ready to leave the building. He learns from the Hindu that Karswell's mother called: her son is taking the train to Southampton at 8:45. "She kept saying that all evil must end." Holden rushes out: it's tonight at 10:00 that Karswell has predicted that he will die.

Holden has finally become that spectator who believes in the truth of the image. What is interesting is first that in order to finish the film ("all evil must end"), the narrative evidently must repeat, and second that the announced scene, simultaneously endlessly deferred and constantly reiterated, must finally happen. Holden's belief (like Harrington's, earlier) precipitates the arrival of the demon. This occurs in a literal fashion and according to the strictest rules of suspense. Holden says to Karswell, in the train where he has joined him: "I believe that in five minutes something monstrous is going to happen." Like Harrington, Holden confesses his error to Karswell; he even thanks him explicitly for having convinced him of the existence of a world that he had never believed possible (the world, of course, of the cinema). He even offers to make a public apology. The only difference is that his own parchment didn't burn and that he has learned the rules of the game. Holden manages to pass it on to Karswell who becomes the victim that we expected him to become.

There are three reasons for this denouement. Holden-Dana Andrews is the star, the man in the couple that he forms with Joanna (a couple treated with a surprising reserve which increases the mystery of the film and allows it to be somewhat free of cinematic convention). Holden also incarnates, as we have seen, the spectator: specifically, that aspect of the spectator who cannot believe in spectacle and finally, totally, accepts it only because the spectacle comes to its end. Spectators, in fact, play all the more freely with the fact of belief the more they already anticipate the moment when, with the film over, they can have a lesser belief. Finally, Karswell is the director, the man of illusions, of evil, of instinct [*la pulsion*]. The "true believers" that he controls invert the order of good and evil; they believe in the virtues of evil. Karswell is thus the person who cannot avoid the image: he produces it, he recognizes it as a mortal, and he can only die from this.

But for the apparition of the monster in this scene, Karswell's death is one of the hardest moments in cinema that I have ever come across—at least of that cinema that recognizes a mortal power in the image. As soon as the parchment comes back into his hands, Karswell becomes nothing but movement. His hands outstretched, he chases, in unchanging direction, after the piece of paper which escapes him: first, in the corridors of the train and then, when the train stops, on the tracks along which the effect is carried out to the point of vertigo, until the moment that the parchment bangs up against the edge of the rail and is burned up. Then, on the darkened horizon, at the exact point where Karswell's bug-eyed look sees the train disappearing, there appears the whirl of light that announces the arrival of the monster. The monstrous image thus seems to be born out of the vanishing point that Karswell's look follows out along the line of the tracks. Karswell turns back in order to escape. But, from the other side, from the opposed axis, there appears a second train that advances toward him. What is extraordinary here is that Karswell never leaves the rails (except at the very last moment only to avoid being hit by the train and only to be grabbed up by the monster.) He stays on the tracks, following the line along which the parchment led him and on which the monster-light and the train are facing off against each other. At this end of the film, Karswell becomes the hero of fascination. The one who really believes in the cinema. To the point of dying in order to make us believe in it. He is fascinated by the image, by shadow and light (incarnated by the train and by the monster-light) as pure forms of movement. These forms would blur into each other in destroying him if the genre exigencies of the film's production didn't cause the train to pass under the demon who rips into Karswell's body before throwing him onto the side of the track.

By contagion, the effect of the train carries through to the very last shots, beyond Karswell's look. After approaching the tracks where the body is, Holden returns to the station platform where he finds Joanna. They finally agree to a common viewpoint; Holden repeats what Joanna suggests to him: "Maybe it's better not to know" (let us leave intact that aspect of mystery proper to the cinema, let us leave it that way so that we can better take pleasure in it.) They move forward on the platform in medium shot; then, with the camera having moved back, they are framed in the last shot in long shot. It is at this moment that a train goes by, the third one. Its whistle recalls the sonorous vibration that underlined the arrival of the monster. It invades the image and literally effaces the couple. After the passage of the train, there remains nothing but an empty shot, offered to the pure look of fascination.

The parchment is that which translates to the greatest degree this power of the look. Why does the parchment more than the monster-light or the train which, each in its own way, so strongly express the properties of the cinema-apparatus [*dispositif-cinéma*]? Because it is a fragment. A book is at the center of the film: it orients the itinerary of the hero, from the British Museum (where the book is missing and where Holden receives in return a visiting card whose words disappear) to Karswell's house (where he doesn't get the book, confronting in its place a tornado, a leopard, and the monster-light). The book thus leads to the fantastic itself: the hallucinated image. It becomes the secret of the film. It could be supposed to express the meaning of the film, if only it was decodable. But in remaining elusive, the question of the book shows that the only meaning of the book is to incarnate Karswell's power. His power at engendering belief, at creating images, at producing fascination. In this respect, the book is the metaphor of the film: a volume of images and signs, it expresses the virtuality of the film.[3] It is here that the parchment intervenes, as mysterious in its runic symbols as is the book which is supposed to contain, in a language indecipherable to non-initiates, the key to the final meaning of life. But this meaning, as we have seen, is meaningless: it concerns only the development of the film and reduces all discourse to the production of the image, of the figure. This is what the parchment expresses, the scrap, the fragment of the book. The explosion [*éclat*] of the figure. If the book represents the film as a virtual body, the volume of all the images, the manuscript incarnates the circulation of the image as a fragment. We have to imagine its movement, simultaneously concrete and abstract. The manuscript is this object which circulates and whose circuit the heros must pass over again and again like a "who's got the bobbin game." But it is also and especially that which in the image itself moves, cannot stay in place, its vanishing point and its vibratory aspects. It is simultaneously the secret heart of each image and that which slides between the images: the image of the image, we might say, in what it has of the perpetually undone. The metaphoric insignia of the film, the manuscript produces and reproduces the careening metonymy of the film. It is the image that one never touches. It always escapes and ends by burning up. And one dies from it. As one does in front of the object of fascination.

But why, in the look at the fleeting object, make Holden a hypnotist? What need does this story have of hypnosis? Would it be to give substance to the old idea that sees in the cinema a sort of hypnosis? Undoubtedly. But above all it allows the opposition of two regimes of belief and the look, regimes which are mixed and yet distinct: hypnosis and fascination. They correspond here to the positions of the two principal characters: it is also because it runs the risk of seeming overdone that this film is so delicate. With all the difficulties specific to its genre, the film invites us to project this film onto the whole of cinema.

Hypnosis (real hypnosis) has need of fascination. But in pushing it to its limit, it subjugates fascination and puts it to sleep, if we can put it this way. The subject of hypnosis gives up his/her look under the domination of the double movement which grips it tightly: regression, idealization. The subject-spectator is submitted to a similar domination in that light form of hypnosis which belongs to the spectator: the hypnosis of cinema. But there are two ways of living the look that remains the spectator's, that person who has not really been hypnotized: the identifying look and the look of fascination, one heading toward life and the other toward death (this distinction is Lacan's: between that which he calls "the instant of seeing" and the "*fascinum*").[4]

Holden is that subject who believes, like Mesmer and Freud, that hypnosis increases the field of consciousness and allows one to see more than one sees normally with the eye of simple memory. This is something that the cinema has in common with hypnosis and realizes according to its own proper means. The role of hypnotizer delegated to Holden thus

designates by analogy this power of the cinema-apparatus. But the character is defined in such a way that, through him, this power is freed of
fascination: either because fascination is supposed to become abolished
in hypnosis or because it remains in suspension in the instant of seeing.
Inversely, Karswell believes only in fascination. He indicates in fact that
there is no clear and distinct vision that doesn't carry fascination within
itself as its menacing other side. Karswell holds the truth of this film for
which he is a sort of delegated producer by virtue of the fact that he obliges
Holden to become a spectator for it. A complete spectator which also
means a fascinated spectator. This is why Holden is the only one to have
hallucinations, above and beyond the monster-light that he shares with
Harrington and Karswell (the calling card, Karswell's silhouette which
disappears while wavering in the halls of the British Museum, the cat-
leopard); compare this to Karswell who, for his part, always sees nothing
but a real that is already hallucinated and already fully fascinating (the
monster of the end condenses the image of this). To underline this double
game between the two instances, the narrative, right after the seance where
Holden hypnotizes Hobart, subtly endows Karswell with the power of
hypnosis (he puts Joanna, whom Holden has with him in the train, to
sleep). Karswell is thus assimilated to Holden at the moment when Holden
admits the power attributed to Karswell since the beginning of the film.
The spectator, in turn, sees the film that is born out of this debate; the
spectator gives in with a pleasure mixed with fear to the soft bliss of
fascination that is contained in hypnosis.

The sequence of hypnosis, during which Holden's turnaround is produced, is also the moment when the two regimes converge clearly in the
story just as in the image. Before a crowd of onlookers whose obvious
function is to designate to us our own place, both in and outside of the
drama, Holden, on stage [*sur scène*], is the director [*metteur en scène*].
By chemical means (Pentothal), Hobart is pulled out of his catatonic state.
In front of we spectators, as of the spectators in the auditorium, he becomes
the pure fascinated spectator. He resees the unbearable image that he fled
by paralysis. An extreme closeup of his eyes (the only such closeup other
than that of his deadened eye nine shots earlier): fixed, fixing us, wide
open. Four shots later, there comes an extreme closeup of his face, his
eyes popping out of his face: Hobart screams and lunges toward us.
Hypnosis serves as the means by which Holden puts him back to sleep—
that is, subjugates the pure force of fascination. And it is in the shelter of
hypnosis, as is the case for the real spectator, that Hobart relives the
originary scene. Until the moment when Holden, menaced by the truth
that is born from his position of mastery and which reduces it to nothing,
awakens Hobart and orders him to see. This is the end of the hypnosis,

for the hypnotizer as well as for the hypnotized, and it is the triumph of fascination. Hobart leaps out of the window rather than succumb; and Holden, as we have seen, finally gives in so as to avoid dying. The spectator takes all the more pleasure in being able to recognize in all this the antagonistic forces which work together to make up identity.

7

Historical Trauma and
Male Subjectivity

Kaja Silverman

. . . if there is no virility which
castration does not consecrate then
for the woman it is a castrated
lover or a dead man (or even both
at the same time) who hides behind
the veil where he calls on her
adoration.

(Jacques Lacan)

The dominant narrative film encourages the viewer to substitute its "impression of reality" for the lost object, and so to deny the phenomenal lack which he or she "knows" full well. Cinema's reality-effect consequently derives in part from its perceptual intensity, i.e. from the primacy it gives to the imaginary register.[1] However, that effect is also the outcome of a specific ideological operation. A film's sounds and images will only induce general belief to the degree that they belong to "the privileged mode of representation by which the image of the social consensus is offered to the members of a social formation, and within which they [are not only asked to] identify themselves," but in fact identify themselves. In other words, a cinematic text will satisfy the viewer's desire for reality only if both text and viewer inhabit what Jacques Rancière would call the same "dominant fiction."[2]

The phallus stands or falls with the dominant fiction, since it is there that it assumes the properties of visibility, turgidity, and erectness which more appropriately qualify the penis.[3] In other words, it is merely within a culture's dominant representational and narrative reservoir that the paternal signifier "grows" into an organ, and becomes available to the male subject as his *imago*. Since that *imago* does not so much reflect him as cast its reflection upon him, he will be in a position to deny his castration only so long as he doesn't notice the "frame"—so long as the dominant fiction seems his natural medium. A loss of belief in that fiction will lead to a loss of belief in the phallus as well, and thus to a crisis in male subjectivity.

Unlike its Freudian counterpart, Lacanian psychoanalysis has always been quick to acknowledge that male subjectivity is founded upon lack— to concede that "what might be called a man, the male speaking being, strictly disappears as an effect of discourse . . . by being inscribed within it solely as castration."[4] Unfortunately, it has been equally quick to neutralize the radical implications of this deviation from the Freudian paradigm, and in the process to shore up both sexual difference and the existing symbolic order. Nowhere is that neutralization more explicit than in an interview conducted by Hélène Klibbe with Serge Leclaire, one of the most orthodox of Lacan's followers (at least until the mid-seventies). Although its ostensible topic is homosexual writing, the interview in question is devoted almost exclusively to the topic of castration, which it describes as the necessary and inevitable basis of both male and female subjectivity. Yet far from challenging traditional gender demarcations, this common heritage is immediately negated by anatomy, which dictates a very different relation to the symbolic for man than for woman.

Leclaire argues that because the male subject possesses the penis, he is in a position to deny his castration, and so to aspire to power and privilege. He is on the "right" side of the symbolic, but on the "wrong" side of knowledge. The female subject, on the other hand, has tangible "proof" of her castration, and consequently turns away from what are in the final instance only illusory goals. Although she is on the "wrong" side of the symbolic, she is on the "right" side of knowledge. Leclaire's formulation is sustained throughout by an extended theological analogy, which is evocative in many ways of Lacan's invocation of St. Teresa in *Seminaire XX*:

> Let us call the phallus "god." It's an old tradition, You don't have to see "God," properly speaking, you have no image of him. "God" (the phallus) is invisible; therefore, the relation to the phallus is marked by a nonformalizable relation, a relation of exclusion. At the same time, everything is in relation to the phallus; everything is in relation to "God." Let's suppose that there is a child, Jesus, the son of God, who serves as mediator. Now, let's replace the "child Jesus" with the penis, which happens to be the most convenient representative of the phallus. Because man has in his body a relation with his *penis as the representative of the phallus*, schematically, his natural inclination leads him to forget the fact that the phallus ("God") is invisible, unseizable, unnameable. But woman does not have this representative in her body; therefore her relation to the phallus is less veiled. She is less tempted to forget the fact that the phallus is absent. Consequently, man's and woman's relations to castration are profoundly different. I am referring to castration as the relation to the phallus, to the Invisible, to an unnameable term. In Lacanian language I would say that it is both signifier and object. . . . In the whole evolution of woman, nothing has ever come as a screen between the invisible "God," phallus, and the way she speaks. For man, the possession of the penis, which is

> highly cathected, serves as a screen denying the fundamental character
> of castration. Man comes to believe that the has not been castrated.[5]

This passage is characterized by a major internal contradiction. Its entire
argument rests upon the assertion that the phallus cannot be seen, grasped
or named—that it is, in short, *unrepresentable*. However, the penis (which
can be seen, grasped, and named) is described as both "the most convenient representative of the phallus," and as the latter's incarnation or
"son." The relation between the phallus and the penis is thus totally
mystified; it seems at the same time miraculous (i.e. beyond rational
or secular explanation) and natural (i.e. existentially or ontologically
motivated). In either case the relation seems to escape social determination. We are told that it just "happens to be."

A similar refusal to admit that the phallus could be in any way culture-
bound is evident both in Leclaire's subsequent claim that "Man comes to
believe that he has not been castrated" (in the implication, that is, that this
perception is entirely spontaneous), and in his sweeping generalization
that "In the whole evolution and history of woman, nothing has ever come
as a screen between the invisible 'God,' phallus, and the way she speaks."
Sexual difference and the paternal signifier are situated in a space beyond
historical causation or political intervention—in a kind of "sacred time."
The overriding theological metaphor not only contributes heavily to this
sense of changelessness, but helps to soften the passage's contradictions
into paradox.

The present discussion shares with Lacan and Leclaire the assumption
that male subjectivity is founded on castration. It also shares with those
two theoreticians the view that the lack which the male subject must
somehow disavow is finally his own. However, it takes a very different
position on the relation of gender to that lack—the position that while the
loss of the object and the subordination to a pre-existing symbolic order
may be the necessary "price" of entry into language, no imperative dictates
that lack be exclusively identified with one sex. It is by no means inevitable
that the male subject be constructed through a series of defensive mechanisms calculated to protect him from any knowledge of the terms through
which he enters meaning, nor that the female subject be constituted
through the obligatory assimilation of both her own and the male subject's
castration. As Martin Thom observes, "Both symbolic castration and the
phantasy of the fragmented body are universals of human experience,
since they represent the fact of having been born, embodied, into a world
where language is. [However] their articulation, one with another, in a
particular social formation . . . will differ."[6]

What I am trying to suggest is that Lacanian psychoanalysis has focused
attention on the universal experience of symbolic castration rather than

upon the ways in which it is (variably) articulated. Although it teaches us the vitally important lesson that the penis is not the phallus, it diminishes the value of the lesson by defining that term as "the signifier intended to designate as a whole the effects of the signified, in that the signifier conditions them by its presence as a signifier."[7] It thus deflects critical attention away from the discursive practices which install the phallus not merely as the privileged signifier within our cultural order, but as the signifier of privilege—its status as the marker of a complex of psychic, social, political, and economic differences.

Far from belonging to a kind of "sacred time," beyond the vicissitudes of history and the particularities of different social formations, the phallus is always the product of dominant signifying and representational activities, activities which are vulnerable to interruption and transformation. It is consequently never more than a distillate of the privileged semes and values of a given symbolic order. It is, indeed, often less than this collective "vision," since its meaning and function may vary somewhat even from one discourse to another. What makes the phallus seem somehow "larger" and more "palpable" is the constant representational support the dominant fiction gives to that signifier—the endless circulation of a wide variety of ideal paternal images and sounds. It is also through this image and sound production that the penis "happens" to seem "the most convenient representative of the phallus," since that production asserts over and over again the identity of these two disjunctive terms.

Thus the male subject does not just spontaneously happen to believe that he is not castrated. That belief is instilled in him through the unceasing flow of paternal images and sounds within which he is encouraged to "find" himself; through the externalizing displacement onto the female subject of the losses that afflict him; and last, but by no means least, through his subordination to the dominant fiction by means of which his social formation coordinates its diverse discourses. Since this final operation generally necessitates a series of additional castrations, phallic male subjectivity might also be said to be predicated upon a massive cultural disavowal of the lack upon which it rests.

Classic cinema plays a vital part in the construction of this subjectivity. Not only is it an important supplier of paternal representations, but it orchestrates for the male subject the projections so necessary to his sense of personal potency. Its images, sounds, and narrative structures are drawn from the ideological reserve of the dominant fiction, and its suturing mechanisms function both to insert the viewing subject into that fiction, and to inspire confidence in its capacity to resolve conflict and neutralize opposition. This confidence is a prerequisite both for the male subject's identification with the phallus, and for the female subject's disavowal of male lack.

Not only does a loss of belief in the dominant fiction generally lead to a loss of belief in male adequacy, but the spectacle of male castration may very well result in a destructive questioning of the dominant fiction. Male subjectivity is a kind of stress point, the juncture at which social crisis and turmoil frequently find most dramatic expression. Major rifts between the dominant fiction and the larger social formation can almost always be detected within a classic narrative film through the breakdown of sexual difference—through the disclosure of male lack or impotence.

A number of films made in Hollywood between 1944 and 1947 attest with unusual candor to the castrations through which the male subject is constituted—to the pound of flesh which is his price of entry into the symbolic order, as well as to the losses he subsequently suffers within that order. *Pride of the Marines, Hail the Conquering Hero, State Fair, Those Enduring Young Charms, The Lost Weekend, The Guilt of Janet Ames, Spellbound, It's A Wonderful Life, Gilda,* and *The Best Years of Our Lives* all dramatize the temporary collapse of the mechanisms through which the female subject is "normally" obliged to assume male lack.[8] Indeed, many of these films attribute to a female character the scopic and narrative control which are the usual attributes of a male character. As a contemporary viewer remarked, "The first thing one has to note about these films is that the descriptive term—'boy gets girl'—no longer fits. In *Lost Weekend,* it is the heroine, not the hero who gives the kisses. . . . In *Spellbound* it is *she* who walks into *his* room in the middle of the night. . . . In *Pride of the Marines,* when letters and telephone calls get her nowhere, the heroine resorts to abducting the hero 'bodily' home, there in the face even of his desperate 'Get me out of here!' to insist that they shall be married."[9]

These films are also characterized by a loss of faith in the familiar and self-evident. The hero no longer feels "at home" in the house or town where he grew up, and resists cultural (re)assimilation; he has been dislodged from the narratives and subject-positions which make up the dominant fiction, and he returns to those narratives and subject-positions only under duress. He is unable to align himself with the phallus because he is no longer able to believe in the *vraisemblable*. In a number of instances the revelation of male lack is shown to be the symptom of a larger historical crisis. *Love Letters, Pride of the Marines, Hail the Conquering Hero, The Lost Weekend, The Best Years of Our Lives,* and *The Guilt of Janet Ames* all clearly identify that crisis with World War II and the recovery period. In each case the hero returns from the war with a physical or psychic wound that renders him incapable of functioning smoothly in civilian life.

I will turn in a moment to what is perhaps the most interesting of these films, one which focuses obsessively and at times erotically on the psychic and social castration of its three male protagonists, and which stubbornly refuses to suspend disbelief in the face either of the dominant fiction or its phallic representations, insisting that the ideological formulations of pre-war America are incapable of resolving the contradictions of post-war America, and consequently of concealing male lack—William Wyler's *The Best Years of Our Lives* (1946). First, however, I would like to clarify the theoretical model which will be used to account for the relation between it and its historical "moment."

The textual analysis that follows will rely heavily upon three broad theoretical categories: social formation, dominant fiction, and history. The first of these categories will be understood as the "complex, overdetermined and contradictory nexus of discursive practices, in which the human subject is constituted and lives in a relation of absolute interiority"[10]— as a nexus which includes not only language, literature, cinema, the "academic" discourses, the social sciences, the law, and politics, but *all* social activity and exchange. Far from cohering around a single mode of production, as it ultimately does within the Althusserian paradigm,[11] social formation will here designate the *non-unified totality* of discursive practices within and through which the subjects that make up a given socius conduct their *material* existences.

The second of my categories, dominant fiction, is here opposed neither to an ultimately recoverable reality, nor to the condition of "true" consciousness. "Fiction" underscores the *constructed* rather than the illusory basis of reality, while "dominant" isolates from the whole repertoire of a culture's images, sounds, and narrative elaborations those through which a consensus is established—those which mediate between the often contradictory discourses which comprise a social formation, permitting a group identification and collective desires. For a dominant fiction is more than a set of representational and narratological possibilities for articulating consensus. It is also a libidinal apparatus or "machinery for ideological investment,"[12] an investment which is as vital as labor or exchange to the maintenance of the social formation. Since the plurality of discourses which make up a social formation are unified only within its dominant fiction, social formations depend upon their dominant fictions for their very sense of identity and unity. A dominant fiction is informed by what Ernesto Laclau calls a "will to 'totality' "; it is the mechanism by which a society "tries to institute itself as such on the basis of closure, of the fixation of meaning, of the non-recognition of the infinite play of differences."[13] A particular social formation will thus be able to maintain itself against the antagonistic pressure of external stimuli only so long as the dominant fiction has adequate libidinal resources, and is able to determine the distribution of those resources.

Although no area of the social formation escapes discourse, that formation is under constant siege from what remains outside discourse—from the biological, from the ecological, and from what will here figure as "history." Fredric Jameson at one point in *The Political Unconscious* describes history as what "hurts"—as "what refuses desire and sets limits to individual as well as collective praxis, which its 'ruses' turn into grisly and ironic reversals of their overt intention."[14] Following Jameson's rather unorthodox lead, I will define history as a force capable of tearing a hole in the fabric of the dominant fiction, and so of disrupting its internal economy. In short, I will identify it with *trauma*.

Freud's attempts to account for the behavior of those suffering from war traumas led him in *Beyond the Pleasure Principle* to a scandalously physiological formulation of the human psyche. That formulation may pose more problems than it solves for traditional psychoanalysis, but it proves singularly useful as a model for conceptualizing the relation between history and the dominant fiction. That appropriation would seem justified not only by the thematic similarities linking the present discussion with *Beyond the Pleasure Principle*, but by their theoretical convergence—by their joint assumption that trauma can best be understood as the rupture of an order which aspires to closure and systemic equilibrium by a force directed toward disruption and disintegration.

Like the psyche described by Freud, the social formation develops a "protective shield" by means of which it guards itself against external stimulation—it develops, that is, a dominant fiction. This protective shield or dominant fiction articulates the desires of the socius. To the degree that individual subjects accede to those desires by investing in the requisite representations and narratives, the dominant fiction (like the protective shield within the Freudian formulation), is supplied with "its own store of energy," and so manages "to preserve the special modes of transformation of energy operating in it against the effects threatened by the enormous energies at work in the external world"[15]—effects which tend toward a leveling out of them and hence towards destruction. In other words, the dominant fiction maintains its libidinal economy intact.

The protective shield or dominant fiction also orchestrates sensory perception, converting vision and hearing into apparatuses "for the reception of certain specific effects of stimulation." It subordinates eye and ear to a particular scopic and auditory regime, a regime which determines what can be seen and heard as well as the larger function those activities will serve. The dominant fiction thus isolates the sensory organs both from excessive amounts and "unsuitable kinds" of stimuli (22). It does this in part by negotiating defensive mechanisms such as projection, disavowal, and fetishism.

However, the dominant fiction is helpless to protect either the individual subject or the social formation against any stimulus strong enough to penetrate its walls and interrupt its libidinal economy. History periodically ruptures it, just as fright shatters the protective shield described by Freud. When this happens the social formation and its subjects are flooded with excitations which can neither be ignored nor assimilated, and which are conducive of a profound unpleasure. Freud associates situations of this kind with trauma:

> We describe as "traumatic" any excitations from outside which are powerful enough to break through the protective shield. It seems to me that the concept of trauma necessarily implies a connection of this kind with a breach in an otherwise efficacious barrier against stimuli. Such an event as an external trauma is bound to provoke a disturbance on a large scale in the functioning of the organism's energy and to set in motion every defensive measure. At the same time, the pleasure principle is for the moment put out of action. There is no longer any possibility of preventing the mental apparatus from being flooded with large amounts of stimulus, and another problem arises instead—the problem of mastering the amounts of stimulus which have broken in and of binding them, in the psychical sense, so that they can then be disposed of. (24)

The verb "to bind" has of course a very specific sense in Freud's writings. It refers to the process whereby memories characterized by a high degree of affective and sensory intensity are brought within linguistic control—the process whereby they are anchored to signifiers, and consequently to meaning. The memories in question are totally transformed by this binding operation[16]; indeed, it might be more accurate to say that something else is put in place of the original, hallucinatory mnemic traces. That "something else" is a signified, or rather a cluster of potential signifieds. Between the profoundly affective and sensory memory and the signified there is an instant of complete discontinuity—the instant at which the signifier intervenes.

However, history (at least as it figures both within *The Political Unconscious* and the present discussion) cannot be bound; it is always both absent and unrepresentable. What *can* be brought within linguistic control is the trauma it generates *within the established systems of representation and signification*, a trauma which is experienced by the subjects who depend upon those systems for their sense of identity. History makes itself felt through the crises it creates and the changes it "inspires" in the dominant fiction and the social formation—crises and changes which are ultimately mastered through the very articulations which first make them available to thought. In other words, history is accessible only through texts, to whose very organization it is antipathetic. It passes into the cultural domain through the agency of the signifier, i.e. through that very register whose functioning it most threatens.

It is precisely *because* history threatens signification that its force is felt so strongly there. That force disrupts the equilibrium of the dominant fiction, generating temporary irregularities and sometimes even radical change within textual practice. It is at the level of these irregularities and changes, as Jameson suggests, that we should look for its traces, since "the deviation of the individual text from some deeper narrative structure directs our attention to those determinate changes in the historical situation which block a full manifestation or replication of the structure."[17]

For *The Best Years of Our Lives* history is synonymous with World War II. However, that event is at no point directly represented; it can be read only in its after-effects—in missing limbs, alcoholism, recurrent nightmares, unemployment, home-breaking women, disabled bombers, and the claustrophobia of small-town life, to all of which it gives a privileged place. *The Best Years of Our Lives* also makes a self-conscious departure from what were then the conventional formal strategies of Hollywood cinema. Finally, it makes no effort to align male subjectivity with phallic values. Instead, the film identifies its central male characters with junk—with what cannot be absorbed by the dominant fiction. It is characterized by what Siegfried Kracauer was to call "ideological fatigue"[18]; by a loss of belief in the family, small-town life, and the adequacy of the male subject.

> Characters of this kind have rarely been seen before on the screen. Visionless, at the mercy of any wind, benumbed even in their lovemaking, they drift about in a daze bordering on stupor. . . . It is as if those Innocents had been dragged out of their enchanted universe to face the world as it actually is—a world not in the least responsive to their candid dreams and hopes. The guise of the discharged soldier assures us that they are now average individuals, stunned by the shock of readjustment. (p. 572)

The Best Years of Our Lives is one of the films through which André Bazin pursues his realist dream. To a certain extent the case he makes for Wyler also resembles the case he makes for Vittorio De Sica. In the essay on *The Best Years of Our Lives*, as in the essay on *Bicycle Thief*, he praises what might be called the "authenticity" of the pro-filmic event.[19] However, whereas Bazin attributes the realism of De Sica's film to its transparent reflection of the pro-filmic event, he attributes the realism of Wyler's film to the technical difficulties that event created—to the tactical problems posed by the use of a complete, life-sized set and non-theatrical makeup:

In concentric value, I will first cite the realism of the decor, built in actual dimension and in its entirety (which I suspect would complicate the shooting since it would be necessary to raise the "sections" to give the camera proper perspective). The actors wore clothes exactly like their characters would have worn in reality, and their faces were no more made up than in any town. No doubt this quasi-superstitious but scrupulous regard for the truthfulness of the everyday is uncommonly strange to Hollywood, but its true importance rests not so much on its tangible convincingness for the spectator as in the disruptions it must inevitably introduce into the mise-en-scène: the lighting, the camera angle, the direction of the actors.[20]

Bazin thus equates the realism of *The Best Years of Our Lives* with its *traumatic* qualities—with its deviations from a cinematic practice which was no longer capable of passing representational muster after the upheavals of the 1940s. Not only was the film's break with the formal conventions of Hollywood motivated by those upheavals, but "something of the inundation, the cyclone of realities which [the war] had unfurled upon the world" finds "interpretation" through it.[21]

Wyler also establishes an intimate connection between history and the film's articulation. Indeed, he remarks not only that "the picture came out of its period, and was the result of the social forces at work when the war ended," but that it was "written by events"[22]—i.e. that its enunciation was coerced by an external stimulus. Like Bazin, Wyler distinguishes sharply here between his own film and conventional Hollywood cinema. For those who had seen the corpses at Dachau, he writes, Hollywood seemed not only "divided from the main currents of our time," but "a long way from the world."[23]

The force of the events which coerced the "writing" of *The Best Years of Our Lives* manifests itself in part through the formal markings (deep focus, the long take) which differentiate that work from most Hollywood films of the period. It also manifests itself through the film's realist aim—through its evident desire to connect the viewer with "the main currents of our time." Finally, history makes itself felt through the systematic demystification of the "preexisting inherited traditional or sacred narrative paradigms which are its initial givens," a demystification Jameson associates with "realistic representation."[24] (I hasten to add that I do not mean to valorize realism, or to impute to it any truth-value. Nor do I mean to privilege the long take and deep focus as somehow capable of delivering "more" than classical editing or conventional focus. Their historical value resides merely in their deviation from an established norm.)

The inherited narrative paradigms which *The Best Years of Our Lives* most systematically demystifies are those which serve to construct the adequate male subject. Far from obliging the female subject to display her lack to the gaze of her sexual other, it repeatedly calls upon her to look acceptingly at his lack—to acknowledge and embrace male castration. It thus radically reorders the libidinal economy of classic cinema, an economy which organizes the viewer's desires around the masochism of women and the magnanimity of men.[25]

As I suggested above, a number of other films from this period also invert the classic paradigm, but that inversion is ultimately justified by the physical, psychic, or social restoration of the injured male subject (even *Pride of the Marines*, which is unusually blunt about its hero's blindness, shows him beginning to recover his vision at the end.) *The Best Years of Our Lives*, however, offers no such easy resolution, nor does it account for its deviation from gender orthodoxy by promising that the female subject's healing touch will restore the wounded male subject to his former potency. Instead, it attributes the social and psychic estrangement of the returning veteran to an ideological unraveling—an unraveling which it shows to be due in part to the massive exposure of the male populace to death and dissolution (i.e. to that force which threatens all forms of cultural coherence), and in part to the social contradictions of post-war America.

The first of the many scopic traumas which punctuate *The Best Years of Our Lives* occurs in the military airport where Al (Fredric March), Homer (Harold Russell), and Fred (Dana Andrews) wait for a flight back to Boone City. Homer reveals his hooks, which have been concealed until now, when he and Fred go to the desk to sign the passenger list. Fred and the ground attendant exchange a look of shock across the metal implements. Homer exposes his hooks again on board the plane, as he offers cigarettes and a light to Al and Fred. This time reactions are much more muted, but Homer begins almost immediately to talk about what it will mean to return to his family and girlfriend (Cathy O'Donnell) without his hands. "They don't know what these [hooks] look like," he worries. "You'll be all right—wait and see," responds Al with false reassurance. "Yeah . . . wait and see," Homer says bitterly. "Wilma's only a kid. She's never seen anything like these hooks."

Homer here articulates the thematics of his amputation—the thematics of an intolerable difference, accessible to vision, which positions its carrier as both other and inferior, and which confers upon its viewer an unwanted knowledge. His hooks function much like the female genitals within Freud's account of disavowal[26]; they too attest to an intolerable absence or loss. The comparison between Homer's disfigured arms and the female body within the classic psychoanalytic account of sexual difference becomes even more striking when he associates Wilma's scopic ignorance with her youthfulness, and imagines that her affection will be unable to survive the unveiling. Over and over again the film insists upon this equation making the spectacle of Homer's hooks (and, even more, his stumps) something primal and traumatic, and stressing that to the civilian eye he is a "mutilated creature."

However, the first and only time we see the amputated limbs is also the moment at which Wilma most ardently embraces Homer. The sequence in question begins with Wilma coming into the Parish kitchen where Homer is eating a late-night snack, and pressing him to clarify the terms of their relationship. Homer self-protectively rebuffs her at first, but eventually allows her to go to his bedroom and help him undress. After the harness and hooks have been removed, he compares himself to "a baby that doesn't know how to get anything except by crying for it," and averts his eyes from what he expects will be a gaze of recoil. But Wilma's look contains nothing but tenderness, and as she puts him to bed (a ritual earlier performed by Peggy [Teresa Wright] for Fred, and by Millie [Myrna Loy] for Al) the lovers embrace.

Because Homer's lack is localized at the level of the body, and because it manifests itself in the guise of stunted limbs and physical helplessness, it also situates him in the position usually reserved for the female subject within classical cinema. Not only is he the object of a probing social gaze, obliged to account for his appearance to strangers at drugstore counters, but his undressing becomes the occasion for an intense erotic investment. In an essay published in 1947, Robert Warshow remarks upon the sexual charge of the sequence where Homer discloses his stumps to Wilma, and attributes that sexual charge to a "feminization":

> He . . . has lost his hands—and with them his power to be sexually aggressive. . . . Every night, his wife will have to put him to bed, and then it will be her hands that must be used in making love. Beneath the pathos of the scene . . . one feels a current of excitement, in which the sailor's misfortune becomes a kind of wish-fulfillment, as one might actually dream it: he *must* be passive; therefore he can be passive without guilt.[27]

Homer's stumps and compensatory hooks constitute a crisis not only of vision but of representation—a crisis which is the result of combining documentary detail with the spectacle of male castration. As Wyler himself observes, the decision to cast an actual amputee for the part of the disabled sailor gives the image of that character a credibility it would not otherwise have had, and so implicates the viewer more fully than usual in all visual transactions within which it figures ("We wanted Russell himself to play the part, rather than an actor. No matter how good a performance an actor gave of a man without hands, an audience could reassure itself by saying, 'It's only a movie.' With Russell playing Homer, so such reassurance was possible").[28] Warshow makes a similar point, but he complains that the casting gives the film too much authenticity—that it erases the boundary between cinema and life:

> Everything about the sailor is especially affecting because the part is played by a man who really did lose his hands in the war. There was nothing else to be done, I suppose, but this is one of the elements that help to make the movie spill over into the real world, carrying its falsehood with it.[29]

Despite their varying assessments of its success, Wyler and Warshow agree that the casting of Harold Russell for the part of Homer Parish was a choice on behalf of belief. There are at least two important issues here, one of which pertains to classic cinema's "impression of reality," and the other of which bears upon the process of disavowal through which that cinema has traditionally constructed the male subject. Harold Russell's double amputation does not "make the movie spill over into the real world," but it does situate the image of Homer Parish's arms on a different level of representation than the rest of the film. At every other point, including Russell's acting, there is a dimension of performance or simulation to which the stumps and hooks cannot be subsumed. Russell's injury is no more "present" than any other pro-filmic event; it too is recorded, and its "unfolding" is purely "fictive."[30] However, in this instance the filmic representation exercises a strong referential pull, seeming to point beyond the text and Russell's acting to his body and the traces left there by the war.

Because of this, there is a sort of doubling up of belief, a reinforcement of the disavowal Metz and Comolli identify with the cinematic experience. The image of Russell's stumps and hooks functions further to minimize "the gap which the 'yes-I-know/but-all-the-same' has to fill."[31] It negates the cinematic signifier, inclining the spectacle even more precipitously than usual toward the referent or object. Yet at the same time what most passes for "the real thing" in *The Best Years of Our Lives*—what provokes the representational "lurch" toward the pro-filmic event—is precisely what classic cinema is generally at most pains to deny, and against which it marshals the defensive mechanisms of projection, disavowal, and fetishism: male lack. The peculiar doubling up of belief around the castration of the male subject may well be the most traumatic feature of Wyler's intensely traumatic film.

Homer is not the only exhibit of male lack in *The Best Years of Our Lives*. Fred's castration is also on permanent display, particularly after he removes his air force uniform. When he finally manages to track down his wife (Virginia Mayo) the day after his return to Boone City, she greets him enthusiastically, much taken with the ribbons decorating his chest. Indeed, she responds to him *as spectacle*—as a glamorous and heroic image. "Come on in, honey, where I can take a look at you," she exclaims, "Oh, *marvelous!*" However, the first time she sees him in civilian clothes she visibly recoils, appalled by his shabby and unfashionable suit, with its working-class connotations. She literally begs him to change back into his uniform, exclaiming with satisfaction after he complies: "Now you look wonderful . . . now you look yourself. . . . now we're back where we started."

Fred soon resumes civilian dress, becoming an even more pitiful spectacle when he is forced to return to the drug store where he worked before the war, and to don the white overcoat of a salesman and soda jerk. On the only occasion we see him at work in the first of these capacities a small boy releases a toy plane into the air above Fred's head, and pretends to shoot it. The plane is an ironic reminder of the heights from which he has fallen since his return. As it noisily circles around the cosmetic counter of the crowded store, it is also indicative of the way in which ideology attempts to recuperate the trauma of history through trivializing representation.

A woman's hand reaches into the air and grounds the spinning plane. The camera cuts to Peggy, owner of the hand, who has been standing quietly out of frame watching the little drama. The expression on her face, which registers both sympathy and bemusement, suggests that her gaze has taken in all the manifold complexity of the scene. Once again the female subject is given a privileged access to the spectacle of male lack. Here, as in the nocturnal exchange between Wilma and Homer, that spectacle is highly eroticized, saturated with female desire. Later the same day Peggy confides to her parents, Al and Millie, her intention to break up Fred's marriage to Marie, revealing in the process her investment not only in the former bombardier, but in the disintegration he increasingly comes to represent.

Peggy is introduced to Fred the night of his return to Boone City, when they both turn up at Butch's Bar. Because he has no place to sleep, the Stevensons take him home with them, and Peggy gives him her bed. Awakened during the night by Fred's cries, she goes into the bedroom and rescues him from a recurrent nightmare about a burning plane—a nightmare which replays his worst war experience. Fred is sitting bolt upright as she enters, his eyes wide open. Peggy's immediate response is to cover his eyes, as if to protect him from in intolerable sight—a gesture which locates him again on the side of the spectacle. She then induces him to lie down, and wipes his face with a cloth as she whispers over and over: "Go to sleep." Peggy performs these nursing gestures with an even more passionate tenderness than that with which Wilma regards Homer's mutilated body. Her desire for Fred can be traced to this moment of unveiling.

Marie adopts a very different attitude toward what she regards as Fred's "difference." She is embarrassed by his nightmares, viewing them as symptoms of psychological abnormality and social failure. They are also further evidence of what she already suspects—that Fred has been "contaminated" by a force antagonistic to the "good times" she seeks. "Are you alright in your mind?" she irritably asks, "Can't you get those things out of your system? Maybe that's what's holding you back. You know, the war's over. You won't get anyplace till you stop thinking about it. Come on—snap out of it!" (Ironically, the film here entrusts Marie with its clearest articulation of the dysfunction which results when history invades the dominant fiction and its subjects with massive quantities of external stimulation. The war has indeed infiltrated Fred's "system," and that trauma has not yet been "bound.")

When Fred loses his job because of a drugstore brawl, and Marie announces she wants a separation, he decides to leave Boone City. On his way to the military airport he stops by his father's shack to collect the clothes Hortense has washed for him. While there he discards various war souvenirs, including a commendation for distinguished flying. These once-prized possessions have been relegated to the status of junk; they attest to experiences which are not only unassimilable to the *vraisemblable*, but threatening to its positivity. After Fred leaves, his father picks up the commendation with trembling hands and reads aloud from it. What emerges is an account of the purest negativity—of a death drive unleashed equally on enemy and self:

> Despite intense pain, shock, and loss of blood, with complete disregard of his personal safety, Captain Derry crawled back to his bomb site, guided his formation on a perfect run over the objective and released his bomb with great accuracy. The heroism, devotion to duty, professional skill and coolness under fire displayed by Captain Derry under the most difficult conditions reflect the highest honor upon himself and the armed forces of the United States of America.

Immediately before the reading of Fred's war commendation, we see him arriving at the military airport, trying to catch a plane out of Boone City. When asked whether he wants to fly east or west he says it doesn't matter; because the war has invaded his unconscious, his homelessness will be equally acute wherever he goes.

While Fred waits for the next plane he walks down to a field filled with hundreds of World War II bombers. The planes have all been stripped of their engines and propellers, and are waiting to be scrapped. Like Homer and Fred they are disabled and unwanted, a "defilement" which must be jettisoned because it "escapes that social rationality, that logical order on which a social aggregate is based."[32] Fred climbs into one of the planes, and moves through the litter of dust and worn maps to the bombardier's seat. The camera cuts to an exterior reverse shot of the nose, showing Fred in a low-angle, medium close-up through the plexiglass window. As he looks to the viewer's right the camera cuts again, moving with Fred's gaze to one of the outer engine nacelles. It then pans from right to left across the surface of the bomber, pausing momentarily at each of the other three nacelles, as if to emphasize their readiness for departure. A third exterior shot follows, dollying in rapidly from a long shot to a direct close-up of the nose, and then tilting slightly to disclose Fred, still sitting motionless behind the window. The last two exterior shots effect a di-vision, denying what they at the same time assert. In the first of those shots the absence of engines and propellers is belied by the musical score, which evokes the sounds of take-off. In the second the low angle of the camera and its head-on approach simulate the movements of a plane preparing for flight, even as the image of the disabled B-17 attests to the impossibility of any such event.

This extraordinary disavowal does not so much cover over a lack as push negativity to the limits. When Fred imagines himself aloft once again on a bombing mission, he detonates the *vraisemblable*. At that moment he escapes social rationality, opting for the non-ego over the ego, the threatening outside over the coherent inside, and death over life.[33] The film throws its formal weight behind this negativity through the di-visions described above. When it pits sound against image, or camera angle and movement against iconic meaning, it too invests in junk, privileging what falls beyond the social pale over what remains within.

In the exterior close-up of the bomber's nose with which the sequence ends, Fred's face seems to have surrendered all consistency, and to have become part of the texture of the plexiglass window. And although he is called back to life and work by the salvage man, he never really leaves the scrap yard. In the final sequence of the film, when Peggy meets Fred at Homer's wedding and remarks that she's heard that he's "in some kind of building work," he responds: "That's a hopeful way of putting it. I'm really in the junk business—an occupation for which many people feel I'm well qualified by temperament and training. It's fascinating work." Moreover, when Fred proposes to Peggy in the concluding moments of the film, he does so entirely through the delineation of his lack ("You know what it'll be, don't you Peggy? It'll take us years to get anywhere. We'll have no money, no place to live. We'll have to work . . . be kicked around").

The Best Years of Our Lives ends with one marriage, and with the promise of another. However, those marriages do not have the usual metaphoric value; rather than affirming the cultural order, they further dramatize (and eroticize) male castration. Moreover, the two sets of lovers remain remarkably alone in the middle of this ostensibly social ceremony, an isolation which indicates their isolation not only from their families and neighbors, but from the dominant fiction.

When Homer slips the ring on Wilma's finger, and she lovingly places her hand on the cold metal of his hooks, the onlookers recoil from the severely denaturalized spectacle. The contact of flesh and steel evokes yet another crisis of vision, eliciting fear, anxiety, and pain. Al, standing in rear center frame, holds tightly onto Millie's arm, a gesture which attests not only to the tension in the room, but to the difficulties in his own marriage, and his barely contained desire to break the phallic contract.

In left frame another scopic exchange occurs, unwitnessed by anyone within the diegesis. Fred (in medium close-up) looks toward Peggy (in long shot), and she returns his gaze. This visual transaction resonates with the affect generated by the "main event"—a displacement motivated in part by Fred's proximity to Homer, and his status as best man, and in part by Peggy's (and the viewer's) knowledge that he too is marked by castration. Since Fred and Peggy effect their scopic reunion during the reading of the marriage vows, those vows also perform double duty, binding them together in anticipation of the kiss and the declaration of lack which are soon to follow.

Because they so closely approximate the reactions attributed by Freud to the male subject at the sight of the female genitals,[34] two kinds of critical response to *The Best Years of Our Lives* warrant attention here. One of these responses disavows the conspicuous display of male castration, insisting upon the film's conformity to the classic paradigm. Thus Roger Manvell argues (against a strong but unspecified opposition) that it "staunchly upholds the sacred stability of home and family, and even . . . of free enterprise and the virtues of big business,"[35] while Michael Wood characterizes it as "an evasive and cosy tale."[36] The other response acknowledges not only the film's negativity, but the concentration of that negativity at the site of male subjectivity. However, it defends itself against that unpleasurable spectacle through moral disapprobation—through a horror of the mutilated creatures who populate *The Best Years of Our Lives*. Kracauer, for instance, discovers in Wyler's film "a common man reluctant to heed the voice of reason and a liberal spokesman unable to run the emotional blockade around him."[37] Similarly Warshow writes that "the sexual relations of the characters form an unusually clear projection of the familiar Hollywood (and American) dream of male passivity. The men are inept, nervous, inarticulate, and childishly willful."[38]

Warshow's choice of the word "projection" is more than a little relevant to the present discussion, but his use of it runs completely counter to that which has been touched here, and which I have discussed at length elsewhere.[39] He associates projection with Hollywood's construction of the *male* rather than the *female* subject, and he identifies the former with qualities that are more conventionally identified with the latter. Furthermore, Warshow represents *The Best Years of Our Lives* as a typical example of Hollywood film, rather than as a text which breaks in certain key respects with the normative model. What this bizarre logic ultimately points toward is his recognition of the lack which continues to afflict classic cinema's male subject, despite the numerous projections and disavowals which are marshaled against that lack—a recognition forced upon him by *The Best Years of Our Lives*, and which he counters with a sweeping condemnation of Hollywood.

If there were space, I would discuss two other films from the war period, Henry Levin's *The Guilt of Janet Ames* (1947) and Frank Capra's *It's A Wonderful Life* (1946).[40] The first of these films calls upon the female spectator to look at the male subject with her "imagination" rather than her eyes—to disavow her knowledge of his lack, and to "make-believe" that the penis is the phallus. The second acknowledges not only male castration, but male masochism. Together, *The Best Years of Our Lives, The Guilt of Janet Ames,* and *It's A Wonderful Life* provide a powerful demonstration that the phallus is always the product of the dominant fiction, and that when that fiction proves incapable of mastering the stimulus of historical trauma, the male subject will no longer be able to find himself within its idealizing configuration. I have focused here upon Wyler's film not only because it inverts classic cinema's scopic regime (a regime which turns upon woman's castration), but because it openly eroticizes male lack. Moreover, unlike the other films with which it might be grouped, *The Best Years of Our Lives* makes no attempt to contain the negativity which it unleashes, nor does it at any point facilitate a phallic identification on the part either of its male characters or its male viewers. Something of "the inundation" or "cyclone" of the war is indeed "unfurled" there.

8

Motherhood and Representation: From Postwar Freudian Figurations to Postmodernism

E. Ann Kaplan

Freud's contribution in relation to the mother is his discovery of the mother in the unconscious. The phallocentric aspects of his theories are a problem for feminists, but this should not be confused with a second problem, namely the neo-Freudian collapsing of the level of the social (the historical mother) and the psychic (the mother in the unconscious). Helene Deutsch's theories of the woman psychically satisfied only in mothering buttressed images abounding in fiction and film of the saintly "angel" mother-figure; Karen Horney's study of maternal narcissism— i.e. of the mother's projecting onto the child her own unfulfilled desires, or of her use of the child to play out problems with her own mother, was reduced in the post-Freud period to notions of masculine identity and penis envy inhibiting successful mothering. Melanie Klein's important theory of the two internalized unconscious (imaginary) mothers arising from the child's experience at the breast was later literalized in the alternate "idealized" nurturing mother and the dominating "phallic" one that popular materials featured.[1]

Film is perhaps more guilty than other art forms of literalizing and reducing Freudian motherhood theory. But the desire to confine the mother within restricted pop-Freudian stereotypes is itself a symptom of the mother's increasing cultural threat in the post-war period. The 1940s arguably represent a transitional phase between a cultural motherhood role that prescribed a stern presence, and the Freudian "attentive" mother, whose image was to evoke the polar opposite, an hysterical "phallic" mother. If we compare a film like *Now Voyager* (Irving Rapper, 1942) with *Marnie* (Alfred Hitchcock, 1964) the change will be clear: significantly, however, we are talking about degrees of difference rather than substantive change. On some levels, *Now Voyager* and *Marnie* are only too similar in their representations of mother-daughter relations. But shifts in the cultural motherhood discourse resulting from the films' different historical contexts and cinematic genres produce significant alterations in emphasis and point of view.

In between *Now Voyager* and *Marnie* are the immediately post-World War II films—*The Locket* (John Brahm, 1946), *Secret Beyond the Door* (Fritz Lang, 1948), *The Snake Pit* (Anatole Litvak, 1948)—where the evil mother has less prominence or where the stress is not so much on the mother's specific damage to the child's psyche. We can see these films, however, as marking the first impact of women's move into the work force during the war. The increased level of women's threat to returning veterans began to stimulate a deeper kind of reaction for which Freud's theories became a convenient conduit.

It is then the uses of the newly popularized Freudian discourse that I will analyze in looking first at *Now Voyager*. I will argue for its status as a text transitional between a cultural-role focus on the mother and later "hysterical" texts like Hitchcock's *Marnie*. *Now Voyager* arguably still works with the 19th-century concept of the mother as educator, teacher, purveyor of Christian moral values, but it combines this stance with the new Freudian awareness of oedipality and of the psychic damage that mothers may inflict. Because Freudian theory is only just being assimilated culturally, the text does not yet *embody* the level of the psychoanalytic; it rather *uses* psychoanalysis as a narrative discourse, as a means for producing character-change and explaining mother-daughter interactions. Generically a "woman's melodrama," the text asks the spectator to identify with, and to appreciate, the daughter Charlotte Vale's development to maturity and autonomy—her triumphing over her oppressive mother.

Marnie rejects this cognitive-constructive level and rather positions the spectator between identifying with the heroine's terrifying mother-related neurosis and the hero's self-confident analysis and mastery of Marnie's neurosis (a "mastery" also of both Marnie and her mother). Although the film also pays lip service to a popularized Freudian discourse in its analysis of the mother's impact on the girl-child, the text has more to do with a deeper level of reaction to the mother described by Julia Kristeva in *Powers of Horror*. Generically a thriller of sorts, *Marnie* speaks mainly from the patriarchal position.

Most analyses of *Now Voyager* focus, naturally enough, on the heroine, Charlotte Vale, played by Bette Davis. While there are issues relevant to mother images in the Bette Davis figure, Mrs. Vale, Charlotte's mother (Gladys Young), is more pertinent to my immediate concerns since she exemplifies the negative (possessive, controlling) pole of the split-mother in the popularized Freudian discourse of the time. Charlotte herself comes to embody the other "positive" mother-pole in her self-denying nurturing of her lover's child, Tina. In this way, the film sets up the mother-duality (phallic/angelic) of Freudian theory that was not evident in earlier films.

In the first part, the text (relying on psychoanalysis as a discourse) presents as "true" the notion of the possessive mother as unmediated cause of her daughter, Charlotte's, mental illness. The representation of Mrs. Vale in the opening sequence mimics one of Karen Horney's "masculine" mothers, suffering from penis envy and an unconscious overattachment to her daughter. Her figure is harsh, rigid, severe; her hair is scraped back from her face, highlighting the long thin nose and high cheekbones, while her dress is pulled tightly up to the neck. Her loud, dominating voice with its sharp, clipped tone seals the image of a non-nurturing, unyielding mother-figure, far from the idealized patriarchal feminine.

The confrontation with the psychiatrist, Dr. Jaquith (Claude Rains, as one of a long line of such Hollywood figures to follow[2]), who has been called in by her sister-in-law to help Charlotte, merely authorizes the "reading" of Mrs. Vale for the spectator: Jaquith quickly makes a bond with Charlotte and turns his "medical" gaze onto Mrs. Vale as well; only now this gaze is thoroughly negative: "If you had deliberately and maliciously planned to destroy your daughter's life, you couldn't have done it more completely," he tells her. This statement supports images provided the spectator in a flashback sequence to a shipboard romance Charlotte had when on vacation with her mother. Mrs. Vale's icy manner and unrelenting demands on Charlotte climax in her brutal severing of Charlotte's affair with a petty officer.

Unlike Charlotte, Mrs. Vale refuses to surrender to Dr. Jaquith and to accept his power to help and cure her daughter. For this refusal, she must be punished, just as, in a parallel move, Charlotte will flourish because of her submission to Dr. Jaquith, her entry into the (repressed) erotic relationship that will act as a lever to pry her from her mother. It is only through the text's dehumanization of Mrs. Vale—its refusal of any sympathy or sensitivity to her subjectivity, her unconscious, her history/memory—that the text makes possible Charlotte's "freedom." The text insists on the central relationships being those of Charlotte and the surrogate fathers (the psychiatrist, the lovers); only by punishing Mrs. Vale sadistically, and forcing the spectator to hate her, can the narrative pry Charlotte and her mother apart, sever the mother-daughter bonding.

As in Freud's famous case history of Dora, the mother becomes not an entity to be *worked through* in the "proper" psychoanalytic sense, but rather a figure in the background who is dismissed as an object, positioned as an obstacle that must be gotten around rather than as part of a central and dual relationship.

Here we see how psychoanalysis is used as a discourse to repress any feminine that refuses to submit to patriarchal law. For, reading against the grain of the film, we could hypothesize that Mrs. Vale's oppressive behavior arises, in the first place, from her own oppressive positioning in patriarchy. In accord with Monique Plaza's analysis, her possessiveness could be seen as her only way of getting something for herself; her distaste for the patriarchal feminine (and her desire to keep Charlotte away from it) may have legitimacy, given Mrs. Vale's possible knowledge of its oppressive function.[3] The text itself, however, cannot see Mrs. Vale's behavior in this manner, and is not interested in its origins. It is precisely such constraints that enable us to see the force of patriarchal law, even in films made for the female spectator and focusing on women's issues.

To this extent, *Now Voyager* would seem to address the popularized Freudian type of mother. Mrs. Vale's possessive, controlling behavior serves as a displacement for social anxiety at the very moment (1942) when America's entry into the War entailed women's entry into the work force in large numbers. The fear of the mother that such a social situation re-evokes (i.e. the mother's power spilling out into the public sphere, not safely confined within the home) on the unconscious level feeds into the production of the hated, controlling figure. Further, for a short space during the opening sequence, the film touches on deeper psychoanalytic (even Lacanian) levels, showing Mrs. Vale as a mother who tries to keep her daughter down with her in the Imaginary—who refuses to release her child into the patriarchal Symbolic. In the first scene, Charlotte, although technically adult, barely has access to language, especially when in the presence of her overpowering mother. The psychiatrist's role is to represent the Third Term (the Father, the Law) that has to come between mother and daughter. This achieved, Charlotte is able to separate and to form an adult sexual relationship of her own.

It is significant that *Now Voyager* represses any attention to the mother's, Mrs. Vale's, experience of the releasing of Charlotte into the patriarchal Symbolic. This betrays the patriarchal bias of the film: Instead of exploring the pathos of our human condition (that the separation from the mother is necessary)—something that Kristeva and other French feminists in particular have begun to explore—the text behaves sadistically toward Mrs. Vale, acting out a childlike hatred rather than empathizing with both parties in the dyad.

It is precisely the refusal to address the poignancy of Mrs. Vale's (and any mother's) position which allows us to see that patriarchal fear of the mother remains; this suggests an arrested desire for the mother—a desire for subjection to her masked as fear. At the start particularly, the film speaks from a position of incomplete entry into the Symbolic, which, if smoothly accomplished, should eliminate any need to fear the mother.

But the film does not continue to function on this level: it quickly accomplishes Charlotte's separation from her mother, and works to distance not only the mother but the psychoanalytic terrain: first, the film uses the Freudian discourse to "psychoanalyze" the prior 19th-century "stern" mother, showing the negative aspects of this sort of command over the child. In this way, the text positions the mother safely for us: it explains her behavior as wrong and as deserving the punishment it gets.

Second, since it is a woman's melodrama, the film situates itself in Charlotte's point of view and grants her increasing subjectivity (in the sense of controlling the narrative, making things happen and forming her own decisions). The film allows us to follow Charlotte's triumph over her mother through her increasing autonomy. We see Charlotte overcoming her fears, and achieving a degree of independence with the help of the various male "fathers" referred to. The fearsome mother is reduced to a whining, bedridden, almost comic object. And meanwhile the text replaces her outmoded mothering with Charlotte's new, self-consciously Freudian "attentive" surrogate mothering, which has positive and "strong" aspects to it.

Nevertheless, this mothering involves (as required in the paradigm) personal sacrifices in that Charlotte cannot have both the child and the man she loves: in this way, if Charlotte can be seen as maturing into an increasingly self-reliant woman,[4] it is important to note that it is a "maturing" into a predictable patriarchal feminine which exposes the absence of any alternate tradition or perspective with which to identify. The film does however raise the problem of female independence—it allows us perhaps to glimpse its parameters, its constraints—in a way quite impossible in a film like *Marnie*.

Here, *Now Voyager* follows the conventions of most women's melodramas: these films allow exploration of women's desires, wishes, and conflicts, and often involve a struggle between the male and the female discourse, as here Charlotte contests the discourses of all three men in her life to some degree. (The struggle between mother and daughter, however, involves a patriarchal construction of these relations and thus functions on a more complicit level). But while these narrative aspects provide some satisfaction to the female viewer, narrative resolutions usually insist on the woman being positioned as subservient to the male. *Now Voyager* provides Charlotte with slightly more autonomy than usual, but her desires are still conventionally patriarchal.

Now Voyager is, then, a transitional film in that it keeps fear about the mother under control through its "analysis" and "placing" of her, and through introducing Charlotte as a counterbalancing figure. This ability to control fears about the mother is increasingly rare in the next two decades, when films manifest what can only be described as a kind of hysteria in relation to the phallic mother.

Hysteria about the mother—evident in the "monstrous" mother image—

was perhaps foreshadowed already in a book written in the same year that *Now Voyager* was released, namely Phillip Wylie's *Generation of Vipers*. Wylie's book betrays the sort of slippage from the unconscious to the social mother that prevails in Hollywood images: that is, he purports to be writing about the social scene (just as films *pretend* to be mimicking "reality"), when the book's language indicates the transferring of unconscious hostility to the mother into a generalized depiction of a *social* mother-figure. Although Wylie is remembered as the one to conceptualize "momism," the virulence of his attack may be forgotten.[5]

But obviously, Wylie's legitimate social anxiety is confused with a deeper cultural problem regarding the mother—perhaps the dread of her body that Horney discussed already in 1932,[6] or what Kristeva has called the "abject" associated with the mother. Kristeva's theory of the abject illuminates the kind of horror toward the mother that we find in Hitchcock—and particularly his 1964 film *Marnie*—by delineating the place that the mother occupies in patriarchal culture as that which "disturbs identity, system, order. What does not respect borders, positions, rules. The in-between, the ambiguous, the composite."[7]

Kristeva links the phenomenon of abject being to "our earliest attempts to release the hold of *maternal* entity even before ex-isting outside of her" (p. 13). The mother becomes for the child the realm of the abject that must constantly be struggled against through identification with the Father in the Symbolic. Kristeva notes that one can hardly expect the mother to help the child "become authentic and autonomous in its turn," given her own problems with the phallus that her husband represents (p. 13). Important for my project here is Kristeva's noting that the breaking away from the maternal (the abject) is violent and clumsy "with the constant risk of falling back under the sway of a power as securing as it is stifling" (p. 13).

The mother, then, becomes a sort of phobic object: A form of the abject, the phobic object has to do with uncertainty over boundaries ("all the more determining as the paternal function was weak or even nonexistent," p. 63), and with the tenuousness of the symbolic. The cross-cultural importance of the mother, socially and symbolically, results in the need to separate the sexes (a need which is often expressed through rituals of defilement); this means giving men rights over women (p. 70). But the very victorious masculine, Kristeva notes, "confesses through its very relentlessness against the other, the feminine, that it is threatened by an asymmetrical, irrational, wily, uncontrollable power. . . . That other sex, the feminine, becomes synonymous with a radical evil that is to be suppressed" (p. 70).

In addition to this already awesome fear of the mother, the mother is the authority that maps out the bodily areas and impresses "differentiation of proper-clean and improper-dirty, possible and impossible . . ." (p. 72). Kristeva importantly distinguishes this "maternal authority" of bodily "mapping" from the paternal laws, within which, "with the phallic phase and acquisition of language, the destiny of man will take shape" (p. 72). It is precisely this repressed maternal authority from the pre-oedipal, early moment, that is responsible for the culturally pervasive, and for Kristeva, universal, phenomenon of the mother as "abject" (p. 68).

Kristeva's analysis moves far beyond the classical Freudian formulations found in theorists like Deutsch and Horney; nevertheless, these formulations are important not only because of the use that Hollywood made of them in the war and post-World War II period, but because of their continued use to conceal the deeper horror to do with the abject. In other words, Freudian psychoanalysis, as a discourse, was a means through which culture attempted to articulate and defray the fears regarding the abject maternal. The angel and evil mother paradigms that pop-Freudianism articulated were an easy and useful tool for representing deep unconscious fears of falling back into the horror of the mother's being, where boundaries are elided.

I will argue that this pull toward the abject maternal underlies representations of the mother in film; it cannot be made conscious yet constantly threatens the subject. Perhaps Luce Irigaray describes this pull in her haunting essay "This Sex Which Is Not One"; and it is the horror of the abject maternal that perhaps accounts for the "monstrous" mother image so prevalent in Hollywood melodramas like Marnie.

The comparison with Now Voyager interestingly exposes the new hysteria toward the mother evident in the genre differences between the films. Now Voyager, as we saw, was a woman's melodrama, the form explicitly addressing the female spectator and permitting the insertion of female subjectivity in however tenuous a form. Marnie significantly legitimates the horror that it is dealing with by situating itself partly within the thriller genre that is associated with the male look. In fact, the film intermixes the stuff of melodrama (Marnie's family history) with the thriller (Marnie as the criminal whose deeds must be investigated) so as to permit a patriarchal investigation into the very mystery of woman herself. The film then, unlike the woman's melodrama, speaks from the male position, very much as does most film noir. (Indeed, the intermixture of melodrama and thriller evokes Mildred Pierce [Michael Curtiz, 1945] and The Blue Gardenia [Fritz Lang, 1953][8].)

In Marnie, the real horror displaced into the thriller genre is produced by Kristeva's "phobic object" which in turn (as noted above) involves early pulsations in the mother-child relationship. One could see the film as constructed precisely as an attempt to articulate and then control the terror of the mother via a clever narrative structure. That is, the actual experience of terror/love in relation to the mother (that duality whereby the child at once desires the mother *and* fears being swamped by the dual relationship which risks, in Kristeva's words, "the loss not of a part [castration] but of the totality of his living being" [p. 64]) is (as in *Now Voyager*) located in the figure of the heroine, not the hero. Here, however, the film dwells far longer on the daughter's hysterical, panic reaction to her mother. Whereas the institution of psychoanalysis quickly "saves" the daughter from the mother in *Now Voyager*, in *Marnie* this "saving" constitutes the film's *aporia*, its climax and resolution.

Marnie's (Tippi Hedren) relationship to her mother, Mrs. Edgar (Louise Latham), is then the one that involves terror/love; Mark Rutland's (Sean Connery) mother is, usefully, dead, and he is fully in control of his relationship with his father. In this way, the depiction of the mother as abject does not implicate the hero. On the contrary, the hero appropriates the role of the Law/the Father/the Symbolic—the sphere through which the mother can be overcome, or in which such a conquest can *appear* to have been made. Indeed, Rutland's function, like that of Jaquith in the earlier film, is to exorcise the heroine's terror of the mother. But, unlike *Now Voyager*, Mrs. Edgar is never actually controlled or rendered harmless as is Mrs. Vale: in the climactic final scene, *Marnie* still longs for her mother, still wants something from her (perhaps the illusory oneness?), and is still refused. The spectator is denied the satisfaction of the mother's emotional acceptance of Marnie; Marnie has rather to be pulled brutally away from the mother by Mark Rutland. His tool, the *discourse* of psychoanalysis, has not "worked" for Marnie, as it did so easily and smoothly for Charlotte Vale. Mrs. Edgar resists *total* control—something excess remains, and it is the threat of that excess that brings Mark to drag Marnie away brusquely.

In terms of *genre*, the film's combination of the woman's melodrama and the thriller, is, like the psychoanalytic discourse, a device that attempts to erase the trouble that the mother causes in the narrative. For the introduction of the thriller plot into the melodrama usually results in the repression of the female discourse and of female subjectivity; it legitimizes the ultimate control of the narrative by a male protagonist, who is responsible for unraveling the mystery, which, as noted above, turns out to be the mystery of Woman herself. It is through assuming the function of investigator of both Marnie and her mother—through his interference in their relationship—that the two women are finally brought under Rutland's control: or, more accurately, the device brings Marnie under his control, and ensures Marnie's separation from her mother; but the mother as noted is not entirely defeated.

The cinematic devices used in relation to Mrs. Edgar indicate that the text itself is working on a primal level in relation to her figure. She is an unattractive, awesome, and negative presence from the start—the deliberate antithesis, it would seem, to any dominant ideal-mother code. And yet she does not fall neatly into the usual mythic opposite of the "evil" or "possessive" mother like Mrs. Vale; or, in Hitchcock's own *oeuvre,* the surrogate-mother figure Mrs. Danvers (Judith Anderson) in *Rebecca* (1940). Rather, she occupies some other terrain—more mysterious, more ambiguous and contradictory. The spectator is torn between hatred toward her, for her rejection of Marnie who adores her, and pity for her: this pity emerges once we understand her tragic life, her taking upon herself the murder Marnie accidentally committed as a child, and— on some level—her love for Marnie. And it leaves us confused as to how we are to position her—it means that the question about the mother is never satisfactorily resolved, never quite closed.

We experience Mrs. Edgar through Marnie's consciousness (including her unconscious dream images). Marnie's recurring dream and daytime hallucination (set off whenever she sees the color red) revolves around the traumatic, primal scene of her mother's lovemaking with a sailor, which the child innocently interrupts when a thunderstorm frightens her; the drunken sailor begins to fondle the child, and the mother, taking it for rape, beats him with a poker. When the mother is overcome, Marnie picks up the poker to protect her, and the sailor dies of the child's blows.

The beloved mother is, then, associated with primal terror, sex, blood, and death. And the text itself takes Marnie's stance toward her: the screen is suffused with red whenever Marnie has her hallucination; the mother's image is sinister—backlit, silhouetted and shot from a low angle; the eery, rhythmic banging in Marnie's dreams always refers to the walking stick which represents her "castration" in the fight with the sailor (literally, her leg was broken and never properly healed).

At the same time, Marnie loves her mother with a pathetic, slave-like longing that betrays her uncertainty about boundaries and that exposes the tenuousness of the Symbolic which precisely strives to establish clear boundaries. The tenuousness of the Symbolic is underscored in another frequently posited binary opposition in the film—that between "nature" and "civilization." Rutland, a parttime zoologist, is attracted to Marnie precisely because she represents the wild animal in the jungle that always threatens to overcome society. (This analogy is made literal in the scene in Rutland's office when the thunderstorm brings on one of Marnie's hallucinations and transforms the place into a temporary "jungle.")

It is this danger of lack of boundaries that Mark Rutland eradicates through his use of a popularized Freudian discourse. Rutland, on the one hand, acts like the zoologist with a wild animal, hunting Marnie down, following her tracks until he captures her; on the other, he reads psychoanalytic books, like *Sexual Aberrations of the Criminal Female.* He interrogates Marnie in the manner of the psychoanalyst searching for psychic clues to her disorder, piecing together bits of the puzzle: and he is not above betraying his word in the service of unlocking Marnie's enigma. This is most brutally clear in Mark's forcing himself sexually on Marnie during the boat trip, after having promised not to, apparently with a view to finding out what her "sexual aberrations" are (he knows she is a criminal!). The result, far from "unlocking" anything, it seems, is Marnie's suicide attempt.

Marnie does resist Mark's efforts to control her, but all her attempts seem only to increase his determination to gain her subjugation. For instance, after one of Mark's attempts at psychoanalyzing her, Marnie aptly (and ironically) notes: "You Freud, me Jane?" But these gestures fail to hold Mark at bay: indeed, shortly after this comment, Mark manages to bring Marnie to such a pitch of anxiety that she tells him about the killing of the sailor. As a result, Mark locates the mother as the "criminal" who has "ruined" Marnie. In order to "free" Marnie of her, Rutland orchestrates a confrontation, under his supportive, analyst presence. Rutland is waiting in the wings to "possess" Marnie, once the mother is dislodged from her dangerously close position. He thereby restores a patriarchal order that Marnie had severely challenged.

The film works with a simplistic and reductive Freudian scheme of revelation of the "trauma" followed by the instant "catharsis" and "cure"—a pattern familiar from many Hollywood films of the post-war period. Once again, the psychoanalytic discourse simplifies and refuses any understanding of the mother-daughter relationship in all its pathos and difficulty—for the mother as well as the child.[9] It brings under control the dangerously independent stance of both mother and daughter, who articulate hatred of men, who despise sex, and who want to live without men. Indeed, as we saw, Marnie defends herself well against Rutland's controlling attempts, until he finally brings on her neurotic panic and elicits her cry for help. Theoretically, had Mrs. Edgar been able to return Marnie's love openly (she loves her child but cannot express it, for reasons that remain unclear[10]), the two might have formed a unit unto themselves. The potential for this is enough to cause "trouble" in the film that must be eradicated: it is an option that is interestingly also refused in *Now Voyager*, but within a different configuration. There, it is Charlotte's love for Jerry (Paul Henreid) that remains unfulfilled: she and Tina do not constitute a threat because the *child* is not what Charlotte *really* wants: she substitutes for Jerry. But Marnie does want her mother, and it is this desire that the film wrenches away from her.

Marnie's terror has to do with her fear of losing her mother—either through sex with a man, through her being hurt by a man, or through not being lovable herself. Her terror is linked to desperate need of the mother on a primal level that precedes the entry into language. The historical

Hitchcock's own experience with this sort of fear (mentioned by Donald Spoto in his biography of the film director) is merely one example of something that is culturally pervasive.[11]

Kristeva's question, "What is it about this representation (of the patriarchal or Christian Maternal) that fails to take account of what a woman might say or want of the Maternal?," suggests the gap between lived mothering and the Symbolic order. Let me briefly focus on this gap, moving then from discussion of the mother in the unconscious to the historical mother who "lives" mothering. This shift is problematic since above all I want to avoid the collapsing of the psychic and the social that has caused theoretical confusion. I believe that lived mothering, like history, is non-representable: my discussion then aims not to represent *the mother-subject* but to tease out contemporary discourses about her. I hypothesize a subject caught in the middle of contradictory discourses.

Let me begin by pointing to some important changes in the gap between the non-representable level of lived mothering and the mother in the Symbolic in recent years. Indeed, in the postmodern era, we might well ask how relevant Kristeva's question still is. Jean Baudrillard has speculated that "The Faustian, Promethean (perhaps Oedipal) period of production and consumption" has given way to "the narcissistic and protean era of connections, contact, contiguity, feedback and generalized interface that goes with the universe of communication."[12] If he is right (or if he were to be right by the year 2000), what implications does this have for the mother on the levels of both (a posited) lived experience and the Symbolic? Hitchcock's 1960s films (like *Marnie*) embodied motherhood discourses from earlier generations—but weren't they being articulated in their most extreme form at the very moment when their relevance was being eroded by the new high-tech industrial developments?

One of the characteristics of the postmodern moment is the proliferation of subject positions that historical individuals occupy. Whereas in earlier eras, the sound-image "woman" was more or less congruent with "mother" (the only other possibility was "whore"), now things are far more complex. If we accept the visions of Arthur Kroker and David Cook, indeed, gender will no longer be the problem per se: both men and women become victims in an era in which the human body of either kind is no longer adequate to technological speed and sophistication.[13] Women's bodies are again being appropriated, this time by new reproductive technologies,[13] and the whole concept and practice of mothering is being revolutionized in the process. As Shulamith Firestone predicted long ago, reproduction will eventually be mechanized, rendering biological motherhood obsolete. What happens to psychoanalytic processes in such a situation?

Obviously, American culture is not yet at such a point, and thus the question does not have to be answered now; the unconscious is still very much with us, but things are changing. The complexity of the contemporary situation arises in part because new motherhood discourses (the result of feminism and other sixties liberation movements—gay and minority liberation, the sexual "revolution") and their accompanying technologies (test-tube babies, surrogate mothering, in-vitro fertilization, gene manipulation) enter into a culture already laden with the older myths represented in *Now Voyager* and *Marnie*. The new discourses do not overnight sweep aside the old order of things, or found a totally new motherhood-language, but rather cause a disruption and dislocation. What we then have today is a scene of struggle between opposing concepts with often bitter, hostile, and violent results.

Technologies have been developing in such an accelerated manner that culture seems unable to keep up. Historical women are faced with a plethora of often conflicting mother images in the mass media, from the new "Super-Mom" and "Executive-Mother," to the newly redeemed stay-at-home mother, to the bravely independent or selfish childless woman.

While television Soaps and Serials have for some years been constructing narratives that include mothering "problems," there has been little real exploration of the deep, underlying cultural dilemmas that motherhood involves on both an economic/social/institutional level and on the psychoanalytic one. Hollywood mother images betray a bewildering series of contradictory images, if we consider films over the past twenty years. There was the late seventies *Unmarried Woman* (Paul Mazursky, 1978) cycle that at least dealt with the new increase in divorce and the resulting problems for the middle-aged mother; there was the reactive *Kramer vs. Kramer* (Robert Benton, 1979) cycle in the early eighties, that figured the new nurturing father (all to the good) but at the expense of the now masculinized career-crazy mother; there was the *Frances* (Graeme Clifford, 1982)/*Mommie Dearest* (Frank Perry, 1981) cycle a bit later on that showed a deeper reaction to the Woman's Movement in its reversion to the "monstrous" mother who had been eclipsed in the later sixties and seventies; and finally, there has been a second "opening up" (parallel to that in the late seventies) to narratives of contemporary mothering dilemmas in films such as *Terms of Endearment* (James Brooks, 1983), *Heartburn* (Mike Nichols, 1986), and *Baby Boom* (Charles Shyer, 1988).[14]

Extremely complicated adjustments are evidently being made on the Symbolic level in response to women's finally declared irreversible move from the domestic to the public sphere—a move that has been going on since the turn of the century. While from a consumerist point of view this move is being welcomed (women wage-earners at the new high levels are clearly a rich source of markets, and advertisements therefore depict no trouble in the new roles), things are obviously more complex on the deeper cultural levels.

The complexities of the current situation, however, suggest the need for a new theoretical paradigm. We are arguably confronting a post-feminist historical moment, i.e. a moment in which prior feminist interventions, having had their effects, can no longer be undertaken in the old ways. For the various feminist discourses, as developed from 1960 to 1980, are partly responsible for the current changes in women's actual institutional situations. Capitalism has also found ways to co-opt, integrate, and thereby subtly reverse the very discourses that have benefitted women, thus putting those discourses into question.

If post-structuralist feminism demonstrated the need to analyze the language order through which we learn to be what our culture calls "women" as against "men," as we sought to bring about change, now we need to re-evaluate the usefulness of "feminist" as a concept since it has been appropriated by dominant consumerist culture. "Feminism" may be seen as an essentializing term that looks back to the individualist frameworks of early feminist positions and that may no longer serve in the postmodern era. The concept of an oppositional cultural stance like feminism becomes more and more difficult once society's *rhetoric* has integrated what were earlier feminist demands.

For instance, in 1986, a lot of fuss was still made about Mother's Day, although there was a significant alteration in mother images in ads for presents: instead of household goods, as before, ads suggested sexy nightgowns and dresses, or glamorous perfume as presents—objects that were previously only linked to pre-marital romance. We had evidently by then won the right to be a "mother" and to be "sexy." In 1987, however, the whole "Mother's Day" business was muted: there were few ads at all. Women appeared to have won the right not to be pigeon-holed as "mothers."

What does this all mean? While some feminists are arguing that the mother should begin to represent herself, many historical mothers are rather trying to avoid the category altogether. This latter effort betrays the inadequacy of our social institutions to the new developments. For America retains the 19th-century nuclear family as its predominant concept for child-rearing, despite the fact that the social roles and the division of labor that such a family entailed no longer routinely apply. Technology combined with the new liberation movements have made possible forms of relating that move far beyond the traditional nuclear family.

It is largely women who bear the brunt of the gaps and imbalances on the daily level. A few men are now rearing their children from birth, and certainly men are sharing in child-rearing tasks in an unprecedented fashion. Women who combine mothering and career continue to feel that they do neither job adequately. So many mothers regularly work that categories have become confused—a confusion most extreme in the middle classes and in intellectuals and artists.

Lower-class women have been forced to work since the first industrial revolution, but, due to the type of work—usually manual labor of some kind—there was little identity confusion (i.e. a working-class wife/mother would continue to locate her main self-concept in those roles rather than in her piece-work at the factory). As middle-class women have begun to enter the professions in the wake of the sixties movements, and as women intellectuals and artists have increasingly begun to make scholarship and artistic creation their main goals in life, so for the historical female subject it has become more and more difficult (and perhaps undesirable) to develop and retain an identity as "mother."

On the level of cultural constructs, child-care discourses continue to be contradictory, some still claiming that the young child's psychic needs call for a constant, reassuring *maternal* presence if the child is to develop a sense of security and a stable identity. Recent debates about the effects of day-care centers on children include data that show very early day care may have harmful psychic results.[15] This data can be used to improve day care, but it can also encourage the old habit of "blaming the mother."

In filmic representations, if the myth of the "angel-in-the-house" and her corollary "phallic" opposite no longer prevail, we have an equally disturbing recoiling from the obscenity of biological mothering (as may be found, for example, in a film like *Aliens* [James Cameron, 1986]), that dove-tails with the notion of the "clean machine" which will one day produce babies without all the offensive, female biological messiness.

Meanwhile, there is evidence that the mother in the unconscious (the Imaginary mother) persists: psychically, the mother still never satisfies, the phallus is still longed for. Young mothers do not want to be identified with the construct "mother,"[16] and express even more hostility toward their own mothers.

What can motherhood mean in the post-feminist, postmodern era? As its specificity wanes in the light of women's new, multiple social roles, are motherhood's traditional qualities also waning? Is this beneficial or harmful? Can we have a society that bases itself on healthy nurturing values (as Charlotte Perkins Gilman envisaged in *Herland* [1915]) while at the same time freeing individual historical female subjects from the burden of representing the nurturing mode? Is there a crisis in the area of nurturing in general in the sense that no one wants to undertake that role now that women are no longer mandated to do so? Can we alter social organization to deal with the changed attitude toward nurturing?

Further, is it useful to encourage women to release their repressed aggression and hatred?[17] Is this merely a predictable antithesis to the constraints of nurturing and self-sacrifice so long forced on women rather than a thought-out strategy for moving forward? Shouldn't we rather be insisting that *society* undertake the responsibility for nurturing the young since individual parents no longer seem to take pleasure in that role?

The call for women to express hatred and aggression is bound up with the postmodern era and with fundamental alterations in the motherhood discourse. As developed by Fredric Jameson and Jean Baudrillard, the postmodern involves the blurring of hitherto sacrosanct boundaries and polarities, the elimination of any position from which to speak, the reduction of all to one level, often seen as that of the *simulacra*. American capitalism, in this view, in its desperate search for ever new markets and its uncanny ability to co-opt subversive discourses, has incorporated many that were oppositional in the sixties, into dominant ones, blurring distinctions. If Rousseau can be seen as initiating the first modern motherhood (moral, social) discourse in the 18th century; and Freud the second motherhood discourse (the mother in the unconscious) in the 19th century; is the late 20th century witnessing the demise of both forms of motherhood discourse? If so, who is it that desires the end of the discourse? Women? Capitalism?

Motherhood is perhaps a victim of capitalism's postmodern attempt to blame women for not nurturing while it develops reproductive technologies that complicate the biological mother-child relation and keep women in the labor force (viz, surrogacy). Capitalism thus can exploit woman as worker and consumer while bemoaning her absence from the home. The "crisis in mothering" may be a patriarchal construction to deflect attention from the economic, political, and cultural ills no one knows how to cure. Once again, as in Wylie's hysterical text, "Mother" (just because of its unconscious power, its emotional pull) is the sign around which to mobilize discontents whose origins may in fact lie elsewhere. And meanwhile, what *woman* may want of the maternal remains unknown—or is it merely still unspoken?

9

Couching Resistance: Women, Film, and Postwar Psychoanalytic Psychiatry

Janet Walker

Juliet Mitchell's defense of Freudian psychoanalytic theory for feminism (*Psycho-Analysis and Feminism,* 1974) and the large body of psychoanalytically informed feminist textual analyses of film notwithstanding, the question of the legitimacy of psychoanalytic ideas for feminist study is still subject to debate.[1] In fact many of the aforementioned textual analyses of film have integrated the very debate itself into their psychoanalytic methodology, so that the analytical work proceeds self-consciously through a critique of psychoanalysis' own limitations or contradictions to illuminate the corresponding contradictions of its textual object. The debate, then, does not seem one that should be resolved as much as one that should be pursued, "worked through" perhaps but not "worked out." Here I would like to approach the question of the legitimacy of psychoanalytic theory for feminist inquiry not so much by way of a psychoanalytically informed textual reading, but by way of psychoanalytic history and its filmic representation.[2]

The period from World War II to the mid-1960s defines the social historical crux of the relationship between women and psychiatry[3] precisely because it is the most suspect from a feminist perspective. Two landmark books, *The Feminine Mystique* (1963) by Betty Friedan and *Women and Madness* (1972) by Phyllis Chesler, are in large part responsible for this indictment of an age, having disseminated the view that post-World War II American psychoanalytic and psychiatric practices served as agencies of women's adjustment to stereotypically conceived roles prescribed by society.[4] And here even Juliet Mitchell would agree, having based her defense of Freudian psychoanalytic theory for feminism and feminist textual study precisely on its distinction from American "pseudopsychoanalysis" which she regards as having "done much to re-adapt discontented women to a conservative feminine status quo, to an inferiorized psychology and to a contentment with serving and servicing men and children."[5] Nevertheless, while trying not to minimize the significance of American psychiatry's oppression of women (indeed part of my project here is to bring to light further evidence of that oppression), I would submit that American psychiatry stood in this period as an institution whose internal debates opened profound contradictions with regard to the adjustment of deviant women, and that the path of these contradictions may be followed into textual activity.

The second part of this article, then, will examine the recirculation of American psychiatry's contradictory impulses, "adjustment" and "resistance," in two Hollywood films thematically concerned with the relationship between psychoanalytic ideas and practice and mental illness in women: *The Three Faces of Eve* (Nunnally Johnson, 1957) and *Tender is the Night* (Henry King, 1962).[6] While on one hand, these films depict psychiatrists leading deviant women back to the path of "normal femininity," reaffirming in filmic terms the status of psychiatry as a guarantor of psycho-sexual and narrative adjustment,[7] they also employ psychoanalytic ideas to *resist* the totalizing tendency of the adjustment impulse. Thus, a rhetoric of resistance is established, a rhetoric motivated by the wider and quite complicated cultural context of women and psychiatry.

If psychoanalytically informed textual analyses of Hollywood cinema in general tend to bring out its characteristic contradictions, my project here is to specify certain of those contradictions, notably those residing in the filmic representation of the relations between women and American psychiatry from World War II through the mid-1960s. And, following a kind of Foucauldian logic which assumes that social institutions and cultural practices are both articulated through (albeit different) discursive formations, I will attempt to read the passage of these contradictions back and forth from social historical to filmic texts.[8]

Psychiatric Adjustment and Resistance

> There is *no* vagueness about the goals, functions, and needs of the normal woman. Science in recent years has thrown a bright light on her, and that is why we can be certain of many fundamental details about her.—Marie N. Robinson, M.D., *The Power of Sexual Surrender* (1959)

As a psychiatric term, adjustment is defined as the "functional, often transitory, alteration or accommodation by which one can adapt himself better to the immediate environment."[9] As a feminist term, this word implies the imposition of socially legislated behavior on a reluctant person

by an authority figure so that feminine adjustment becomes a process of
gender normalization. While not to be conflated, the two meanings are
related. It is precisely that shift from supposedly objective benevolent
science to the imposition of partisan interest which is at stake in this
interpretation of postwar American psychiatry's adjustment of women.

The treatment during World War II of "emotional stress of the war,"
"combat fatigue," and neurotic recruits catapulted Army psychiatry to
professional and popular heights. The search for the *cause* of these ills
led to renewed attention to the psychology of women—as the mothers of
neurotic recruits. The rise of psychiatry in the post-World War II period,
then, was every bit as dependent on the figuration of the patient-mother
(in both senses of the word patient: she who is ill and she who waits for
the return of her soldier husband or son and later for her breadwinner
husband) as on the illness of draftees. A chapter in William Menninger's
Psychiatry in a Troubled World: Yesterday's War and Today's Challenge
(1948), where Menninger noted that the postwar family was in crisis
and argued that the importance of the "healthy, happy home life" was
immeasurable, evidences psychiatry's new concentration on home, family, parents, and hence, on mothers.[10]

While Menninger did not blame women or proscribe women's work
outside the home,[11] two best-selling popular books did: psychiatrist Edward Strecker's *Their Mother's Sons* (1946); and *Modern Women: The
Lost Sex* (1947), by Ferdinand Lundberg, a sociologist, and Marynia
Farnham, a psychoanalyst.[12] Strecker, and Lundberg and Farnham all
found women to be *neurotic,* which was for them synonymous with being
maladjusted. Furthermore, they argued that, as neurotics, women were
consequently carriers and *disseminators* of neurosis. These books illustrate
the way the original call to *study* the mother-child relationship, of which
Menninger's work is an example, gets shifted, in popular literature (and
in some, though not all, professional literature), to a justification for
reducing the advised role of the woman to exclusive maternity.[13]

In the United States at this time virtually all practicing psychoanalysts
were required to be medical doctors, psychoanalysis was the theoretical
core of psychiatric residency training, and 82% of the members of the
American Psychoanalytic Association were also members of the American
Psychiatric Association.[14] Reflecting this thorough imbrication, one prominent historian dubbed his subject American "psychoanalytic psychiatry."[15] It is not surprising, then, that the adjustment orientation of American psychiatry may also be located in American psychoanalysis. For
example, psychoanalyst Franz Alexander advocated what he called "supportive procedures," meaning a kind of therapy in which the psychoanalyst
actively advises and encourages his patient. According to Alexander,
"supportive measures knowingly or inadvertently are used in all forms

of psychotherapy."[16] In fact, he argued that transference, the principal psychoanalytic therapeutic tool, consists precisely in a kind of support necessitated by the patient's regression to dependent attitudes of infancy and childhood. Phyllis Greenacre also pointed to a form of the transference relationship being practiced in which the analyst takes an *active, directive stance* toward current events in the patient's life. This form of the transference relationship does not rely on the process of "working through" but on the process of "working out," of "carrying into reality actively new behavior patterns under the suggestion and support of the analyst."[17]

It would of course be incorrect to say that women alone were subject to the American "supportive" or"adjustment" impulse in psychoanalysis, but the supportive impulse is singularly consistent with the arrangement of power in American society that locates the female as dependent. The following example suggests one interesting avenue whereby supportive technique was advocated for the female patient in particular. In the face of the relatively small number of practitioners and number of patients for whom psychoanalytic treatment was deemed appropriate, analysts became interested in "widening [the] scope of indications for psychoanalysis," and Leo Stone undertook to explore the use of psychoanalysis with "borderline" cases.[18] The patients Stone discusses are allied as a diagnostic group by their narcissism,[19] even though narcissism and transference are usually mutually exclusive, the incapacity for transference in narcissistic neurosis having been what originally led Freud to deem such neurosis inaccessible to psychoanalysis. Yet, drawing on the work of Karl Abraham and others, Stone included among his recommendations for the special management of these patients "prolonged preliminary periods of supportive therapy."[20]

But who are these patients with narcissistic neurosis for whom supportive therapy is specially indicated? They are women. Freud associates narcissistic object-choice with women and anaclitic object-choice with men, yet he points out that this distinction is merely "schematic" and that "both kinds of object-choice are open to each individual."[21] Stone, however, mentions six of his own cases as examples of narcissistic transference and all six "happen" to be women. The case on which Stone elaborated is that of a "gifted woman composer" who "in an atmosphere of a mildly friendly positive transference" was able to "swing for a time from a highly personal and recondite musical idiom, which brought her little of the recognition which she so desperately needed, into a routine but secure effort, quite remote in character from her original work." This career change "paralleled efforts to establish a genuine relationship with her husband."[22] One cannot overlook the similarity between this "success" in supportive analysis and the larger social impulse to discourage professional careers for women in favor of happy marriages to which the women devote their all.

Popular case histories by psychotherapists and psychoanalysts and analytic autobiographies by patients themselves provide additional evidence for the adjustment impulse. Probably the most famous case history from the postwar period is that of Laura, the woman described by Robert Lindner.[23] Lindner's successful analysis revealed that Laura, normally a "fashionably thin" (Lindner's phrase), attractive woman who would eat to the point of falling unconscious, was consuming food to fill the emptiness within her in order to simulate pregnancy by her father. In the terms of the narrative that Lindner weaves, his analysis makes perfect sense. Yet we might also ask what psychoanalytic traditions are furthered by its content and what it implies about female roles. I don't disbelieve the case history; I "merely" find it ideologically charged. The extreme "classicism" of the analytic interpretation, in which the patient is determined to be acting out the little girl's fantasy (described by Freud) of having a baby by her father, strikes me as a convenient reaffirmation of a basic psychoanalytic explanation. The choice to popularize this particular case history reveals that there was a great stake in such a literal "proof" of theory, and conversely, that the theory being proven met a perceived social need to see women as professional mothers. Here I would argue about this case history what Karen Horney argued about the psychoanalytic account of female development—its outline recreates the pattern of how men view women complete with their fears and desires about women. Like the popular "marriage manuals" of the time, including *The Power of Sexual Surrender* from which the opening epigraph was extracted, Lindner subscribes to the view that a woman must be married to be happy. He titled the case history "Solitaire," implying not only the isolation of illness, but that Laura's unmarried state was a tragic consequence of her illness. Bursting into her apartment during one of her eating binges (an act hardly in keeping with psychoanalytic neutrality), he discovers the pillow apparatus she had fashioned to simulate pregnancy. This holds the clue to her cure, which, presumably, will lead to marriage to her "eligible" boyfriend Ben.

In the 1970s and 1980s, bulimia has been reinterpreted by media critics as an understandable if self-destructive response to the rigid social standards of female attractiveness furthered by the media.[24] Lindner's analysis ignores such cultural determinations of neuroses even though the study itself reveals the marks of their operation. For example, Lindner's characterization of Laura's situation as all the more tragic for the fact that she is pretty and thin is only logical to the extent that one adopts the standard that "thin is beautiful" and the common wisdom that personal appearance is the criterion by which people, especially wives, should be judged.

So far I have read professional psychiatric literature and its popular offshoots with a view toward highlighting the adjustment impulse couched in certain psychiatric therapeutic practices. Yet, as I indicated at the start, it would be an oversimplification to say that the adjustment impulse was the only one articulated by postwar psychiatry. The theories and practices of American psychiatry, most notably American psychoanalysis, were also articulated through discourses of resistance to the work of normalizing therapy so disastrous for women. Within American psychoanalytic litera-ture several characteristic areas of research taken together constitute, in effect, if not on purpose, a terrain of feminist resistance to the work of normalizing therapy. One such area is the *re*assertion of interpretation rather than manipulation as the core of psychoanalytic technique. Another area is the increasing interest evident in the literature of the period in the transference and especially countertransference relationship.

While the tendency to advise or manipulate was present and in fact seemed always to be on the verge of dominating American practice, its presence simultaneously fueled the opposite tendency. American psycho-analysis drew on Freudian models that admonished the analyst to *resist* the temptation to mold the patient to his own image or world view. According to Freud:

> The analyst reflects the patient's individuality and does not seek to remold him in accordance with his own—that is, according to the physician's—personal ideals; he is glad to avoid giving advice and instead to arouse the patient's power of initiative.[25]

And according to Merton Gill, writing in the *Journal of the American Psychoanalytic Association,* such Freudian-derived analytic neutrality was important to the "essence of psychoanalytic technique."[26] For Gill and others, "neutrality" did not mean perfect objectivity; that was recognized as impossible. The analyst was not to strive for the unrealistic goal of providing an inanimate reflective surface for the patient. Rather, "neutral-ity" meant precisely that the analyst should refuse "supportive" or "direc-tive" techniques, in favor of "explorative" or "interpretive" ones based on the transference relationship. The analyst is neither a director of behavior nor an inert sounding board, but rather a human being who is "alert for the development of patterns of emotional response in himself (sic) to the patient."[27]

It is important to point out here that this disavowal of adjustment therapy does not necessarily mean that American analysis really was free of the adjustment impetus. These analysts need not be taken at their word in terms of actual practical application. Obviously, adjustment therapy was applied in varying degrees both within the practice of an individual analyst and by different analysts at different times. But, in a way, it is necessary literally to take these protestors-against-the-adjustment-model *at their*

words. The presence of the debate itself, and the presence of anti-adjust-
ment agitators themselves, indicates that the conformist psychiatry identified by Friedan, Chesler, and others as *the* practical model of the era was
not actually so conceptually or practically exhaustive as it seemed.

Even in popular accounts a discourse of resistance to the adjustment
model was present—although here the discourse often exists more as a
line of defense against impossible expectations than as an integrated part
of the theory. For example, in a discussion of what psychoanalysis can
do for "you" in *Are You Considering Psychoanalysis?* (1946), Alexander
Martin says that analysis draws back from advisement.

> Analysis is not the kind of treatment one ordinarily associates with a
> doctor-patient relationship. A condition is treated, it is true, but it is
> not treated by a prescription, a formula, or a blueprint from the analyst.
> This must be understood very clearly, for many individuals expect
> the analyst to advise them, to tell them how to lead their lives. The
> experienced analyst does not set out to do this . . . To the question
> "What should I do?" the analyst would be inclined to say "First let us
> find out all of what you *are* doing."[28]

Marriage manuals also reveal certain resistances to psychoanalytic adjustment. No psychoanalyst, it was said, should or would prescribe or proscribe marriage or divorce. Predictably, popular discourses did not express
fear of psychoanalytic advisement in the form of a feminist critique of psychoanalysis's justification of the (oppressive) institution of marriage, but
they did express it—as the fear that psychoanalysis would *disrupt* existing
marriages. A 1950 issue of *The Nation* published a testimony by a woman
who began with the statement, "My husband and I were recently divorced
upon the suggestion of his psychiatrist."[29] The next issue contained responses from two well-known psychiatrists. Gregory Zilboorg, the author
of one, takes a defensive position. He goes so far as to question the woman's
veracity (while denying he does so) in order to assert that "no true psychoanalyst ever advises marriage or divorce as part of the therapy."[30]

As the least manipulative of psychotherapies, psychoanalysis often
refused to be an enforcer of socially prescribed female roles. Of course
this avenue of resistance could never be complete. As a female resident
analyst puts it in *Mademoiselle* (1947), "Values? . . . I decided during
residency that I had better be clear on what I thought the good life was
because every word the analyst says to a patient carries a value judg-
ment."[31] The practitioner and the patient both operate within the context of
the wider social system held together by ideological glue which constantly
constructs individuality. Yet wouldn't another avenue of resistance to
normalizing models of femininity be the very *acknowledgment* of the

consenting role of psychoanalysis within the status quo? This acknowledgment itself is evidence of psychoanalysis's ability to critique its own authoritative status, and in so doing to perform analysis other than adjustment therapy.

The concept of countertransference, like that of interpretation, is pivotal to reflections on the work of the analyst, for countertransference is the mechanism through which we can conceptualize the analyst as an active participant without seeing him or her as an advisor. Unlike transference, always a prominent concept in psychoanalytic literature from Freud on, countertransference only became a topic of extended discussion as late as the postwar period. Jean Laplanche and J.-B. Pontalis indicate in their definition of the term that Freud very rarely used it.[32] As they go on to say, countertransference received much more attention as psychoanalysis came more and more to be understood as a *relationship*. This occurred particularly in America where the cultural interpersonal school, which looked at the doctor-patient experience, was well rooted. Countertransference literature was different from transference literature in another respect as well. Unlike the relative agreement in the literature on the definition of transference, the literature on countertransference recognized wide *disagreement* as to what the term comprises. Is it the analyst's response to the patient's transference? If so, does this refer just to the analyst's unconscious response or to his or her conscious response as well?

I read this increased interest in countertransference in the 1950s, and the divergence of opinion over its meaning, as evidence of the centrality of the role of the analyst *as a problem,* and of the concomitant weakening of psychoanalytic authority in this period. Analysts obviously felt a need to reassess the status of the analyst with particular reference to his or her position of dominance in the doctor-patient relationship. While American psychoanalysis is not a clearly subversive institution, the capability and, indeed, the inexorable requirement of psychoanalysis to deal with such a volatile issue as countertransference, are quite potentially radical from the point of view of a critical reading. The problematic notion of countertransference figures the problems of dominance and submission under patriarchy.

On the one hand countertransference was sometimes regarded as an abnormal and unwanted characteristic of the analytic relationship.

> Countertransference is the same as transference—it is then immediately obvious that countertransference is undesirable and a hindrance.

> It is not safe to let even subtle manifestations of the countertransference creep inadvertently into the interpersonal climate. The analyst must recognize and control these reactions.[33]

Here the analyst's fear reveals a desire to reaffirm the omnipotence and objectivity of the analyst—and a belief in the so-called "sterile" analysis, a fantasy which allowed analysts to deny the real power imbalance of the analyst-analysand relation.

A differing viewpoint held that countertransference was *normal* and constantly present in analytic work, yet defined countertransference as desexualized and sublimated in nature. The emotional role of the analyst could be allowed, but only when construed as completely without erotic content.[34] Proponents of this point of view refused to use the term transference *neurosis* which implies incomplete sublimation of unconscious material. They advocated the notion of "abstinence" developed by Freud to describe the necessary atmosphere of the treatment.[35] The analyst in this latter view is still quite controlled and controlling.

In addition to this considerable equivocation, itself an indicator of the instability of authoritative psychoanalysis, some accounts of countertransference do seem to open to radical readings. Lucia Tower, for example, emphasizes that "no analyst has ever been presumed to have been so perfectly analyzed that he no longer has an unconscious, or is without the susceptibility to the stirring up of instinctual impulses and defenses against them."[36] In place of the silent, omniscient, unemotional model of the analyst as a paragon of health and virtue, this model of countertransference can reveal an analyst who is human, emotional, and not so thoroughly analyzed himself or herself as to be free of any resistance to the transference relationship—he or she might be a superior analyst, but not a more authoritative one.

For Tower, the countertransference is specifically a response to the patient's transference and is made up of unconscious phenomena derived largely from the analyst's childhood. She describes how countertransference elements, the emotional material that has emerged in the context of the ongoing intimate relationship of the doctor and patient, may be used to further the analysis after having been subject to a process of self-analysis. Crucially, Tower admits the erotic nature of countertransference response, arguing that the great number of writers who say such libidinal material should not be tolerated testifies, paradoxically, to its very presence.[37] The issue of countertransference, then, directly brings into question the mental health of the analyst himself or herself.

Filmic Adjustment and Resistance

The analyst, and in particular the analyst *him*self, is the main figure through which psychiatry is introduced as a theme into Hollywood cinema. And following Hollywood's fundamental concern with sexual difference and family formation, where the psychiatrist is a man, the patient is often a woman. The doctor-patient couple doubles, then, for the traditional romantic couple, and represents wider socio-cultural discourses on psychiatry and women in the Hollywood narrative.

In the films under discussion here, as well as in many other films—including *Whirlpool* (Otto Preminger, 1949), *The Snake Pit* (Anatole Litvak, 1948), *The Cobweb* (Vincente Minnelli, 1955), *Lady in the Dark* (Mitchell Leisen, 1944), *Lady in a Jam* (Gregory La Cava, 1942), *The Dark Mirror* (Robert Siodmak, 1946), *Oh, Men! Oh, Women!* (Nunnally Johnson, 1957), and *Lilith* (Robert Rossen, 1964)—the narrativized doctor-patient unit reiterates a configuration of power where the doctor is the authority who adjusts the help-seeking patient to a traditional marriage that she has somehow threatened, guiding her on the one path to both mental and marital health. In *The Three Faces of Eve* the authoritative power of the psychiatrist is textually overdetermined as I will show.

Nevertheless, in these same films the representation of the doctor-patient unit also enables a critique of its ideological ramifications. In *The Three Faces of Eve* this critique may be discerned in the lessening enunciative power attributed to the psychiatrist as the narrative unfolds. In other films the doctor's authority is undermined by the erosion of his sanity and by one of the same narrative devices through which it is established, the romantic involvement between doctor and patient. In *Tender is the Night,* for example, the woman's psychiatrist is also her husband. This crude parody of the transference-countertransference relation breaches a central taboo of psychoanalysis, renders the doctor vulnerable to the same emotional foibles as any unwitting husband, and suggests that the doctor has a personal rather than objective stake in the maintenance of traditional marriage. The relationship between a fictional male psychiatrist and his fictional female patient, then, is a key narrative representation of both adjustment and resistance.

The Three Faces of Eve is a primer for the narrativization of the psychiatric adjustment impulse, articulating it through various cinematic figures of authorial control (the discourse of scientific rationality, enunciation, the rhetoric of vision) that have been theorized in contemporary film studies since the early 1970s. Virtually all such figures are exemplified in the person of Alistair Cook, who opens the film with a non-diegetic assertion that this film is based on a true story, "a classic of psychiatric literature," and whose voice-over introduces the first narrative action: the delivery of Eve (Joanne Woodward) to her psychiatrist, Dr. Luther (Lee J. Cobb).

The fictional psychiatrist then takes up the role of narrator (though his "narration" takes the form of expository conversations with his colleague,

Dr. Day), describing Eve's problem of multiple personality in terms of sex role stereotypes for women and the underlying premise that anatomy is destiny. Neither Eve Black, "the rollicking and irresponsible playgirl," nor Eve White, "the defeated wife," is "really qualified to fill the role of wife and mother or even responsible human being," he despairs. "What in short," he asks, "had *nature* intended this young woman to be?"

The narrative of Eve's three personalities (including the synthetic personality, Jane) resonates in even broader ways with professional precedents which are themselves based on cultural archetypes. The range of female roles presented by the film conform fairly closely to those described in its source book, *The Three Faces of Eve,*[38] and the roles presented in the book, in their turn, bear great resemblance to the three primary personalities identified by Morton Prince in his patient Miss Sally Beauchamp in *The Dissociation of a Personality* (1905).[39] Neither is Prince's own lengthy work without precedent. A quote from the preface, "If this were not a serious psychological study, I might feel tempted to entitle this volume, 'The Saint, The Woman, and The Devil,' " indicates the extent to which Prince is relying on cultural mythology, where the flip sides of the coin of femininity are the mother and the whore, and reworking this conceptualization through the Judeo-Christian tradition, so that mother and whore become Saint and Devil.

That the film works to define femininity in narrow terms, is made even clearer by the discrepancy between the number of personalities "discovered" by Dr. Luther and the account by "Eve" herself. Chris Costner Sizemore's 1977 autobiography, *I'm Eve,* identifies twenty-two separate personalities.[40] There is also a crucial difference in the *kind* of personalities described. Where the eponymous connotations of Eve White and Eve Black include the biblical Eve and reach into the archetypal arsenal of descriptions of femininity as described, the twenty-two separate personalities of *I'm Eve* substantially broaden the range of possibilities so that the personalities—the lying girl, the purple lady, the big-eyed girl, the freckle girl, the turtle lady, among others, are not reducible to archetypes nor solely to sexual connotations.[41]

With the flashback to the trauma that precipitated Eve's illness, a flashback that reintegrates her personalities and ends the narrative, the choices open to women are further narrowed, now to exclusively familial ones. Other female characters are here present for the first time, but, embedded in a flashback narrated by Jane, they become structural representations of one woman's psyche: daughter, mother, grandmother. Psychologized as they are, and confined to the context of the traditional family, the female roles depicted echo the aspect of Freud's essays on femininity in which discussions of the girl child conflate her with her mother and speak of her future (inevitable) maternity while discussions of the boy child concentrate on his *relationship* to his mother.[42] Thus, I would argue that this flashback condenses an historical tendency (the characteristically 1950s reduction of social problems to female psychical problems), and a psychoanalytic justification (the limitations in Freud's account of feminine psycho-sexuality).

The course of the conscientious psychiatric treatment Eve receives results in maternal, exemplary femininity in the form of Jane, whose insertion into the nuclear family is visualized as a *tableau vivant* with which the film ends. In this final image we see Jane, her new husband Earl, and her daughter, Bonnie, driving off together to start anew—the reunited family. Earl is in the driver's seat, Bonnie in the back, and all are happily licking ice cream cones—the perfect symbolic condensation of oral sexuality and storybook familiality. Here, then is fulfilled the postwar dream of prosperity and togetherness.

In considering an institution such as American psychiatry jointly with that of cinema around the troubled place of femininity, one longs for a visual disposition of the psychiatric rhetoric. This is provided in the pharmaceutical ads which began to appear in force in *The American Journal of Psychiatry* in July of 1952. The imagery of these ads betrays an ideological consistency with adjustment-oriented psychiatric practice: the male doctor depicted as an authority figure (a man among male colleagues—I did not come across one female psychiatrist); the housewife overburdened by routinized tasks; and the working woman laboring in women's service jobs such as secretary or teacher. Drug therapy promises help in carrying out these roles. A representative ad from 1960 shows the progress of a woman's treatment in six photodocumentary frames.[43] The first frame depicts the kindly physician in white listening across his desk as the "tense, nervous" patient discusses her "emotional problems." Her hands are clasped together and her head is bowed. After taking a capsule in frame two, the patient is able to stay calm "even under the pressure of busy, crowded supermarket shopping." In frame four she enjoys her evening meal with her husband and two children and in frame five "she is able to listen carefully to P.T.A. proposals." Frame six finds her "peacefully asleep." Here, then, is the woman's day—the goal of psychiatric prescription.

Notably, these drug ads do not deny real world problems, but instead refer frequently to the pressures of modernity. But of course, in their own interest, they do not admit of any cooperative social actions that could be taken to alleviate these problems. The cure they promise is individual and cosmetic. It does not relieve the problem, but only makes the patient better able to cope. For example, Dexamyl may be prescribed "to help the

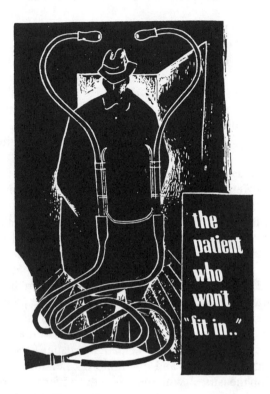

The mentally depressed patient who will neither "fit in" with his surroundings nor cooperate in treatment presents an increasingly wide-spread problem in these anxiety-ridden times. 'Methedrine', given orally, has a remarkable stimulant effect which elevates the patient's mood and produces a sense of well-being.

'Methedrine'® brand

Methamphetamine Hydrochloride, 5 mg.

COMPRESSED

 BURROUGHS WELLCOME & CO. (U. S. A.) INC. · TUCKAHOE 7, NEW YORK

depressed and anxiety-ridden housewife who is surrounded by a monoto-
nous routine of daily problems, disappointments and responsibilities . . .
with 'Dexamyl' you [the prescribing psychiatrist] can often help her to
face her problems."[44]

Men don't escape this prescription of drugs to ameliorate social problems. A ubiquitous image is that of the harried businessman. One ad
picturing a man in a business suit, hat, and overcoat and carrying a
portfolio claims that "in these times of accelerated activity, strife, and
resulting mental tension, appropriate dosage of 'Seconal Sodium' . . .
fully answers the problem."[45] Another ad depicts a drawing of a man in
hat and overcoat silhouetted against a lighted doorway. Superimposed
over this image is a giant stethoscope and the words, "the patient who
won't 'fit in.' "[46]

But while male as well as female roles are rigidified in these ads, there
is a significant difference in the visual representations of men and women
in relation to their (always male) doctors. In ad after ad figuring a woman
patient, the point of view of the photograph or drawing is that of the male
psychiatrist: through his eyeglasses, over his shoulder, from behind his
desk. The ads address the psychiatrist subscriber to the *The American
Journal of Psychiatry,* encouraging identification with the authoritative
doctors pictured. In one ad a beam of light shines from an unseen source
behind the whitehaired, white-coated doctor onto the anxious woman.[47]
Clearly, science throws a "bright light" on her. The ad copy enumerates
the "goals, functions and needs of the normal woman" and recounts
how "raging, combative, unsociable patients usually become more co-
operative, friendlier, quieter, and much more amenable to psychotherapy
and rehabilitation measures" with the use of the advertised drug. Unacceptable angry behavior is replaced by socially acceptable docility.

Compare this to an image of the male patient. He is someone we may
identify with. We generally see almost his whole body as he verbalizes
his problem. Significantly he is usually seated next to, rather than across
the desk from, his physician. In appearance he could almost *be* his physician. In a representative ad from 1958, both doctor and patient wear
business suits and glasses.[48] Where there is a male patient, the point of
view is from the *patient's* side of the desk.

This visual scheme for distinguishing the sexes coincides remarkably
with the representational strategies of sexual difference in classical Hollywood film which place the woman as the object of the gaze of male
characters in the narrative, of the directorial agents of the film, of the
filmic apparatus itself, and of the male spectator, inscribed in the work of
the text through processes illuminated by psychoanalytic theory.[49]

The Three Faces of Eve figures a specialized case of this domination
through vision in the crucial moments of transition from one personality

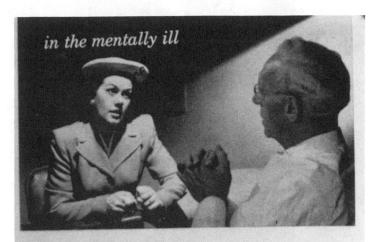

in the mentally ill

'Sandril'

(RESERPINE, LILLY)

... *facilitates psychiatric treatment*

'Sandril' calms, diminishes anxiety and tension, improves sleep pattern in psychoneurotic states.

'Sandril' frequently produces relaxation, decrease in hallucinations and delusions, improved communication, and increased depth of effect in psychotic patients. Raging, combative, unsociable patients usually become more co-operative, friendlier, quieter, and much more amenable to psychotherapy and rehabilitation measures.

'Sandril' is virtually nontoxic; does not produce liver damage or severe orthostatic hypotension.

Lilly

QUALITY / RESEARCH / INTEGRITY

DOSAGE: Usually 0.5 to 1 mg. twice daily.
SUPPLIED: Tablets, 1 mg., yellow (scored), and 5 mg., buff (cross-scored). Ampoules, 2.5 and 5 mg. per cc., 10 cc. Also, tablets, 0.1 mg., orange, and 0.25 mg., green (scored); elixir, 0.25 mg. per 5 cc.

ELI LILLY AND COMPANY

80TH ANNIVERSARY 1876 · 1956

to another. The film presents nearly twenty transitions among the various personalities of Eve, most of which occur in the office of her psychiatrist. The first emergence of Eve Black in the presence of Dr. Luther occurs as Eve White is seated in his office. In despair, she covers her face with her hands and purse. The film cuts to a close-up of Dr. Luther who asks "feeling better now?" When we return to the shot of Eve, she is no longer Eve White but Eve Black . . . who feels fine. Thus, the cutaway to Dr. Luther's point of view serves as a point of identification for the spectator who sees the transition through the incredulity of the doctor's gaze.

By now Dr. Luther has gotten the idea that he may "call up" the dormant personality who will then appear on demand. Later when he attempts to explain the rare situation to Eve White's husband, Ralph, Dr. Luther opts for a visual demonstration: the transition to Eve Black and back to Eve White is repeated with cutaways to dumbstruck close-ups of Ralph. Prior to the scene with Ralph, a disbelieving Dr. Luther had corralled his psychiatrist colleague to witness the spectacle. Although this time there is no insert of the doctor at the actual point of transition, the visual paradigm remains in force since the transition occurs across a cut and in response to a verbal suggestion from Dr. Day. Eve Black slouches on the couch as the two doctors look on in a three-shot. Dr. Day mentions Mrs. White's name and the film cuts to a close-up of her lifting her head. Four shots follow which alternate between the staring doctors and Eve White. The power of Drs. Luther and Day is here figured as superior even to Eve's own powers of self-determination. Moreover, Dr. Luther's psychiatric abilities, proposed by the plot, link up with the visual levels of filmic narration. His control over the woman is that of a narrator—a narrator of personality and cure.

Yet psychiatry is not *only* an authoritarian regime in *The Three Faces of Eve*. Since the presence of psychiatry as a fictional theme also requires the joint presence of mental illness, thematized psychiatry can also *enable* this film and others to broach troubling issues of problematic female psycho-sexuality. Psychiatry promises to guarantee the regulation of these narrative "problems," but once broached, the discordant views of femininity are not completely controlled. Under the guise of mental disturbance, *The Three Faces of Eve* presents female roles that correspond to the limited range of roles offered in the socio-historical context of postwar America. Yet because women's roles were also being widely discussed and challenged at the time, the symptom of Eve's illness—the different personalities—may be read alternatively as the narrative refiguration of ideological contradictions surfacing in the debates on women's place.[50]

An effective disturbance also exists at the level of the visual rhetoric of control in *The Three Faces of Eve,* a disturbance in the psychiatrist character's authority and in the spectator's scopophilic pleasure. The early transitions between "Eve's" different personalities occur across the cut, motivated by the psychiatrist's call and accompanied by non-diegetic music used to identify each personality. But as the film progresses, this rule changes and the change is crucial. The majority of transitions between personalities, and especially the later ones, are handled (without cues or cutaways) by the body language and acting of Joanne Woodward. Dr. Luther has hypnotized Eve White who is seated in a chair to the right of the frame. To the left of the frame Dr. Luther sits at his desk, turned away from her, making notes. When the transition occurs, not only is there no cutaway, but it is clear to the audience that Dr. Luther, who is visible on-screen, has not participated in the emergence of Jane.

Unlike case histories published by psychiatrists in which the author has full descriptive control over the patient, here the patient is depicted by less clear-cut means, and I would argue that the very complexity of the shell of authorial agencies around the fictional mentally ill woman allows a certain representational play. Through the loosening of classic editorial structures, in the context of a portrayal of role options for women, the real contradictions of "problematic femininity" become accessible to the reader open to them.

Tender is the Night thoroughly disturbs the thematic matrix, a matrix that at least partially held the element of ideal femininity in place in *The Three Faces of Eve*, by moving beyond female to male pathology, and specifically to the pathology of the male psychiatrist/husband. It is not the woman's mental problem which is at sake in *Tender is the Night*, but rather the problem of the analyst-analysand relationship itself, and in particular the problem of the countertransference.

Because Nicole Warren (Jennifer Jones) has inherited from her father a huge fortune, "so big as the Morgan's Bank and Rockefeller," she is in a position to challenge Dr. Diver's (Jason Robards, Jr.) authoritative status as analyst, researcher, and husband. But perhaps more importantly, it is Nicole's increasing mental health that threatens Dr. Diver's professional and emotional life. While she was ill, at least he could rationalize cutting down on his practice because he was giving so much attention to Nicole. When the American *vedette* asks, "Are you still practicing?" Dick can roll his eyes to the upper floors of the Villa Diana, where presumably his intimate relations with Nicole are lived out, and answer, "Never stopped." But as Nicole mends she removes the last vestiges of his professional affectations. As Dr. Diver puts it, "perhaps I'm going crazy myself." Significantly, the book he can't finish writing is called "Psychology for Psychiatrists," a title which doesn't only imply use by psychiatrists, but a treatise on psychiatrists as well.

According to the narrative, it is possible for a male psychiatrist to maintain a good marriage with his female patient only so long as the distribution of power in the husband-wife coupling is congruent to that within the doctor-patient relation. Once the roles are reversed in male illness or female economic power, the resonance between the marital and analytic situations ceases and both fall apart. In *Tender is the Night* this cessation of viability is predicted by Dr. Diver's counselor, the wise Dr. Dohmler:

Dohmler: When she finds out that she married a human being, a fallible human being and not a God . . .
Dohmler: Of course all things are possible, but what will you be by that time? Will you be still what she wants or what you want? What has already happened to you? Ours is a strange profession. Many of us come into it because we ourselves are a little broken up, a little bit crippled. We've become clinical before we can fight our own battles with life . . .
Dohmler: Nicole could be helped were it not for you. You could be helped were it not for Nicole.

The script's own dialogue describes this shift as a movement from "transference" to "countertransference," an explanation which is a particularly 1960s addition since it is not present in the 1932 source novel by F. Scott Fitzgerald. The following dialogue between Dr. Franz Gregorovius and Dr. Dick Diver is presented as a correct explanation of the state of affairs near the end of the film:

Gregorovius: Wonderful, Nicole is cured, there's no doubt about that.
Diver: Oh, I'm very happy to have your diagnosis Dr. Gregorovius. And to what do you attribute this cure?
Gregorovius: You know from where comes her new ego strength.
Diver: Ah, you think it's anaclitic do you? Transference of strength between doctor and patient?
Gregorovius: Why are you so bitter Dick?
Diver: Ah, come now Franz, you can tell me. What you also mean is that it has worked in reverse.
Gregorovius: What I mean is that Nicole is no longer dependent on you.
Diver: You imply the transference is over, the countertransference has begun and I am the weak one.

The countertransference is presented as a morass into which Dr. Diver, regardless of having been forewarned, must fall. Having fallen, he loses his effectivity as an analyst, his sanity, and his desirability as a mate.

This narrative exemplifies the way analytic authority may be linked both to the ghettoization of mental illness in women characters and to the avoidance of countertransference by male psychiatrist characters. Thus, *Tender is the Night*'s presentation of a countertransference that threatens the male psychiatrist's power may be read as the representational transposition of psychiatry's disinclination to acknowledge the Oedipal conflicts of the psychiatrist himself. In spite of this disinclination, the conflicts embodied in the concept of countertransference are nevertheless broached in both narrative and professional literary terms. In this guise they become the very subject of these respective discourses.

The pervasive tendency of American psychiatry including psychoanalytic theory and practice to authorize and publicize itself with recourse to a model of adjustment therapy for women affects the narrative and textual strategies of Hollywood films which overtly invite incorporation. Yet this cultural complex is not a monolithic but a hegemonic process. The specific form of the debates within American psychoanalysis, as well as their very existence, reveal currents of resistance to normalizing models of femininity—currents of resistance whose drift may also be observed transferred to filmic representation.

10

Psychological Explanation
in the Films of Lang and Pabst

Janet Bergstrom

Introduction

Psychological manipulation, disastrous shifts in self-image, madness: these are recurrent, even obsessive motifs in Weimar cinema, from Robert Wiene's *The Cabinet of Dr. Caligari* (1919) to Fritz Lang's *The Testament of Dr. Mabuse* (1932). Both Lang and G.W. Pabst emphasize psychology in their Weimar films, but I would like to argue that the function of psychology is quite different, both thematically and structurally. My original point of departure was the observation that detail shots (or inserts, sometimes including enlarged close-ups of faces) serve a very different purpose in *Pandora's Box* (Pabst, 1928) than they do in *M* (Lang, 1931), and it is this difference in the use of a stylistic feature that I would like to pursue. In this paper, I use three films—*Pandora's Box, M,* and *Secrets of a Soul* (Pabst, 1926)—to show opposing tendencies within Weimar cinema that pivot on the representation of psychology. On the one hand, with *Pandora's Box* and most of Pabst's Weimar films after the Expressionist *Der Schatz* (1923), there is an increasing emphasis on "realistic" characters who are carefully individuated through psychological depth; on the other, in Lang's films, we find an abstract use of characters as types with almost no attention to "depth" or "development." The emphasis instead is on the relationship of the type to various institutional structures that play prominent roles in Lang's films, such as the legal system, the media, and the family.

Pabst's explicitly psychoanalytic film, *Secrets of a Soul,* occupies a midpoint between *Pandora's Box* and *M* conceptually. *Secrets of a Soul* investigates a character's hidden desires and fears, but in a highly reductive manner. The psychological dimension is represented through a variation on the use of available types. The character's actions, dreams, and emotional states are reduced to bits of "typical" information that become completely comprehensible as they are transformed into a case study, that is, in the translation of the character's behavior into conventionalized symptoms that become rationalized as a nameable and curable neurosis.

Lang and Pabst are not unique in the ways they chose to represent psychology and psychological explanation (or its absence), but their films provide strong examples of tendencies which were practiced commonly in a more or less mixed form within Weimar cinema.[1] Considering their films from this perspective allows us to observe and analyze significant variations in theme, structure, and style within the same national cinema, with a view toward a more detailed understanding of the function and development of its conventions.[2] Moreover, the opposing tendencies that can be seen in their films are central to an issue that goes beyond the description of any national cinema. It is my hope that these examples contribute to a demonstration of the ways identification at the level of characters relates to identification at a more abstract and structural level, and, perhaps most importantly, how level shifts back and forth are internalized by the spectator. Much of contemporary film theory has revolved around ways the spectator (or types of spectators) identify with characters. My analysis attempts to move away from this tendency.

This paper does not attempt a psychoanalytic interpretation (or reinterpretation) of these films; instead, my objective is to consider how psychology is used at the narrative level, within the story itself, similarly to the ways that other conventional systems were available for use in Weimar cinema and could be adapted to various ends. The broad term "psychology" is preferred to "psychoanalysis" because its relative lack of precision gives it the advantage of being able to refer to actions and motifs that are designated as "psychological" by the plots of the films themselves, whether or not they are portrayed consistently, whether or not they are intended to convey the structural logic and cultural resonance of psychoanalytic theory. In the cinema, the representation of psychoanalysis, even when named, is rarely, if ever, consistent with psychoanalytic theory. Having stated this, however, I do believe that there is an important connection between this study of "psychology"—how it is conveyed and understood—and contemporary psychoanalytic theory. Because it is the process of internalization of "narrative" information by the spectator that is under investigation, "psychology" and "psychological explanation" as terms of analysis crisscross traditional issues of psychoanalytic interpretation of specific films and the *dispositif* of cinema. I want to argue that Lang, in his difference from Pabst in these examples, negotiates between characters and abstract levels of the narrative in a way that resists the traditional conceptualization of character identification. Characters are used as abstract types or sites where different structural levels of the film can intersect. This is accomplished through the orchestration of cinematic and narrative conventions across the presumably conceptually separate levels of primary and secondary identification, as formulated in the seminal studies of Christian Metz and Jean-Louis Baudry.

First, the role of psychology will be discussed: what is its narrative function, and its relative importance; how varied are its representations; how closely is it related to (a) dramatic resolution and (b) symbolic resolution? Next, the role of psychological explanation will be examined: is a given psychological state explainable; if so, to what extent and in what terms? What weight is given to psychological explanation relative to other forms of explanation which might be represented in the narrative by institutions such as the law, the media, and the family?

The Function of Psychology

The aim of Expressionism is commonly said to be the external representation of internal states. In Weimar cinema, *The Cabinet of Dr. Caligari* provides an extreme example of how exaggerated set designs, costumes, and makeup, and a correspondingly limited repertoire of dramatic actions, characters, and acting styles represent the fundamental instability of society as projected by the characters who belong to it. The Expressionist character is a "type" dispossessed of psychological depth. The psychological dimension isn't absent; it is displaced, externalized through different registers of design and typology. What is assumed to begin with, however, is that there *are* internal states that need to be represented. As the heritage of Expressionism becomes more diffuse and eclectic in Weimar cinema, the representation of internal states moves ahead in two different directions: one tendency conserves and transforms the more stereotypical, conventionalized representation of internal states in order to use characters as "types" who undergo, or exemplify, a limited number of "typical states," and where character development is not pursued. The other leads to more "realistic" characters individuated by an increasing emphasis on psychological depth, and stories that are motivated primarily by emotional conflict and reactions to dramatic events. According to this line of thought, Pabst becomes a psychological director, close to his actors, concerned to motivate their actions in terms of psychological realism, to make them "live" their characters (Louise Brooks *is* Lulu), and to move his plot forward by means of his characters' dilemmas, actions, and reactions. Pabst is also, not incidently, famous as a director of women, such as Asta Nielsen and Greta Garbo in *The Joyless Street* (1925) and Louise Brooks in *Pandora's Box* and *Diary of a Lost Girl* (1929). He gained a reputation for understanding and portraying feminine psychology as it could be seen during the Weimar period.

Lang exemplifies the opposite tendency. He was rarely interested in particular characters and there is virtually no character development in his films. A character could change into his opposite (Beckert [Peter Lorre] describes this phenomenon during his long speech at the end of *M*), but this familiar use of the figure of the double simply flips a character type to expose its reverse side, rather than basing drama on the evolution of internal states. Although a number of attempts have been made to match Lang's division of the sexes and his story dynamics with the familiar Oedipal model in which female characters play specific symbolic roles with respect to male characters, in fact his direction didn't favor either male or female characters, dramatically or symbolically, nor did his story material, developed with Thea von Harbou.[3] His narratives tend to shift back and forth from the individual character's dilemma to a broader level of society, which absorbs and transforms that problem into a larger one, somewhat differently defined as a result. Lang investigates individuals as representatives of groups, and group psychological behavior as an integral part of the way the social system works— through both formal and informal institutions, in Michel Foucault's sense—such as the legal system, the press, and the family on the one hand, and "ordinary" or everyday social behavior among members of a community on the other.

One way this distinction may be seen is by looking at the way detail shots are used: how, why, what do they mean? *Pandora's Box* and *M* are remarkably consistent internally and different from each other in their deployment of this stylistic feature. First we will examine two examples from *Pandora's Box* and then two examples from *M*.

In the first sequence of *Pandora's Box,* Dr. Schön (Fritz Kortner) comes to Lulu's apartment to tell her of his impending marriage to a woman of his own class. In so doing, he intends to end his relationship with her. As he enters, Lulu runs happily to meet him and puts her arms around his neck, kissing him. Schön pulls away from her, walks across the room, and sits with his back to her. Another shot of Lulu shows her puzzled reaction. The montage alternates between Schön, who tries to keep a distance between them and cannot bring himself to speak, and Lulu, who reacts with subtle changes of expression. Inserted into this series are two detail shots of a figurine on the mantelpiece. Schön toys with it aimlessly, betraying his nervousness.

These detail shots have no function beyond signaling Dr. Schön's emotional state. The figurine is never seen again, lost among decorations which have a clear significance, such as the large painting of Lulu dressed as Pierrot that connects her with performance.[4]

The focus of the scene is immediately psychological: it is constructed around Schön's inner struggle and Lulu's reactions. The detail shot of the figurine, turning in Schön's fingers, emphasizes this relationship: we see Schön before the detail shot, followed by Lulu's reaction.

At the end of the film, we see a large poster warning the women of London about Jack the Ripper. The shadow of a man emerges alongside it, introducing abnormal psychology as a fact or a given of the plot in the form of this character. (This is similar to the introduction of the child-murderer in Lang's *M* some three years later, and serves the same purpose.)

In the following shot, Lulu encounters this man, and invites him to come with her out of the cold to her room. In sharp contrast to the luxurious apartment she had at the beginning of the film, she now lives in a filthy, drafty attic with the two men from her past who seem to be dependent on her earnings as a prostitute. As Lulu and the stranger climb the stairs to her room, the man opens a knife behind his back. A long series of close-up shots between them (twenty-one shots) seems to reveal an inner transformation in him through the generosity Lulu expresses with the warmth of her eyes and smile. Her attitude toward him and her bearing are the opposite of the cynical prostitute "type," and this is reinforced when she wants him to come with her after he says he has no money. In reply, he drops the knife and a close-up of his face reveals a change in his expression: he smiles, as if relieved of a burden. In this scene, dramatic changes have been cued by internal, emotional states: it is the inner drama that constitutes the major action.

Once inside, he pulls Lulu onto his lap, and they hug each other affectionately. As she lights a candle on a little table in front of them and watches the flame, a detail shot shows her hand reaching up to hold his, another sign of affection. But a moment later, the man's eyes lose their expression completely as the light flickers, drawing his eyes to the reflection of the candlelight off the blade of a knife lying next to it. As the man holds Lulu against him, her back to us, his eyes suddenly widen in fear or horror. An extreme close-up of his eyes, like the detail shots, emphasizes his emotional state. A detail shot of the gleaming knife follows, which reinforces the reversal of his interior state.

His reaction is the opposite of, and symmetrical to, the smile of relief cued by the detail shots outside on the stairs when he dropped the knife. Lulu's head is tilted back, her eyes closed peacefully, waiting for him to kiss her. Her radiant look is no longer drawing his eyes, as it had before, to counteract his compulsion to murder, and she becomes his victim.

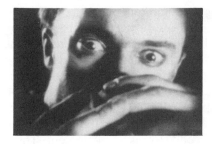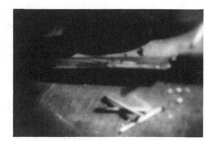

In these examples, taken from the beginning and the end of *Pandora's Box,* we have a long series of shots alternating between two characters, showing the drama of their emotional interaction. Detail shots are used in connection with close-ups of characters' expressive faces in order to reveal greater depth and complexity of character psychology, where characters are motivated by passion—the irrational—not reason. This, to a large extent, is what the narrative is about at its most basic level. There is no "outside" explanation of the mechanisms of psychology in these scenes, and no need for it because of the clarity of the causal relationships that advance the narrative, established by the redundantly emphatic montage (objects, expressive faces).

Psychology is just as important a concern for Lang as for Pabst, but character psychology plays a different role in Fritz Lang's films. Detail shots, which are used extensively and systematically by Lang, also serve a different purpose in connection with the way he uses individual characters. Although Lang often turned to abnormal psychology for story material, and although he shows psychological mechanisms operating at a more abstract level, he is much closer to the various theatrical and melodramatic traditions that used characters as representatives of types than he is to the psychological novel, with its interest in developing highly individualized characters, and the "psychological" cinema that developed its own conventions toward the same ends.

In *M* detail shots enter into an elaborate system of clues or signs to be deciphered, as opposed to providing indications of a character's emotional state; correct interpretation of these signs leads to the identity of the child-murderer and his eventual capture. The significance of objects emphasized by magnified detail shots shifts levels continuously between the concrete and the abstract, the individual and social institutions, demonstrating how the relationships among them are so closely intertwined as to be indistinguishable from one another, or to seem like extensions of one another in the ordinary course of events.

Near the beginning of the second sequence of *M,* we see a detail shot of a letter that the murderer is writing to a newspaper.

"Because the police didn't make my first letter available to the public, I am going directly to the press. . . . I haven't finished yet." A second insert shot of the letter appears in the third sequence in a slightly different form, reproduced on the front page of the newspaper. A hand holding a monocle passes over it, momentarily enlarging each word.

The monocle is held by a Minister in the government, who is on the telephone to the Chief of Police because of the scandal caused by this negative publicity. The phone call motivates a cut to police headquarters where the Chief of Police responds by explaining how his investigators are handling the evidence—the original letter turned over to them by the newspaper. We see a detail shot of a set of fingerprints on an official police card, and then a closer detail shot of one print. A heavy magnifying glass, reminiscent of the monocle, is held over the print, enclosing and enlarging it as a separate object of attention.

Next we see a huge fingerprint projected onto a screen, where it is being studied by an expert seated with his back to us, dwarfed by this unreadable clue.

The murderer's letter, containing the trace of the person who wrote it, circulates from the press to the law both as a material clue and as news which casts the police in a negative light, which in turn has political ramifications. At this point, we are no longer concerned about who is actually studying the evidence. We have moved back and forth between individual characters and a more abstract level of the narrative that intertwines social institutions.

The fingerprint projected onto a screen for the anonymous police investigator has an abstract corollary in a map of the city being marked with concentric circles to indicate the murderer's sphere and the tightening movement of the investigation. The underworld figures have their own map which gives an analogous dimension of abstraction to the elaborate details of their own method of tracing and interpreting clues in order to track down the murderer. (These will be displayed for us much as the police's methods had been.)

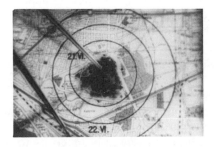

This movement from the individual (specific) to the abstract is essential in *M*. It may be seen in its relationship to character psychology already in the first sequence of the film, which has been analyzed frequently to show aspects of Lang's style.[5] I would like to review the last part of the sequence to point out exactly where this shift in levels is activated by the way the spectator "internalizes" or comprehends the narrative.

Frau Beckmann is working in the kitchen, waiting for her daughter to come home from school. Tension increases as time passes: the meal is ready, other children in the building have returned. Detail shots initially represent the mother's literal point of view, such as the repeated shots of the clock. However, by the end of the sequence, they have become detached from her person. The transition is almost imperceptible from the specific (Frau Beckmann, Elsie) to the abstract (a detached point of view, "another child murdered").

After Frau Beckmann opens her apartment door to the man selling an adventure serial, she moves into the hallway and looks down the stairwell. An insert shot of the empty stairs follows. She turns back to her apartment and looks again toward the clock. A detail shot of the clock follows. Then she walks over to the kitchen window, opens it, and leans out, calling Elsie's name. Another insert shot of the empty stairs follows, identical to the shot seen moments before from Frau Beckmann's point of view. But the window she looks out is on the opposite side of the kitchen from the door that opens onto the stairway. The cut between window and stairway creates an impossible space, and, more importantly, it marks an almost imperceptible shift in levels, from literal to metaphorical point of view. It is expertly executed, following continuity conventions of editing. Frau Beckmann is looking down, out the window. From the strong pattern of repetition based on point of view shots in this sequence, we *expect* a point of view shot. Because we see an exact repetition of an earlier shot, which *had already represented her point of view* looking down the stairwell, the montage moves forward without any sense of spatial violation. It is "as if" Frau Beckmann had actually looked down the empty stairs again, or "as if" she were looking at the series of images that follows in quick succession, redundantly pointing to the inevitability of Elsie's death: the empty attic with the laundry hung up to dry, Elsie's plate set at the kitchen table, her ball rolling out from behind a bush, her balloon catching in the telephone wires before it disappears.

By shifting from literal to metaphorical point of view in a way so strongly tied to the spectator's reaction to cinematic conventions (alternation, repetition, point of view editing), Lang not only makes us see Elsie's murder as a tragedy from the mother's point of view, but he carries us beyond the psychological reaction of this particular mother to this particular child's murder. The logic of the editing has already taken us to an

abstract level of identification, or psychological involvement, while still within the terms of an individualized story. As in the sequence involving Beckert's letter, it is notable that the level shift is imperceptible and that it must be comprehensible as part of the story development in order for subsequent parts to make sense.

The film moves on from here (the first sequence) to indicate a change in its level of generality. From an individual and private reaction (and a proleptic reaction, insofar as we know *before* Frau Beckmann and *for* her), the film moves to the reaction of the public.[6] After a fade to black, voices are heard calling out a special edition of the newspaper, confirming the new murder. A number of vignettes are shown, indicating that the public is in a state of panic. Elsie's murder is no longer something personal. It represents *another* murder in a unpredictable series. Social institutions are not playing the protective, stabilizing role that provides their rationale. The police have been unable to find the psychopath. The media plays an ambiguous role: the press, the radio, and the official reward notices for the murderer inform and warn the public. However, the media simultaneously cashes in on the public's dependence on this news, helping create and benefitting from crowd hysteria. As we pass from the sound of the newsboy calling out a special edition of the newspaper, to the reward poster, to the radio account of the new murder and the absence of clues about the murderer, a causal relationship is set up for the first example of false accusation. Sitting with colleagues around a table, smoking, drinking beer, and reading the newspaper, one man is inexplicably suspected and challenged. This leads to a similar incident on the street and so on.

One might say that Frau Beckmann's reactions are, at every stage, to be expected, normal. By contrast, the public is shown reacting irrationally in the face of the greater irrational force represented by the serial child-murderer. To control this double threat to stability, there is a second shift to a higher level of abstraction. Where first the film changed its level of address (and psychological interest and explanation) from the individual to the public, now the film moves from the public to the institutional level. The bulwark of social order, the law, becomes the focus of attention, organization, explanation, and psychological manipulation. In *M* the law is represented by the mirror-like organizations of the law enforcers and the law breakers, each with its own interest in preserving the status quo. The police are mobilized under Lohmann (Otto Wernicke), and the underworld mobilizes, in parallel fashion, under the orders of Schänker (Gustaf Gründgens). While there are colorful characterizations, there is virtually no character development. This level of abstraction dominates the rest of the film. However, level shifts between literal and metaphorical point of view continue throughout the film, marking its system of enunciation.

Both *Pandora's Box* and *M* use psychology in ways that emphasize fluidity, instability, inherent reversibility, and even contamination among characters or across different levels of social organization. I am arguing that psychology serves different purposes in these two cases, the first increasing depth and complexity of characterization, the second implicating the spectator in scenarios where the individual character is subsumed by the institutions that he or she somehow continually helps to constitute and legitimate. In *M* this causes reflection on the relationship between the individual and social institutions because of the doubt and fear that these institutions are themselves unstable or that they are inadequate in the face of contemporary events, as represented by the irrational in the form of the child-murderer. Obvious parallels could be drawn to actual events in Germany, and not just to the well-known case of the Düsseldorf murderer, which the film took as a point of departure. To understand these two tendencies better, we can look at the ways psychological explanation is used in these films. What seems to demand a psychological explanation? And to what end?

Psychological Explanation

Madness recurs frequently in Weimar cinema, and with nightmarish connotations. There are two rather different kinds of mad characters: those who become mentally deranged during the course of the narrative and those who embody the very principle of madness from the outset. In the first case, madness can be caused by the kind of symbolic fall from a secure position in society to powerlessness, humiliation, and impotence that Siegfried Kracauer describes, a sudden and unacceptable change.[7] This results in the destruction of a positive self-image, and at its most extreme, a loss of identity in every sense, loss of contact with the world around the character. This is frequently represented by the inability of this character to see the external world any longer, staggering as if in a trance. In the second and more radical case, the character is irreducibly irrational from the outset, and therefore is outside social institutions, because social institutions are regulated on the basis of rational behavior. This kind of madness can't be explained, and often can't be contained. Madness threatens to contaminate already unstable social structures in Weimar films. When cornered by the forces of reason, madness doesn't recognize its terms.

In Lang's *Dr. Mabuse, the Gambler* (1922), there is a contest between the primary adversaries up until the very end of the film, when von Wenk (Bernhard Goetzke), representative of the law, finally catches up with Mabuse (Rudolf Klein-Rogge), who has been trapped in his own counterfeiting den. However, although the great chase that has dominated the structure of the film has an ending, in the sense that von Wenk has captured Mabuse and saved the Countess from his clutches, the symbolic resolution that should accompany his victory is undercut by the nature of the victory. For by the time Mabuse has been caught, he is insane. Von Wenk looks at him, and shrugs his shoulders in resignation. This is no longer a matter for the police.

The second Mabuse film, *The Testament of Dr. Mabuse,* opens with the same Mabuse (again, Klein-Rogge) even more powerful within his cell in the mental asylum. He scribbles plans for social domination that are executed by an intermediary, or a medium, who is himself a psychoanalyst, Dr. Baum (Oskar Beregi). The ending is very similar to the technical victory at the end of *Dr. Mabuse, the Gambler.* The films have a conclusion, and, unlike many Weimar films, a positive one. But this only holds true for the resolution of the narrative, which anyway trails off after the knowledge that victory has come by default, granted by the enemy himself, so to speak. As Kracauer put it, writing about both Mabuse films: "As so often with Lang, the law triumphs and the lawless glitters."[8] In other words, there may be an end to the story, but it is dissatisfying and unstable because the crucial element of symbolic resolution is missing. There is no moral victory where the stakes are not primarily those of right and wrong. When the irrational is personified, as in *M* and *Dr. Mabuse, the Gambler,* it is unclear how to redefine the terms of the conflict so as to have meaningful opposition, and therefore, a meaningful conclusion.

When comparing the use of psychology in the films of Lang and Pabst, particularly that area of psychological ambiguity exploited with such interesting results within the Weimar cinema generally, *Secrets of a Soul* stands out in contradistinction not only to the rather abstracted interest in psychology in Lang's films, but also to a number of other important films directed by Pabst during this period, especially *Pandora's Box.* While the case history presented and explained in the film can be interpreted along other lines,[9] just as people have offered alternative explanations for Freud's dream interpretations and case studies, the film was intended to serve a specific, didactic purpose, which entailed a popularizing or reductive operation.

A psychoanalyst explains to his patient, gradually and in simple steps, that he suffers from a knife phobia (although he doesn't use the word). During the course of the treatment, the analyst does introduce a few technical terms, which appear in inter-titles, such as unconscious drives (*unbewussten Triebe*), resistance (*Widerstand*), and parapraxis (*Fehlhandlung*). Care is taken not to overwhelm the "patient" with an unusual vocabulary (the patient meaning either the character in the film or the "student"-spectator interested in learning about the new mental science). Without naming them, the film illustrates important concepts in Freudian dream interpretation such as condensation, displacement, repression, and its sexual etiology. The meaning of these concepts becomes redundantly clear through the way the elaborate photomontage imagery is juxtaposed with the doctor's questions, on the one hand, and the many reaction shots of the patient, on the other. The analyst expresses directly (in an intertitle) the key importance of dream interpretation in curing neuroses, and he relies on the method of free association to arrive at an explanation and a cure.

Clearly, then, not only psychology but also psychological explanation are at the center of the film, more directly than in *Pandora's Box* or *M*. Although *Secrets of a Soul* seems to accomplish its stated objectives as an educational film,[10] paradoxically it is the least satisfying of the three films under consideration here in terms of the use or function of psychology. The entire project of *Secrets of a Soul* is founded on the idea of certainty, and even simplicity, presumably in order to popularize Freudian psychoanalysis in the idiom of Hanns Sachs.[11] Aside from many other serious reductions that give an air of superficiality and false optimism to the case history, two aspects of its presentation that relate directly to conventions of Weimar cinema, and Pabst's own area of experimentation with psychological conflict, should be mentioned. First, the air of semantic stability emphasized in the film is directly at odds with the tendency toward ambiguity and abstraction that characterized such important areas of innovation in Weimar cinema as disjunctive and associative montage sequences, as well as more ordinary narrative exposition, where one often has indirect knowledge of events and causal relationships. The photomontage sequences are the most strikingly avant-garde or experimental aspects of *Secrets of a Soul* in formal terms, yet paradoxically they contribute to the one-dimensional quality of the film. Even if many details in them are not directly explained, they are understood to be distorted memories of a symbolic nature, and most importantly, they are all organized from the point of view of one character, the husband—as dreamer, as the patient in analysis. Detail shots, which are frequent, emphasize a specific psychological meaning for him, such as the many detail shots of knives. They function as clues or signs to be interpreted, but not in the same way as in *M*. Here clues are symptoms which can all rather easily be accommodated into a single explanatory system. Where in *M* explanatory systems such as the law, medical opinion, and the media are themselves the objects of uncertainty, here the idea is to convince the audience that psychoanalysis is an important addition to medical science. In other words, *Secrets of a Soul* is a project of legitimization, where the strength of psychoanalytic explanation is demonstrated by showing a correct diagnosis and a cure. Paradoxically, this could well have the opposite effect, given the conventions of representation in Weimar cinema, where psychoanalytic processes were commonly seen in a conflictual and structural manner, and without the guarantee of satisfaction. The film doesn't really fit into either the *Kulturfilm* pattern (conventionally educational) or the expectations associated with fiction films of its day, although it features a major star, Werner Krauss, and Pabst was a fiction film director with some prominence after the success of *The Joyless Street* the previous year.

Only one character (one character's psychology) is the focus of attention, and it is a male character. This is unexpected from the emphasis on female characters in *The Joyless Street,* which shows the structural and environmental determinants on psychological character development, and would not seem to anticipate films so fundamentally ambiguous as *The Loves of Jeanne Ney* (1927) and *Pandora's Box,* made during the next two years. In *Secrets of a Soul* the wife and her attractive male cousin are important secondary characters, but only through the husband's dream representations, fantasies, and memories. Both of them are central to his cure because they have been causally related to the origin of his phobia. Their screen presence as "real" characters is negligible.[12] One might say that they are fictionalized by the patient's account, as secondary characters are fictionalized (or narrativized) in Freud's case studies. However, they are rendered devoid of psychological depth in a way uncharacteristic of Freud or these other films directed by Pabst.

Not only are the other characters reduced to the husband's point of view in the memory or fantasy sequences, but their function is also strictly limited in the framing story. The narrative overdetermines certainty to a remarkable degree. For example, when the husband returns to his living room after being cured, his attractive, younger wife, who we have been led to understand has been sexually deprived because of her husband's psychological block, comes happily to meet him. Immediately after their embrace, the cousin who has provoked the husband's unconscious jealousy emerges from the back of the living room to greet him, as if he and the wife had been together in a room off-screen. This image seems coded by melodramatic convention, but the narrative doesn't allow for uncertainty about the stability of the original couple. There is an immediate cut from the reunion to an epilogue, with redundant signs of idyllic happiness made possible by the cure of the husband's neurosis. A complete family, now with its own baby, has become a reality, safe from intrusion, as opposed to the husband's nightmare where his wife gives a baby doll to the cousin. (One might speculate that just as the cousin had been the husband's best friend *and*—meaning *because*—he left for the Far East just after the husband's marriage, in symmetrical terms, immediately after his cure, the husband and wife move to a similarly remote place, with no trace of the cousin.)

In contrast to *Secrets of a Soul,* both *M* and *Pandora's Box* revolve around characters who stand outside the ordinary expectations of explanation and accountability. They are introduced as irreducible facts. They are catalysts who change the course of the narrative by causing characters around them to react. This is not to say that Beckert and Lulu function in exactly the same way in their respective narratives. Because the status of characters is so different in *M* and *Pandora's Box*, they can't. Nonetheless, there *is* something importantly the same about their function.

Psychological explanation in *Pandora's Box* is complicated in large part because of the unresolved contradiction of Lulu's character. She, herself, is the enigma, not the rather complicated twists and turns of the narrative. She brings out the dimension of psychological vulnerability in others around her, and in ways that highlight unusual or perverse sexual tensions (such as the relationship between Dr. Schön and his son, or the indirect pathways of the Countess Geschwitz's desire), tensions which are explicable, and even conform to many other-directed, self-destructive scenarios in Weimar cinema. But Lulu, unlike the protagonist of *Secrets of a Soul,* is not reducible either to symptoms or a cure.[13] Lulu is solved as a dramatic problem for the narrative only by the introduction of a parallel character, Jack the Ripper, who is like Lulu in being irreducible; he does not need an explanation because he is defined from the outset as a psychopath, an insane killer of women, as Lulu had been said to bring men to their destruction. The dramatic resolution of the film involves the cancellation of one character who is radically beyond society's conventions in a way that is inexplicable—she is innocent, yet she is destructive— by another irrational force, personified by a second character.

This action, however, does not affect a symbolic resolution. The film trails off, leaving the male characters isolated from each other, irresolute: Jack the Ripper disappears into the fog, still a victim of his compulsion; Schigolch, oblivious of other narrative events, is ironically happy with his Christmas pudding; Alva cries when he sees the stranger leave Lulu's room, assuming it is another act of prostitution, partly to support him, that he is powerless to stop. He wanders aimlessly, head down, into the fog. This lack of resolution emphasizes the psychological dimension, consistent with the rest of the film, and renders an important part of it beyond explanation.[14] There are constant references to class and social constraints, but their purpose seems to be to bring out psychological states within the different characters.

M has a similar structure in terms of symbolic and narrative resolution. If the capture of the child-murderer—whether by the underworld or by the law—would seem to resolve the plot, the manner in which the murderer's case is presented, including his own convincing testimony to the underworld tribunal about his powerlessness in the face of his compulsion to kill, forces the question of resolution to a different and more abstract level. As in *Pandora's Box,* the ending is rendered less satisfying because it occurs in stages which seem to reduce the importance of the dramatic resolution. On the other hand, in *M*, the ending in stages helps mask the frustration or non-resolution of the problem of the film, which is defined as a paradox of social institutions that are shown to be inherently inadequate: (a) Beckert is caught and confesses; (b) the underworld is forced to surrender Beckert to the police; (c) judges file into an abstract courtroom but we hear no verdict; (d) three women, Frau Beckmann in the center, sitting on a bench in dark clothing, speak of the futility of death as a solution, saying they need to watch their children more carefully. Unlike *Pandora's Box,* the question of symbolic resolution is moved to the level of the social institutions that are supposed to be maintaining order. All of these institutions are shown to be lacking in the face of the child-killer, because he represents an irreducible fact—madness—which is radically outside social institutions. The law is shown to be ineffectual, just as the individual mother could not provide a solution. The irony of putting Beckert into an mental institution, parallels with Dr. Mabuse and Dr. Caligari aside, is that he had already been released from one. This was the first important clue the police followed. The important question of institutional inadequacy, which seems to be built into the very structure of institutions in this film is directly related to the way psychological manipulation is part of the terrorizing madman, defined as such, outside social conventions. Moreover, psychological skills are shown throughout the film to be fundamental social skills, part of the way people communicate and exercise ordinary power relationships—whether in a cafe or in Lohmann's interrogation room. The irrational filters down to all levels. It is analogous, in some ways, to the invisible shift from literal to metaphorical point of view in the first sequence of *M,* as if fear of the irrational, represented by the public reaction to the child-murderer, is related to contamination by the irrational in more ordinary ways (hence the quickness of neighbor to accuse neighbor of being the murderer.) Here Lang is once again making a bridge between the specific and the abstract, between the individual character and the social conventions through which he relates to others. The correct interpretation of signs that leads to the capture of the child-murderer does not lead to a real solution, because, according to the institutions and systems of explanation shown in the film, there is none.

In this discussion, detail shots have served a symptomatic function, as well as a small demonstration of how psychological themes and structures are internalized in the three films in question, how the specific is related to the general. In *M* detail shots lead to exteriority; they function as clues in a system of social signs, or social signs as they have been internalized. In *Pandora's Box* and, in its more limited way, *Secrets of a Soul,* detail shots are clues to interior states. While Pabst leaves us with unforgettable characters set against the backdrop of the social history of his day, Lang leaves us with the more disquieting, abstract, and unarticulated level of social institutions that seem detached from the needs of the individual characters whose lives are defined by them.

11

Not Speaking with Language/ Speaking with No Language: Leslie Thornton's *Adynata*

Linda Peckham

Adynata: A stringing together of
impossibilities; sometimes a confession that
words fail us

—Richard A. Lanham,
A Handlist of Rhetorical Terms

Leslie Thornton's *Adynata* (1983) assembles images of China and of women, which are, for the West, universal representations of the other, the Orient as feminine and women as exotic. Superimposed as sites of desire, they are fictions, the product of a narrative or quasi-history that has pictured this (their) body of imagery as its utopia. *Adynata* interrogates the apparatus of desire that makes the meaning of the spectacle possible: beginning with the closure which circumscribes women and the Orient, the film works backwards, unraveling the constructions and recuperations of Orientalism and sexuality. The film also poses the problem of how to approach the dominance of a language which invents femininity, simultaneously territorializing and displacing women. Thornton uses this position outside language, a lack of speech, as a response in itself, a form of signification that treats these representations to both an emptying out and redistribution of meaning.

The opening sequence of the film begins with a photograph of a Chinese couple, a formal portrait taken in the nineteenth century by a Western photographer. Bathed in its own moment of history, with sepia tones and fine costumes, the photograph is the "authentic" Orient. However, it is seen as a document faithful only to the Victorian vision. It is a view from an incalculable distance (difference), as if its actuality were an extension of a Victorian fantasy. The source of this gaze is used as the source for the invention of a fictional Orient: Thornton recreates the tableau of the photograph in saturated color, with an actress on the left in costume, gazing like her predecessor into the lens. This is juxtaposed with shots of exotic plants and flowers accompanied by a popular song from the twenties—conspicuously the wrong era—but the right evocation of senti- ment. The photograph could be seen as a point of departure for the whole film in the sense that all of the imitations and inventions derived from it suspend authenticity, obscure the distinction between copy and original, fact and fiction. The soundtrack also plays with the notion of the fidelity to and recuperation of history: recordings of Chinese radio shows and ethnographic music as "essences" which reconstruct traces of the Orient. Sound effects form a tissue of fallacious chinoiserie, souvenirs which do in fact constitute a substantial presence of the imaginary Orient, that of nostalgia. This is exaggerated in the film by exquisite mixes of sentimental music, *objets d'art,* and pastoral settings. Thornton uses nostalgia as a motor of desire to invest (and invent) erotic and fetishistic significance in what could be arbitrary images, such as the tropical flora. This dynamic in the film suggests an unlimited scopophilia; it is also a way of foregrounding not the object of Orientalism but its origin, an empire of memory and fantasy. Thus the order of knowledge of the other is reversed or inverted: in one sequence, filmed in autumn in a Japanese garden, the camera is hand-held in the first person or subjective mode and performs the clichéd "lotus" walk (of Chinese women with bound feet) as it moves through the garden; the cliché and spectacle are framed as constructs of our own cultural vision.

The fictional itinerary—or perhaps detour—of the Orient established in the opening develops into a strategy of intervention between image and identification. The reading of these representations is constantly interrupted: Thornton inserts into the Oriental context found footage images such as the planet Earth revolving, aerial photographs, and frequently, sounds opposite or extraneous to image, for example, the whine of low flying aircraft over a photograph of Victorian men and women. These elements rupture the sense of continuity which envelops one in the conventional narrative or spectacle, by introducing a scale or perspective enormously out of proportion and context. This kind of montage cuts into pleasure, denying the gaze and turning fascination to an exterior and estranged point of view.

Not only does the film interfere with voyeurism, it casts it as a trope, as an active figure built into the progression of the montage. Voyeurism is a mapping of the body, the eye which isolates woman as object. Beginning with the portrait photograph, which inscribes the relation of division and sexuality (the woman to the left, the man to the right), the film constructs a grid of complex spatial (metaphorical) correspondences between woman and gaze. In one sequence, another resonance of the photograph, a woman is introduced, even more elaborately dressed and made up than the others. She enters what appears to be a stage and arranges herself in a chair. With her mask and costume, staring at the camera, she performs a mime of a woman being seen, a parody of the act of looking which is both a resistance to, and an exaggerated embrace of the male look.

Spatial placement of the woman with respect to the voyeur is a direct relation in these shots. The metaphor shifts as the woman's space is developed across the whole film: the association is made between woman and the Orient (represented fictitiously by Japanese gardens) as surfaces progressively penetrated or occupied. The gaze becomes the sound which often accompanies the woman, the approach of heavy footsteps in an echoing interior; the images of the Oriental garden are dominated by the metric rhythm of a Bach piece as the camera tracks through it.

Metaphors of colonization are intercut with images of confinement. A Victorian greenhouse (of derived Oriental style) represents a closed space within which the exotic species is cultivated and preserved in a controlled climate. The sequence with a woman embroidering a slipper brings together the motifs of foot-binding, decoration, and gender roles in tight shots of her nervous activity. Her hands clench and gesture in an ironic sign language of expression without signs, a mime of frustration and immobility.

Throughout the film the greatest sense of confinement is in the silence or muteness of both the woman and the film itself. In the rich layering of music and effects there is no verbal commentary, no spoken word (or rather, no English). The only vestiges of the conventional voiceover are the wordless pre-vocal utterances which sometimes (in)form the presence of a woman on the screen but are more often off-screen, displaced. This sense of absence (which increases in relation to the cacophonies of the soundtrack) adds a dimension to the film which could be described as an insistent, mute presence. Part of the definition of "adynata" becomes clear—"a confession that words fail us." The paradox of confession—or expression—and, simultaneously, the failure of speech is problematized as speaking with no speech or not speaking as speech. This confinement outside language creates a tension in the film at different registers but most constantly as an impotence, inserted between sound and image, between the overdetermined visual representations of women who have no voice and the ubiquitous musical scores, which operate as a kind of rhetoric (as do the Bach *Klavier* pieces, for example), also inscribing cultural and sexual identity (as with the aria from a Chinese opera). The arrested articulation opens a space of doubt and disturbance at the center of the film.

Adynata can be read at one level as a map of the various territorialities of the Western masculine identity. This is suggested by the actions of pursuit and penetration executed in some of the cinematography where the hand-held camera moves through spaces following a woman or zooms in dramatically on objects. The map is also traced in the language of occupation—that which excludes the voice of women, yet circumscribes the body—a discourse in which women and the Orient are receptacles and products of desire, never the agents.

However, reading this film only at this (ideological) register would ascribe to it a certain affirmation of the oppressive nature of this body of imagery with which the work takes issue. (Such a reading would also miss the dark humor being played out in the exaggeration of these sentimental and nostalgic fantasies which also hide violence.) *Adynata* is a more complex experiment with the performance of myths and fictions whose meaning could be miscontrued, but which at the same time opens meaning through a progressive misconstruction. Rather than negating the artifice (as if the West can restore to Asia a real China, or men a true femininity to women), the film subjects this imaginary iconography of the other to a mutation, a denaturing of the codes and bonds which determine "exotic" or "feminine." One of the devices of narrative cinema is, of course, the code of pursuit (of the object/other) and the bond of capture. Thornton's film plays with this pattern of progression towards closure, especially in the theme of colonization, and thus subverts it. Progression toward closure: it happens not once only (the pleasurably deferred climax) but repeatedly, in the various metaphors of confinement, appropriation, and occupation, as if many Sax Rohmer novels (the ultimate pastiche of the detective story format and arcane mysteries of the Far East) were combined into one, with no plot. The absence of a narrative opens a lacuna in the film. No motive or motivation are provided for the overdriven trajectories of desire. Where narrative cinema is structured around concealing the apparatus of desire, *Adynata* strips it bare, revolving on its onanistic axis.

With a space or an absence in place of a narrative, the whole logic of suture, and spatial and temporal continuity is ruptured. It is replaced with a discontinuity that is not simply a strategy of fragmentation, substituting bricolage as an anti-narrative system; rather, the montage still refers to narrative by cutting in a way that denies identification and destabilizes representation. In conventional cinema, suture, or the seamless flow of the image, creates the illusion of continuous space and time, thus preserving the larger illusion of the narrative as real. In other words, seamless editing works with a principle of the same, the illusion of sameness. *Adynata*, however, cuts on difference as a kind of description, unwriting in the play of textuality. One such instance is the upside down image of a lake in the Japanese garden, where the reflection/mirror image is right side up and the "real" inverted. This is simple play with sameness and difference (or disturbance of meaning) but the ambiguity has many resonances in the film's discourse on the representation of the Orient. In the decoupage of sound and image, this difference or dischord often produces a powerful irony: the autumnal paradise of the garden has a soundtrack of delirious organ music and birds twittering; the image then dissolves to illustrations of bound and deformed feet at the crescendo of the music. The conventional role of music—to provide continuity of meaning, to induce specific emotions—takes on an aspect of madness as it forms a parenthesis in which "beauty" and "deformity" are given a certain parity by association, yet counterposed as an oxymoron, a crisis in meaning.

Another way the film works with a non-relation to narrative space is in the use of found footage. This material has multiple meanings: while it has lost the matrix of its original meaning, it still brings this otherness to a new context. Because of this shift in contextuality it would have an impossible spatial and temporal relation to narrative space. This is precisely what *Adynata* explores. Each shot, each sequence, does not build towards a final closure, and the found footage in particular introduces a rupture in the flow of information. Plural interpretations converge, having the effect of simultaneously dispersing or redistributing meaning at different registers elsewhere in the film. A recurring image is the time-lapse photography of a seedling sprouting. Early in the film this image forms part of the association of plants to woman and the Orient, conveying a sense of the propagation and scrutiny of the exotic; its reappearance later has a more acute resonance with the tortured immobility of deformed feet and cloistered women. The footage also inserts an expanded temporality which is only one framing of time amongst others (the historical time of the Victorian photographs and the Twenties music, fake historical time of the imitation, "real" time signified by the hand-held camera, dynastic epochs of China, and so on). Found footage is deployed even more dramatically in the play with space. One of the first images in the film is an animated but realistic image of the planet revolving. This prefaces the contents of the film with a global dimension, an omniscient point of view which characterizes imperialism. Later there is satellite footage of the slow tilt of the earth's surface; the sound-over is again the territorial echo of boots which carries over into the next shot, also found footage, of a chapel or some sacred womb-like space.

The image of the earth turning is also important as a conceptual figure of what the film does not describe: a utopia where a story resolves all of the information into a circumscribed, unified world (utopian because within narrative desires are fulfilled). Where narrative works with the space of realism to construct the imaginary, *Adynata* works with space as a fictional element to deconstruct representation. The Orient is itself already a fictionalized place, essentially an absence, corresponding to the silent space of woman. Around these figures each cut reorders and interferes with certain trajectories of violence, desire, and nostalgia, so that reading the film does not yield a single, finite resolution but effects a perpetual traversal of the simultaneously fractured and augmented space of the text. The site of the film could be described as a "hypertopia," Maurice Blanchot's word to designate "a constantly surplus place," "the recurrence of a moving and otherwise vacant place."[1] Here Blanchot also describes the relation of the text to the author who, in a conventional narrative, is a central consciousness, an invisible agent unfolding and determining the order of information. In *Adynata* the operation of the montage, the caesura, deports the figure of an author: this position is demarcated as the continuous evacuation of an intentional space from which would issue narration and the accretion of the discourse toward closure. The absence of a narrative voice is also a parallel to the absence of woman's voice/presence of silence. Thornton is not (women are not) the author of these representations: they are a mask of the masculine gaze behind which the author is silent, censored.

Another meaning of "adynata" is revealed: "a stringing together of impossibilities" as a means of speaking. Impossible in narrative logic, perhaps, but in Blanchot's words, "here meaning does not escape into another meaning but into the *other* of all meaning,"[2] that which cannot be articulated within language.

For the film's denouement Thornton uses found footage as quotation rather than inscription, leaving it to speak for itself, as well as silence itself. The sequence begins with footage, filmed from TV, of an Oriental wedding ceremony where the bride dances in a circle, brushing the floor with her long hair and finally prostrating herself. The sound is a contemporary pop song with a derivative ethnic beat which more or less is synchronized with the bride's ritual and the beating of drums in the image. Filming from television quotes a medium in which received ideas and appropriated representations are already multiplied, and where Western culture situates knowledge within entertainment, just as fashion in music has consumed the cultures of the other. The bride is produced in her own culture and reproduced in ours, prostrating herself in many weddings of the same wedding.

Her prostration is the foreshadowing of the image of death. As an ironic play on closure, Thornton inserts the final sequence from *Shoot the Piano Player* (1960) where gangsters pursue the heroine through the snow and shoot her. The clip has been rephotographed out of focus so that the figures are skeletal, moving in a field without detail, reduced to the actions of flight and murder. The sound of footsteps threaded through the film and the motifs and metaphors of pursuit converge here in the spectacle of a woman's death. It is not really important to recognize the origin of the clip (although François Truffaut as an "auteur" works with the quotation or imitation of genre films himself, doubling the representation); it is more important to recognize that the clip is generic to our culture. But what is most violent in this sequence is not the murder, or even the distortion lent to it by rephotography; it is the underlying meaning which the soundtrack brings out, the quality of entertainment. The music is an anachronistic mix of (clichéd) television music, themes from melodramas and cop shows played into slapstick or comedy tracks, with tones of nostalgic melodies. Though mixed together, it is a mass of contradictory emotional signals which, in sync with the image, forces the meaning of the clip into a crisis, revealing pleasure in violence, and cruelty in desire.

Ultimately *Adynata* distills from these "absolute" representations of women the same silence that is immanent in their production. Though they seem not to be altered in themselves they have become truly impossible, unspeakable. This shift is what is difficult to describe in writing about the film. Semiosis occurs in the moment of watching, and is quite fluid; at the same time signification is found in the loss of meaning, the process of disengagement. Few films have used powerlessness so powerfully as a way of opening up a critical space in representation.

12

Some Ruminations around the Cinematic Antidotes to the Oedipal Net(les) while Playing with De Lauraedipus Mulvey, or, He May Be Off Screen, but . . .

Yvonne Rainer

The Audience is once more perplexed after viewing my last film, *The Man Who Envied Women* (1985, *TMWEW*).[1] Some of them are once again asking, "What does *she* believe? Where in this welter of ideas, aphorisms, opinions, quotations, ironies, rhetoric, collisions, is *her* voice? Are there really no arguments to follow, no resolutions or conclusions to be gleaned from this overload? Are the meanings so embedded in ambiguity that even the most assiduous concentration is unable to dredge them up, with the various discourses eventually neutralizing each other?" (The Audience of my daydreams, like the voices of my films, is very gabby.)

I hope not. I am not an iconoclast bent on destroying all vestiges of "authorial discourse." (As a "lapsed" anarchist, I am only too aware that when it comes to authority our choices are merely better or worse compromises.) On the contrary, I would like to believe that I subject such discourses to pressures and tests, or dislocations, e.g., a removal from their ordinary contexts—the printed page, the classroom, or the formal lecture—to unexpected physical and psychic spaces. The space of real estate profiteering, for instance, or the space of seduction, or the space of sexual (mis)representation.

In many ways, *TMWEW* lies outside traditional narrative cinema. There is no plot, for instance, and although the voice of the (absent) female protagonist can be construed as a narrator, this voice departs from convention by refusing to push a story forward or promote a singular thesis that would tie up the various strands. In the struggle for the film's truth this equivocal, invisible heroine is not always the victor. Consequently, in relation to the social issues broached within the film, the question of an externally imposed, predetermined and determining coherence looms very large for some. If the process of identification with the trajectory of fictional characters is thwarted, we look for opportunities to identify with an extra-diagetic author or ultimate voice "behind" the film, if not camera. We are still not fluent in reading films that, while seeming to proffer this identification process, undermine it at the same time by setting other processes in motion, processes that involve a more detached kind of recognition and engagement. Rather than repositioning ourselves as spectators in response to cues that indicate we are being multivocally *addressed* and not just worked on by the filmic text, we still attempt to locate a singular author or wait for a conclusive outcome. The Master's Voice Syndrome all over again. And why not? Why else do we go to see narrative cinema than to be confirmed and reinforced in our most atavistic and oedipal mind-sets?

Well, now that I've so precipitously catapulted us into the psychoanalytic soup, I have to admit that I'm not entirely satisfied with the model of spectatorship so flippantly refashioned here. For one thing, who the hell is this "we"? Can this indolent pronoun possibly account for the people who like the movies I myself make? Let's say it includes some or all of us some of the time, or enough of us enough of the time for me to justify, within limits, my own cinematic practice.

But there is another reason for invoking this specter/spectator, and that is to question its *sexual* homogeneity. Over a decade of feminist film theory has taught us the importance of splitting this undifferentiated pronominal mass into two, if not more, component parts. Let us now speak of male and female spectators. The "we" further unravels when "we" think about stories and storytelling. The stories we love the most are those that appeal to our deepest and earliest fears and desires that modulate and determine our placement in society as more, or less, successful adult men and women. The question has come to be asked (and must continue to be asked inasmuch as those with more power and privilege are always inclined to erase both question and answers): within these stories, quoting from Teresa de Lauretis's "Desire in Narrative,"

> . . . whose desire is it that speaks, and whom does that desire address? The received interpretations of the Oedipus story, Freud's among others, leave no doubt. The desire is Oedipus's, and though its object may be woman (or Truth or knowledge or power), its term of reference and address is man: man as social being and mythical subject, founder of the social, and source of mimetic violence. . . .[2]

> . . . [man as] hero, constructed as human . . . the active principle of culture, the establisher of distinction, the creator of differences. Female is what is not susceptible to transformation, to life or death; she (it) is an element of plot-space . . . a resistance, matrix, and matter. (p. 119)

Monster and landscape, she adds elsewhere, Sphinx, Medusa, ovum, earth, nature, Sleeping Beauty, etc.

Given that Oedipus killed his father and married his mother, it can be said that

> . . . the crime of Oedipus is the destruction of differences and that the combined work of myth and narrative is the production of Oedipus . . . a mapping of differences, and specifically, first and foremost, of sexual difference into each text . . . (p. 120)

The consequence for the reader/spectator is that

> each reader—male or female—is constrained and defined within the two positions of a sexual difference thus conceived: male-hero-human, on the side of the subject; and female-obstacle-boundary-space [on the side of the object].

She elaborates:

> . . . in its "making sense" of the world, narrative endlessly reconstructs it as a two-character drama in which the human person creates and recreates *himself* out of an abstract or purely symbolic other—the womb, the earth, the grave, the woman. . . . The drama has the movement of a passage, a crossing, an actively experienced transformation of the human being into—man. This is the sense in which all change, all social and personal—even physical—transformation is finally understood. (p. 121)

Another question that has subsequently arisen is, "What's in it for us ladies?" Do we (ladies) go to the movies to put our minds in the hands of our various Daddies—benign, malevolent, whatever? The oppressed often have a very curious relation to those in power, a perverse identification with the power they lack. Why else would a black taxi driver justify his voting for Reagan with "I want to be on the side that's going to win?" One of my earliest movie-going memories is recounted in *Film About a Woman Who. . . .*:

> She catches herself snorting gleefully at the scene of the two women being totally bitchy to one another. She remembers a similar scene—was it Dorothy Lamour or Betty Grable?—in a movie she saw when she was no more than 9 or 10. One woman had ripped another woman's dress off. She had stayed in the movie theater long after her friends had left until that scene came around again. And she must have felt guilty about it, because she never told anybody, not her mother, nor anybody.[3]

Yvonne Rainer and William Raymond enact an incestuous dream in Rainer's "The Man Who Envied Women." Photo: Abigail Heyman

During this speech, which is uttered by a female voiceover, we are looking at a snapshot of an elderly woman sitting in a field. I have no idea what the original movie was other than its source, Hollywood, and the approximate year, 1944. I can account for my pleasure in watching that scene as vicarious satisfaction in the eruption of female anger on the screen, an anger that I was not permitted to express in my own family. Right now, however, I am more interested in looking at my response as an example of male sadistic identification. The spectacle of two women fighting over a man provoked in me the pleasure that was clearly intended for the male spectator who would "naturally" identify with the absent (from the scene) male character they were fighting over. I don't remember rooting for either woman, neither the one who would eventually "get her man" nor her rival. The perversity of the situation was that I took pleasure in the humiliation of *both* women. Like the taxi driver, I was identifying with the power of the actual "winner," the man, rather than with those with whom I shared the same psycho-social disfranchisement, the women.

How does this response, or my interpretation of it, mesh with De Lauretis's

> . . . If women spectators are to buy their tickets and their popcorn, the work of cinema, unlike "the aim of biology," may be said to require

women's consent; and we may well suspect the narrative cinema in particular must be aimed, like desire, toward *seducing* women into femininity [emphasis added]. (pp. 136–37)

Or with Laura Mulvey's citation of Freud's argument about female sexuality as "an oscillation between 'passive' femininity and regressive 'masculinity' in her effort to account for

. . . the female spectator's phantasy of masculinization [which] is always to some extent at cross purposes with itself, restless in its transvestite clothes.[4]

They are both pointing to a double identification. De Lauretis further specifies the figures of narrative (movement of the male subject) and image (narrative closure/the space and body of the female object) as exerting, in and of themselves, a dual hold on the female spectator.

I have no doubt that I dutifully identified with the more passive, feminine "desire to be desired," in De Lauretis's words, at other points in my 1940s oedipal drama. (And, as a story of one woman replacing another, it was quintessentially oedipal, a recapitulation of the classical Freudian account of normative male sexual development, with its demand for successful repression of infantile desire conflated with the mother.) But those were not the scenes that kept me in that theater until they came around again. Auguring calamitous consequences in my adult life, it was the scene of the two women fighting each other that gripped me most, a scene that almost thirty years later would be transformed and played out as a real life melodrama of internalized misogyny in my private life. In patriarchal terms, I was a wash-out. It wasn't that I had refused to be seduced into dancing on the oedipal stage. I had simply gone to sleep and missed all my cues. Even the prince's kiss could not awaken me. I refused to wake up, and that is what nearly did me in. If the Medusa had not been sleeping in her cave, could Perseus have slain her? Must it always be either the prince or Perseus who gets you in the end? Here's another story:

On October 25, 1896, on the night after the funeral of his father Jakob, Sigmund Freud had a dream. "I found myself in a shop where there was a notice [*Tafel,* German for tablet (of the law) or table] saying 'You are requested to close the eyes'. . . ."[5] Using Marie Balmary's intricately fashioned key from her *Psychoanalyzing Psychoanalysis,* we can interpret this dream as an "injunction to 'close an eye' to the faults of the deceased." What might these faults have been?

Preceding his father's death, Freud was collecting indisputable evidence that pointed to the father as the cause of hysterical symptoms in the child. His theory of seduction was not well-received by the Viennese medical

Amy Schewel in conversation with Mark Rappaport, with Jack Deller (Larry Loonin) wearing headphones a few steps behind from "The Man Who Envied Women," by Yvonne Rainer.

community. Within eleven months after his father's death, he emerged from depression and mourning only to "close an eye" to his accumulated evidence via the Oedipus complex, his new theory that repudiated his patients' stories by consigning them to the realm of repressed unconscious desire. With his father's death he laid to rest his own unconscious knowledge of his father's unacknowledged past. Rather than two marriages there had been three. The town records of Freiberg reveal a second marriage to Rebecca, a mystery woman who is unrecognized in official Freud biographies. The fate of this wife and marriage remains undocumented. Balmary speculates that she committed suicide just before or just after Freud's birth.

Oedipus and Freud's theory conjoin as myth to conceal the "hidden fault of the father." Oedipus's father Laius had seduced his (Laius's) half-brother, Chrysippus, who later committed suicide "from shame." Freud's "closing his eyes" to Jakob's part in Rebecca's suicide (seducer and abandoner) is reenacted in his ignoring the part Laius played in the Oedipus myth (first as seducer of Chrysippus and later as violator of the gods' injunction against procreation), and is echoed yet again in the attitude

Amy Schewel (left) and Nancy Salzer (right) chatting near an unsuspecting Jack Deller (William Raymond) from "The Man Who Envied Women" by Yvonne Rainer.

psychoanalysis brings to the afflicted patient: "The fault is *your* desire rather than that of your father." And rather than that of The Fathers, or patriarchal society.

To varying degrees and from early on, all of us can characterize our lives as a struggle between closing and opening our eyes, sleeping and waking, knowing and refusing to know. If, as De Lauretis and Mulvey say, women oscillate between masculine and feminine positions of spectatorship and identification, then it must be said that we also oscillate between knowing and not knowing that this is what we do. It is not the first oscillation that is in itself dangerous, but rather a state of ignorance of that oscillation that will permit Oedipus (used here to stand for the *dominance* of men's faults, fears, and desires) in some form or another to do you in. My archetypal Hollywood Oedipus waited off-screen to claim his true love in what was for my nine-year-old spectator a no-win situation, a rigged game in which the precondition for participation as a female was the willingness to lose. My pleasure was that of a sleepwalker dreaming a dream of perennial tomboyhood. A more bitter reality lurked in the wings: the father I could neither have nor become, already prompting dialogue from the scenario governing the next phase of my feminine life. But this last was a story that no one was telling, therefore one which I could not know.

By now it must be more than clear that one does not have to probe very far into the psychoanalytic uses of Oedipus to find a phallocentric bias in both myth and theory. The terms of the oedipal formation of the human subject and its cultural expressions all seem to come down on one side, whether we're talking about women as signifiers of castration threat, voyeurism and the controlling gaze, identity and difference, scopic drives, visual pleasure, To Have and Have Not. The problem is that even as we employ these terms for describing and unveiling the workings of patriarchy, we implicate ourselves deeper into those very operations, as into a well-worn track in the forest. The very notion of lack, as proposed by Jacques Lacan, mirrors the prevailing cultural bias by privileging the symbolic threat of loss of the penis over the actual loss of the mother's body. Yes, I know that language is an all-important mediating factor and that loss of the breast predates the acquisition of language. Which then means, of course, that the breast is "less" than the penis. And how can this be otherwise when the clitoris is *nonexistent?* Psychoanalytic hierarchies of sexual synecdoche are mind-boggling and, for psychoanalysis, irrevocable. For women, however, psychoanalysis can only define a site of prolonged struggle.

All of this may seem far afield from my starting place, the authorial voice and fictional subject in cinematic practice, which we may now characterize as our (back to the undifferentiated pronominal mass!) desire for Oedipus in all or most of His manifestations. Although I may have to pay the consequences of breaking the Law of the Father in my daily life, there's no reason I can't give it (the Law) a run for its money as a filmmaker. If I'm going to make a movie about Oedipus, i.e., Eddy and Edy Pussy Foot, I'm going to have to subject him to some calculated narrative screw-ups. It's elementary, dear Eddy: play with signifiers of desire. Have two actors play Jack Deller, the male protagonist in *TMWEW*. Remove the physical presence of Trisha, the female protagonist, and reintroduce her as a voice. Create situations that can accommodate both ambiguity and contradiction without eliminating the possibility of taking specific political stands.

Shift De Lauretis's image/ground of narrative movement by frequent changes in the "production value" of the image, e.g., by utilizing refilming techniques, blown-up super 8, inferior quality video transfers, shooting off of a TV set with bad reception, etc.—not in order to make the usual intra-narrative tropes, however, such as the character's look at a TV show or a shift in meaning of the image to dream, flashback, or inner thoughts of a character. What I'm talking about is a disruption of the glossy, unified surface of professional cinematography by means of optically degenerated shots within an otherwise seamlessly edited narrative sequence.

Play off different, sometimes conflicting, authorial voices. And here I'm not talking about balance or both sides of a question like the nightly news, or about finding a "new language" for women. I'm talking about registers of complicity/protest/acquiescence within a single shot or scene that do not give a message of despair. I'm talking about bad guys making progressive political sense and good girls shooting off their big toe and mouth. I'm talking about uneven development and fit in the departments of consciousness, activism, articulation, and behavior that must be constantly reassessed by the spectator. I'm talking about incongruous juxtapositions of modes of address: recitation, reading, "real" or spontaneous speech, printed texts, quoted texts, *et al.,* all in the same film. I'm talking about representations of divine couplings and (un)holy triads being rescreened only to be used for target practice. I'm talking about not pretending that a life lived in potholes taking potshots will be easy and without cost, on screen or off.

I'm talking about films where in every scene you have to decide anew the priorities of looking and listening. In *TMWEW* there's a scene in which Jack Deller delivers a rambling lecture to a group of students in what is eventually revealed to be a newly renovated loft-condominium. If one doesn't pay particular attention to the insistent, autonomous tracking of the camera around the space, but puts all of one's efforts into deciphering the spoken text with its ellipses, digressions, and dipping in and out of Foucault, Lacan, Chomsky, Piaget, *et al.,* when Trisha's voice finally begins to talk about the disappeared in Central America and New York, you will have missed the meaning of that space, i.e., an expensive piece of real estate, as a crucial link between the lecture and instances of U.S. international and domestic imperialism. The visual track in this instance anticipates the sound track, but also supplies a subtext for the lecture with its retroactive associations of urban university land-grabbing.

Later in the film, texts are played off in a different way. In a scene in a narrow corridor between Jack Deller and his ex-lover, Jackie, the main thesis of Michel Foucault's "power-is-everywhere" is intercut with documentary footage of demonstrations of power "somewhere" in particular, "on this side" and "on that side." Jack Deller's recitation of the Foucault material is further juxtaposed with Jackie's recitation of excerpts from an essay by Meaghan Morris in which she criticizes theory itself for having "no teeth."[6]

Other tensions abound here: the anti-monolithic arguments of Foucault colliding with Trisha's invocation of military/police and medical fraternities, and the disparity between doing and speaking, or image and text, as demonstrated in the seductive moves of Jack and Jackie, a disparity that then collides with Foucault's "There is no opposition between what is said and what is done."[7] At another point Morris's description of Lacan's reign at the "costume ball" of feminine writing "not as lawgiver but as queen" is followed by a dream sequence in which a mother and daughter (played by one performer) play a queen of the kitchen who is alternately romanced by her son-in-law and watches him and her daughter in bed, in a short and shifty oedipal extravaganza caustically narrated by the irate daughter. If these scenes are about a conflict between theory and practice, or a contradiction between theory and everyday life, they can also be read in terms of a "return of the repressed" which, operating as more than cheap subversion, constantly pressures theory into re-examining systems of signification, reinventing its own constraints.

Finally, I'm talking about films that allow for periods of poetic ambiguity, only to unexpectedly erupt into rhetoric, outrage, direct political address or analysis, only to return to a new adventure of Eddy Foot or New Perils of Edy Foot. He may still shoot off his big toe while getting or not getting the girl, but he'll also ask a few questions or wait in the wings a little longer to see how the ladies work it out without him. And this time around she may start to rip off her rival's dress, but then stop to muse, "Hey, we're wearing the same dress aren't we? Why don't we pool our energies and try to figure out what a political myth for socialist feminism might look like?"

So they (she and she) make a movie together and. . . .

13

Dialogue:
Remembering (this memory of)
a film

Raymond Bellour and Guy Rosolato

R.B.   At the outset let me remind you that the pretext here is the following ideal situation: someone—an historian, a musician, or a psychoanalyst—is interested in film, in the cinema, devotes some of his work to it; and this practice in turn affects his primary occupation. When I was asked whether I would be willing to examine the possible effects of film theory or film analysis on psychoanalysis, my natural response was: yes, I have analyzed films, but I am not a psychoanalyst. Then, since there are not really any psychoanalysts who have devoted serious attention to cinema, I thought it might be fun to create a somewhat artificial double figure and then play with it. The figure would consist of myself—someone who has analyzed films with an approach inspired often by psychoanalysis— and you, a psychoanalyst attracted to film, sensitive to that which is inscribed in the cinema. My thinking was that perhaps this montage would allow us to shed some light on certain aspects of the relation between psychoanalysis and cinema or at least to establish a dialogue between them.

G.R.   I was surprised at first when you asked me to participate in this discussion, given that I am only a psychoanalyst and have never done any analysis of film.

Translated by Thomas Y. Levin Translation of an interview entitled "Dialogue: se (ce) souvenir d'un film" published in "Analectures," the first issue of *Hors Cadre (Le cinéma travers champs disciplinaires)* [St. Denis: PUV] (Spring 1983), pp. 150–167. (Back issues of the journal can be ordered from Michele Lagny, 152 Boulevard Magenta, 75010 Paris FRANCE.)

R.B.   You could always refer to work that has already been done on the subject or the possible impact of the cinema on your analytic practice.

G.R.   Not only this: my perspective might also potentially reveal something more profound. I've been thinking a lot about this question since you first raised it and realized the following: I like movies, have been going to the cinema all my life, but when I want to refer to certain technical details of a film, I find that my memory is extremely capricious and weak. It's incredible. I am convinced that to speak of such details with any degree of precision—as one can with other works of art—an analysis with a moviola, i.e. the possibility of seeing a film over and over, is crucial.

R.B.   Do you mean to say that if one cannot re-view a film in this way, it practically does not exist?

G.R.   The cinema appears as a double illusion, a phantasmagoria.[1] On the one hand, it is immediate, visual, and animated with a fascinating—and illusory—life. On the other hand, after the fact, following its efface-ment from memory, it is also more ephemeral than any other art. You yourself say so in one of your essays. I no longer recall which film it was that had been withdrawn from circulation, thereby denying you the possibility of seeing it again. It was a Hitchcock film, I think, but which one?

R.B.   *Notorious.*

G.R.   Yes, that's the one. And you remained interested in it because it was the object of your desire.

R.B.   Yes, it was the one I desired, but the way things turned out, I never really did work on it.

G.R.   Yes, but this desire manifested itself again in relation to Hitch-cock's work as a whole. The last time we saw each other, you pointed out to me that, by a happy coincidence, a few days later *Notorious* was to be shown on television. Well, I realize that since the moment I saw it, forgetting has again done its work. I recall only very little, having lost not so much the events depicted and the characters but primarily the elements that could be useful for a technical examination. But this is due to the way I look at things.

R.B.   What, for example, do you recall?

G.R.   I remember what I thought about while watching the film.

R.B.   Namely?

G.R.   Namely an idea I had about Hitchcock. I would like to know what you think of it. What struck me about *Suspicion*—we already spoke on the telephone about this—is the last sequence.

R.B.   In *Notorious*?

G.R.   In *Notorious* just as much as in *Suspicion*. Both films were shown on television only a few days apart. You asked what struck me and I told you that it was the last sequence, the last sequence *in* Hitchcock. In *Suspicion* it is the about-face made by the car in which the people come back and then disappear; in *Notorious* it's the same thing.

R.B.   But not in the same way.

G.R.   Not in the same way; the difference is a function of the plot.

R.B.   Yes. Can you be more specific about what happens in this last shot of *Notorious*?

G.R.   Claude Rains tries to flee with the lovers, is rejected and the camera pulls back further and further; Rains turns back towards his accomplices in a long shot centered on a door. That's it, isn't it?

R.B.   Yes, the door of the villa in which the action takes place.

G.R.   That's right: one of the main characters disappears. I wonder if in Hitchcock's films there isn't something like a summary of the plot in the last sequence, something which tends towards disappearance, towards loss, towards that which the film will become for me—a sort of forgetting which will make the film itself disappear, thereby giving it its reality through my illusion. What is the last sequence of *The Birds*?

R.B.   The four characters leave the house, get into the car, and drive off into a landscape covered with birds. On the one hand, what you have here is a final reconciliation, a response to the psychological problem raised by the film. On the other hand, one doesn't know whether or not this reconciliation will be followed by a total catastrophe, that is, a renewed attack of the birds.

G.R.   And they drive off into the distance?

R.B.   They drive off into the distance.

G.R.   So it is the same movement.

R.B.   The ending which Hitchcock didn't film had the car arrive at the Golden Gate bridge totally covered with birds.

G.R.   The Golden Gate bridge is yet another road. In *North by Northwest* there is a similar sequence at the end.

R.B.   Yes, the train entering the tunnel.

G.R.   This is really fascinating. But your work explored something else: Hitchcock's own appearances in his films.

R.B.   Yes, moments which are always indicative, always metaphoric, referring back to the filmic system.

G.R.   These appearances are also important. What I would like to ask, then, is whether there might not be a relationship between the endings of the films and Hitchcock's own appearances?

R.B.   From what angle?

G.R.   In terms of an image which is simultaneously enigmatic and very symbolic. You yourself stressed the symbolic value of Hitchcock's appearances.

R.B.   Yes. Take for example his appearance in *Strangers on a Train*: he gets into a train with a cello in his hand. What you have here is condensation: the young woman who will be the victim of the murder works in a music store, and the exchange of murders between the two heros takes place in the train. Hitchcock puts himself at the heart of the metaphorical circuit between the sexes. But what intrigues me about your hypothesis is the relationship to the ending.

G.R.   This may be specific to Hitchcock. But it is not by accident that you became interested in Hitchcock.

R.B.   I had a hunch that there was something in Hitchcock which extended to all of cinema.

G.R.   Which makes it all the more interesting to reflect on Hitchcock. Through this departure, this escape from the realm of the film, Hitchcock prepares us for our departure by means of a final sequence which simultaneously sums up that which is most essential in the film.

R.B.   As if it were a vanishing object.

G.R.   We separate.

R.B.   We separate, left with only this last memory of the film. This puts us in touch with the manner in which the film itself is really a vanishing object, and it simultaneously points us towards another film, yet to be made, yet to be seen.

G.R.   I'll tell you the word which interests me: it is "*object of perspective*" [*objet de perspective*].

R.B.   What do you mean when you use this term?

G.R.   From a psychoanalytic *perspective* focused on castration, it is that which comes to replace the maternal penis. The *object of perspective* is not a representation, a phallic figuration. It has a status of unreality, of the unusual, the uncanny, the striking. In a story or in an image it is somehow enigmatic and gripping, provoking reflection. This, as I said before, leads to *co-gitation* by developing that reality-unreality expressed in the child's history through his/her phantasms of castration—in the past common to all of us—through the exemplary image of the maternal penis, but is then taken up in an idea of elaboration, of curiosity, displaced, symbolized in an *other* domain such as the aesthetic, for example, where the metaphoric and metonymic oscillation can play itself out completely. And I ask myself whether we do not almost see this *object of perspective* represented in Hitchcock's films, because the final sequences in his films *are* perspectives. Furthermore, I wonder whether your judicious emphasis on Hitchcock's appearances in his own films does not also point to another object of perspective in the film.

R.B.   Certainly the manner in which Hitchcock inscribes himself at the heart of the network formed by lines of force in the film makes everything converge towards him and recede from him. And when I say everything, I mean all symbolization and in particular all symbolization linked to the establishment of sexual difference, since this is the axis around which the film turns in an explicit, insistent manner.

G.R.   All the more if one considers the identifications which you demonstrated well in your analysis of *The Birds*.[2] Hitchcock identifies himself just as much with the woman as with the man.

R.B.   But let's get back to memory, to the question raised by analyses of films. You mentioned at the outset the dearth of memory, the lack which you encountered after watching a film. Now consider the practice of those who try to recall films by analyzing them, who engage in the operation—which is slightly artificial—of stopping them, of reappropriating the films in a different manner by creating a sort of other film which is slower and more global: what do you as a psychoanalyst think of this practice and does it compare it with your own analytic procedure?

G.R.   I would say that it gives one a take on the film. Not only in order to reappropriate it in memory but also to understand it better. Don't you think that films have a latent story, a latent content?

R.B.   Without a doubt, but a content which is more or less latent depending on the film.

G.R.   Take what you call "symbolic blockage."[3] There is, if I have understood correctly, something like a miniaturization of the dynamic of the entire film in each sequence that one could analyze.

R.B.   Yes. This is a mode of operation which, it seems to me, is common to a large number of aesthetic or cultural phenomena and which, I feel, as far as cinema is concerned, is particularly strong in American cinema.

G.R.   What does this blockage imply?

R.B.   It suggests that the movement closing the film is simultaneously the movement that opens it, and that the conditions of this opening and closing process function according to a certain process of symbolization just as much at the level of the film in general as at the level of the detail of the operations put into play. This circular effect is obviously manifest in many other films besides those of the American cinema. But for me, it is only in the American cinema that it takes place so clearly and perfectly.

R.B.   Why?

R.B.   Because in the American cinema, just as in the 19th-century novel, there is a continuous relation between the whole and the part: a relation of organicity, of closure, and of mirroring that does not exist in cinemas that are less strong, less structured, or more modern. This is the result of the crystallization of a grand moment of classicism.

G.R.   This also implies a high degree of technical mastery, by which I mean extensive experience with the technology and a large range of means employed.

R.B.   Yes, or at least sufficient repetition of the mechanics of the art so that, over the course of hundreds and thousands of films, a sort of global, cultural corpus is constituted.

G.R.   I spoke of the latent content or latent narrative; you yourself indicate that analytic concepts such as the Oedipal concept form the backbone of this symbolic blockage.

R.B.   Absolutely. To the extent that the Oedipal scenario supports the entire dynamic of the narrative, puts the identifications into play and activates sexual difference, it is an almost universal principle of the operation of the film in the American cinema. But it would be a pity to reduce the latent content to mere content. What is interesting is to see to what extent the film work—along with the secondarization specific to all work of the unconscious—never ceases to work through the latent content in the way that the dream work does for individual experience (I here employ terms taken from two fundamental texts by Thierry Kuntzel— "The Film Work [1]" and "The Film-Work, [2]"[4]—which, in the realm of film, are the terms closest to the work of the unconscious.

G.R.   When one says the work of the unconscious, one is referring to mechanisms described by Freud, such as condensation, displacement, symbolization, and the representation in images. Now the representation in images is specific to the cinema.

R.B.   It is in any case one of the specific qualities of the cinema.

G.R.   Then let me ask you the following question: how do you yourself make your unconscious work? You stop the film; you decide—"this is where I will stop." Or you examine a sequence from point A all the way to point N.

R.B.   I think there are two things which have not been sufficiently differentiated in this experience. On the one hand there is an undeniable desire for a system, a theoretical desire leading to the formulation of intellectual hypotheses in order to bring out the logic of a certain operation. This results in texts in which psychoanalysis is more or less invoked as an instrument of knowledge or even as a global equivalent of the experience under consideration. However, on the other hand, there is another side that is more intimate, more fascinating, and which very few analyses have stressed: the side one encounters at the editing table or, today, with the use of a VCR, when one stops the film. (More than any other analyses, the essays by Thierry Kuntzel have certainly helped to elaborate this dimension and it is precisely this which his video tapes show us today.) I would call it a major disturbance, a major fascination, effects of indulgence, of misrecognition.

G.R.   At the level of a *single* image.

R.B.   At the level of a single image. One image or another. For example, one day, while viewing Hitchcock's *Rebecca*, I stopped at the sequence where the governess of the castle dies admist the flames and, confronted by this image, I was overcome by something I cannot explain. In the relationships of the whites and blacks, in the woman's stance—her mouth open, close to the window, surrounded by flames—there was something which had an incredible effect on me. The same thing occurred in the same way in *Suspicion* with a close-up of Joan Fontaine—one sees only the upper portion of her face, especially the wide open eyes—on which I had stopped.

G.R.   By accident?

R.B.   Almost by accident. Well, alone with this face, I was frightened. It suddenly became an extraordinary force.

G.R.   Because it had been stopped.

R.B.   It was much more violent than when it simply appeared within the diegesis because it had been stopped but also because it was loaded with the entire weight of the film. It is this that one could call the hidden face of film analysis: it leads those who practice such analysis to an experience which is fantasmatic and associative in an extremely direct fashion.

G.R.   Do you remember this line from Lacan: "Immobility similar in its strangeness to the face of the actor when the film stops." In my text "Paranoia and the Primal Scene"[5] I cited it with regard to the primal scene in order to demonstrate the importance of the visual in paranoia, that fixation on something which leads you into another realm.

R.B.   One goes into another realm, lacking any sense of orientation, one finds oneself facing something very profound and, even if one were to discover the reason for this profundity, this reason itself would always remain displaceable and displaced. What is important to me is the violence of the experience, the dimension hidden from the analysis of films which, without a doubt, points most directly to that which you yourself could achieve through or anticipate from a cure.

G.R.   On the one hand, we are led back to the primal scene: the act of stopping the image augments uneasiness and strangeness. But there is something else, on the other hand, which interests me about Kuntzel's experiments and about the article you wrote on him.[6] The semiotic analysis of cinema is of interest to all the other human sciences, and psychoanalysis among others, when it undertakes to define in general the elements which work together to produce meaning. For the study of language, this sort of analysis has been developed quite far: one can identify linguistic signifiers very precisely. But what are the elementary signifiers in (non-linguistic) semiotics? I think that by using video with reference to Kuntzel's experiments—which provide transformations of intensity and duration—one could perhaps begin to isolate or at least better discern the forms that function as elements—(I call them *signifiers of demarcation*)—in the appearance of visual signifiers. Through these processes of transformation these signifiers would be distilled down to their signifying base, or at least to a point which would allow them to be identified.

R.B.   Do you think that these visual signifiers are at all permanent or circumscribed?

G.R.   I think we have become accustomed to recognizing them in silent films. I refer to silent film because it is easier here to seize the purely visual signifiers. We operate with stereotypes that we know how to recognize. But how are we to determine the elements which make up these stereotypes, how are we to know what we have inherited and on what basis we are operating if it is not by transforming these elements, by trying to go towards unfamiliar forms which we will not be able to identify? In the images which you reproduced in your article on Kuntzel, you also speak of writing, I think . . .

R.B.   Of the return of writing.

G.R.   The return of writing: could one say of the signifier as well as of writing?

R.B.   What I meant to say was that in Kuntzel's experiments (as in other experiments manifesting themselves with increasing frequency in video) there is a kinship with the position of the writer by virtue of the liberty of manipulation and invention.

G.R.   One could push the comparison further if one considers that you have the capacity to make much more liberal use of the elements, the signifiers, like a type of writing in which you inscribe each of the letters. When I looked at these images, there were some to which I could give a name, others not. I'm not sure what this might mean. I have to make some kind of an effort to be able to say "oh yes, that's a woman's face," and I'm still not sure. There is something there which is at the limit, and it is this limit which interests me. I think that your research has enabled us to "demarcate" the signifier. I call this the *signifier of demarcation* because it demarcates itself from language and because it demarcates itself from other information received in the visual field and in relation to which it structures itself.

R.B.   When you say "ascertain the signifiers of demarcation" does this presuppose a finite list?

G.R.   Certainly not.

R.B.   Is it in order to situate things in relation to language?

G.R.   That's the difference. In language [*langage*], the signifiers are the phonemes of which there is a finite number in each national language [*langue*]. By contrast, one of the decisive characteristics of signifiers of demarcation is that one cannot draw up a finite list of them.

R.B.   But since in the hypothesis which you are developing you nevertheless refer to visual elements, how do you understand the relation of closure and non-closure?

G.R.   Consider a morphematic writing such as Chinese. I think that if the signifiers of demarcation are not a finite list, they are at least reduced for each human being to a group which forms the constitutive elements of the characters of this writing. These characters are also the vocabulary.

R.B.   Yes, but as soon as you are dealing with vocabulary you are no longer dealing with phonemes.

G.R.   Yes, of course. There is no double articulation here. So what we have are groups: in a representation composed of many elements, we can delimit within these groups the signifiers we recognize. The entire question is to know at which point the signifier is received as such.

R.B.   You mean to say: how it is that one has the feeling that one is facing something which exceeds representation itself because it is what makes such representation possible in the first place, i.e., constitutes it.

G.R.   Exactly. Exceeding is important. Because at that moment the symbolic is at work.

R.B.   In the sense that the symbolic becomes an abstract constituent in the same way that the phonemes relate to words.

G.R.   Yes, although in the former you certainly do not have a double articulation.

R.B.   But if it is not a double articulation, what is it?

G.R.   It's a composition. These signifiers organize themselves into a representation. They have a component function.

R.B.   So we are still confronting something that is relatively imprecise.

G.R.   This imprecision arises from the fact that there is no double articulation and that one cannot make up a finite list of signifiers of demarcation.

R.B.   What you call the identification of the signifier of demarcation appears by definition to be much more singular, hypothetical, and aleatory than the linguist's practice of identifying phonemes.

G.R.   Certainly, compared to the phoneme. And yet, certain significant "traits" of demarcation—a face, for example, which is more easily recognizable and better presented than it could be through words—convey a meaning with an extraordinary precision unique to them by virtue of their very materiality and by means of their composition. Take the example of a painting and a drawing—for in the last analysis it is not such a great leap from the cinema to a fixed representation on a surface. We can produce a painting with many details, in trompe-l'oeil fashion, with spatial effects and we can also depict something in a suggestive manner with as little as two lines. The issue is to know why it is that these two lines suffice to produce a signifying effect. This is quite evident in the images which you provide in your article on Kuntzel.

R.B.   I find it difficult to understand exactly what you mean when you speak of "producing a signifying effect."

G.R.   It is the process by which the signifier gains effects of meaning through its articulation (or composition) with another signifier. In the photos which you presented in that article, where the image is centered on one part of the face, this does not suffice in order to recognize the face. But as soon as one adds the hair and the arm, one can identify the parts involved after the fact (and in such a way that I can name them). You yourself undertake such transformations by means of the processes available to you through video technology.

R.B.   We should note that this too is made possible thanks to the freeze frame (by the photogram or, rather, the video-gram) in tapes which themselves to some extent grow out of the work on the interruption of the movement of the film-strip [*défilement*], on slow motion, in order to bring out the primary elements, an increase in the unconscious.

While listening to you, I have been asking myself for a while now a somewhat polemical question: why are there no psychoanalysts who have taken a more direct interest in this work?

G.R.   I can imagine two reasons. I think, first of all, that the cinema has long been considered a minor art, and psychoanalysts are no exception in this regard. Secondly, I would say that the practical conditions which we spoke of at the outset make it essential to have certain materials and technology for such work: one has to have a projector or a moviola, and above all some films which are readily accessible, which one can project over and over interminably, which one can stop, slow down, etc. All this is not available to everyone: it is much easier to own books or records, musical scores or photos of works of plastic art.

And then there is perhaps something else as well. Consider the case of those who love the cinema without having any technical knowledge of it. Don't you think that what they want above all else is to protect their personal pleasure, a pleasure which, as we have seen, is so unique—simultaneously fascinating, visually *hallucinatory* and ephemeral, both characteristics being linked to, and reinforcing, each other? This pleasure will be all the more hallucinatory and intense the more it remains elusive and disappears without having been grasped, still a secret. In this way one has the illusion of preserving it, just as one does for an intimate fantasy.

R.B.   So it is the pleasure of allowing it to remain elusive.

G.R.   Yes, letting it remain elusive. It is a great pleasure to go to the cinema and to rediscover the same scenes which are decidedly evanescent: the attack on the stagecoach as it attempts to flee. It is also the pleasure of relinquishing oneself without reserve to the flux of the diegesis. You know, there is an important mental mechanism which the cinema encourages: it is the mechanism which the psychoanalysts—especially the Kleinians—call projective identification.

R.B.   Which is what, exactly?

G.R.   We can project into an object elements that we do not want to have in ourselves, the worst elements, which we thereby externalize. In this way we take possession of the object and can, in return, by identifying with it, identify ourselves with other elements of the object which one could call the good elements. This, in turn, allows us to introject. We can also project the best of ourselves towards the exterior, which is another way of appropriating the object and identifying with it. But, as in the preceding case, we can thereby identify ourselves with other elements that were neither expected nor known. This happens in a very intense way in the cinema. It is an incomparable fascination: one enters the cinema and that's it, one is caught and the projective identification begins.

R.B.   Let's approach the matter from another angle: do you often encounter the cinema in your analytic practice and, if so, in what manner?

G.R.   Of course cinema comes up as a topic on the couch. Patients quite frequently manifest the phenomena of identification which I mentioned earlier. They often enter into a transferential game of cultural seduction with the analyst as if to participate in shared pleasures. Furthermore, patients can be led to see a film in an extraordinarily one-sided fashion as soon as they discover a correspondence between their fundamental problems and those displayed by the film. In this case we are not talking about problems in general but about extremely precise situations, character types that resonate and are meticulously described in a film.
There is also, of course, something else which strikes me as important: the phenomenon of the cinematic memory screen.[7]

R.B.   What exactly do you mean when you use this term?

G.R.   Memory screens which activate a cinematographic sequence.

R.B.   Playing on the double meaning of the word "screen."

G.R.   Yes, it is a cinematographic sequence seen in childhood which is included in the memory-screen.

R.B.   And which itself serves as a hiding place . . .

G.R.   As a hiding place and as a revelation. And which, like almost all memory-screens, emphasizes phenomena of seduction.

R.B.   As if the cinema were destined to this role of memory-screen, indeed more so than any other medium, because it implicates the very scenes which can always take the place of other scenes, revealing and concealing them at the same time.

G.R.   And scenes of seduction above all.

R.B.   Yes. But in what form do you encounter this material in the cure? Does the manner in which the films are recounted to you, the way in which the images are evoked, have something to do with that elusive object [*objet de fuite*] which we spoke about earlier, similar to the fixation of certain moments which are privileged by the film analyst?

G.R.   First of all there is the escape provided by the cinema. If cinema seems to be a minor art, perhaps it is because it is perceived as a means of escape and this more than the other arts. One has the impression of being gripped, of being able to flee the world. It is an illusion, perhaps, but an illusion which is very powerful. One can take recourse to it very intensely at certain difficult moments of one's life. There are also the images that have made an impression, which have remained in one's memory: images of horror, erotic images.

R.B.   But which, in this case, no longer have any relation to the film from which they come.

G.R.   Indeed, they have often left little more than a replacement memory. I knew someone who, although unable to recall a single sequence from a film, could nevertheless remember the poster. What he recalled of the poster, however, was not what it depicted but only that it was related to the "perfume of the lady in black." He remembered only one thing and that was that the poster frightened him, to such a degree that upon leaving the cinema, he was somewhat afraid of passing by it again. This is what remained of the memory, which was perhaps entirely fabricated. I did not verify whether the film actually existed.

R.B.   What interests me in the course of this example, is how it points to the division internal to film analysis that I mentioned earlier; that is, the division between the system—intellectual, propped up with the theoretical scaffolding of psychoanalysis—and the wild and unmasterable experience provoked by the encounter with a particular face or with a particular relationship between two shots which suddenly disturbs you. It's like a materialization of one's relationship to the recollection of one's dreams, even if here one is actually dealing with a construction of real images whereas the dream is an attempt to grasp once again things which are in the process of being lost.

G.R.   This would be a huge rush of effects.

R.B.   Yes.

G.R.   Some films provoke an incredible affective discharge, leading people to get up and leave the cinema. As an example of this sort of film I would cite "L'Incompris" [*Incompreso*, directed by Luigi Comencini, 1967] if one is to believe the reports about it given on the couch. It is the story of a young boy who was not understood by his father, who was apparently not loved by him. But what you have here is not *one* image, it is a story which is all the more gripping because it is a story in images.

R.B.   But a story in images is often constructed in such a way that some of its moments are organized according to formal processes which in themselves provoke affective processes. Take the flashback for example. No matter what the flashback actually recounts, by its very nature it provokes an extremely violent emotional shock through the mere fact that it points to the past. One of my friends had a slightly disturbed relationship to his past at one point and flashbacks had an almost automatic effect on him; one could say that it was their form itself that made him cry.

G.R.   It can also be pleasant to return to one's past. But in any case, the flashback does incite one to return to one's own latent memories. Spectators are led to this point seemingly on their own; they are even led to accept images presented in this manner as belonging, at least by analogy, to their own past.

R.B.   I wonder whether in the analysis of films there is not a sort of operation in two temporalities where the very fact of stopping . . .

G.R.   There is more to it than just freezing the image; there's also backing up. One returns to the preceding images in order to verify the number of shots, no?

R.B.   Here again I would separate the two operations. It is true that one counts the shots, yes, but the return to previous images is also something that goes against the meaning of the film, turning it towards its own past, transforming it through the confrontation of the gaps between the film and what one imagined about the object. And here I ask myself once again how this experience is related to that of the cure.

G.R.   In a certain, entirely implicit way the analyst invites patients to recall their past. However, in the process of film analysis this backing up is entirely internal. But there is something else as well: the entire analytic experience demonstrates that the past can change. This is one of the positive aspects of analysis to which not enough attention is paid. One becomes capable of gaining distance from images that were previously inadmissable and painful; one learns to see them in an entirely different light. Thus we have also fabricated a memory about everything that we say about film. And you deconstruct this memory. You modify it. There is a *work of memory*. So, the disappearing into the distance which occurs in the final sequences of *Notorious* and *Suspicion* (but also in Chaplin's films) is accompanied by an affective charge that we did not point out in our previous analyses. This is, without a doubt, separation, the departure. But one leaves a film just as one would depart from someone dear to us, one's mother for example, and thus with the work of mourning which such departures evoke.

R.B.   It is the end of the hypnosis. That which Barthes emphasized so well.

G.R.   I want to say, further, that as a result the image can become uneasy through its strong retention of an emotion both induced and liberated.

R.B.   Now that we have advanced a little, how would you now formulate what the reflection on cinema—and specifically the analysis of film—could contribute to psychoanalysis?

G.R.   This remains difficult to say as long as one has not oneself had any experience at the viewing table. But one could imagine that such experiences could help us understand mental mechanisms and also the functioning of vision. For we have not yet fully distinguished seeing from being seen. There are still many things that need to be established, for example in the domain of what are called the perversions—fetishism, exhibitionism, and voyeurism—in order to understand fascination better.

As regards the way individuals see, in post-autistic children who have had difficult relations of maternal dependence one currently speaks of a "dismantling,"[8] a sort of perceptual errancy, a type of captivation in the moment by the most lively sensations, however they appear, by a suspension of attention. The result is a dependence which is above all *visual* in relation to the external object.

This floating and immediate grasping is a means of substituting a perceptual and particularly *visual excitement* for a relation to the mother.

In this case, the cinema becomes a means of choice.

As a further example I would cite the phobia where the object—which has its counterpart in the fetish—comes to fill a gap, an unknown that is relative to a maternal abyss. This phobic object is related to the object of perspective, which is to say it refers back to the irreality of the maternal penis. One can thus ask how cinema functions in our daily consciousness as an activity that evokes anguish by relating it to certain representations that have a strong emotional impact.

R.B.   Do you have the impression that this entire debate is heading towards new thoughts on the question of the relation between the "thing-presentation" and "word-presentation"?

G.R.   Certainly. I think that the analysis of cinema can help to explore the question of thing-presentation. I mentioned a moment ago the possibility of reducing representations to constitutive elements: thing-presentations consist in a composition of *signifiers of demarcation*. And I think that you have the means, the experimental means, to map out these signifiers. As far as the psychoanalytic argument is concerned, I think that we can also objectify thing-presentations through experiments in the realm of cinema.

Here is how I see the relationship between the representation of things and of words: on the one hand we have material elements which are the signifiers of demarcation and which constitute thing-presentations. On the other hand we have linguistic signifiers which are at the root of *langage* and *langue*. The possibility of establishing a relation between these two domains—which are not of the same order and which can be utterly heterogenous—resides especially in the organizational processes they have in *common,* i.e. metaphor and metonymy. What I mean is that metaphor and metonymy belong equally to the domain of thing-presentation as to the domain of word-presentation. They are the bridge between them.

R.B.   Don't you get the impression that you are privileging the linguistic aspect to the extent that these processes are constituted in verbal rhetoric?

G.R.   Yes, to the extent that everything ultimately is born of language. One could say that what we see is also determined by language. For objects and perceptions are part of the communicational acts of the speaking being and naming helps that being see by situating objects and perceptions in the desire of the other. But I think that metaphoric and metonymic structure is just as inherent in the organization of thing-presentation as it is in word-presentation. To the extent that the signifiers are composed or articulated, there is meaning. When Freud describes the mechanism of primary process, he stresses condensation and displacement, or—as one would say from a Lacanian perspective (to which I adhere entirely)—metaphor and metonymy. If you start with precise definitions of metaphor and metonymy, you can efficiently explore the development of a film by exploring the homogeneity of development in terms of its metonymy and in terms of its metaphoric ruptures. I think, for example, that by mapping shots you could locate the true points of rupture where metaphor is at work. In Hitchcock's films, the appearance of the auteur, for example, would have this status.

R.B.   It is a super-metaphor. A metaphor of metaphor.

G.R.   It is a metaphor and one which works in a subtle fashion because it has to be pointed out, must be discovered. It is a metaphor of the wink of the eye [*clin d' oiel*]—but in the end the wink is the visual at its liveliest.

R.B.   The visual tells us: I am the enunciator and I am pointing it out by this appearance.

G.R.   The analysis of film effectively allows one to get a better grasp of the latent, spectral presence through which things are presented to sight, whether this be the actor or the character represented. And behind this actor there is the model of the ideal actor. It is the star system. David Rodowick discusses this in what he calls the "circuit of desire" which passes through the role; there is a projective identification, sometimes with the role and sometimes with the visible or invisible actor.[9] We await our actor very precisely to put into play the complex game of our identifications. Certain actors capture our interest more than others without our always knowing why. But there is also the auteur of the film who is always invisible as a body but omnipresent in his work. We also have him in mind as a potential for identification. Thus, Hitchcock appears; the director, ordinarily absent, suddenly appears and, what is more, in his own film.

R.B.   Now here what you have is no longer the star system but the system of cinephilia or of culture. The auteur winks at us in order to tell us that he himself is the object of everything he has directed and that he is the receding image with which one can always identify in the last analysis.

G.R.   You know, for a long time I asked myself "why is Bellour so interested in the films of Hitchcock?" Well, I wonder if it is not due to this sly, ironic role of the auteur who inserts himself in his films and plays in such a specific manner. But perhaps there is another reason?

R.B.   Yes, but it is basically the same one phrased differently: my interest lies in the fact that the systematic organization of the visual field in these films truly stages an enunciation of the gaze, a place for the one who looks.

G.R.   More than elsewhere?

R.B.   Yes, in a more precise fashion than elsewhere, and it takes place in an image that amuses and captivates you: the auteur who appears. He thereby signs the place where he locates himself in order to speak, to enounce, to desire.

G.R.   That's true. Film analysis makes one think about the so important function of enunciation and of the utterance, of the position of the subject, in scopic relations (seeing and being seen) where the fetish has a major place. They are at the heart of the perversions but go far beyond them.

Notes

Introduction

1. Cf., for example, *Literature and Psychoanalysis*, eds. Edith Kurzweil and William Phillips (New York: Columbia University Press, 1983); *Literature and Psychoanalysis: The Question of Reading Otherwise*, ed. Shoshana Felman (Baltimore and London: The Johns Hopkins University Press, 1982); *In Dora's Case: Freud-Hysteria-Feminism*, eds. Charles Bernheimer and Claire Kahane (New York: Columbia University Press, 1985); *Discourse in Psychoanalysis and Literature*, ed. Shlomith Rimmon-Kennan (London and New York: Methuen, 1987).

2. I was unable to include all psychoanalytic film approaches, as will be discussed briefly later on.

3. Let me note, however, that the editors of *In Dora's Case* at least mentioned the film about the case and some of the articles written in relation to the film, even though they decided not to include these materials.

4. Some anthologies have recently begun to combine essays on film, literature, and other disciplines. The trend started with *Powers of Desire: The Politics of Sexuality*, eds. Ann Snitow, Christine Stansell, and Sharon Thompson (New York: Monthly Review Press, 1983); and continued with *The Female Body in Western Culture: Contemporary Perspectives*, ed. Susan R. Suleiman (Cambridge, Mass.: Harvard University Press, 1986).

5. Interestingly enough, Joseph W. Krutch's *Edgar Allan Poe: A Study in Genius* (New York: Knopf, 1926) engages in a sort of psychoanalytic reading before Marie Bonaparte's 1933 study. But Krutch uses psychoanalysis now in the service of aesthetics, that is to denounce Poe's work as inferior because "sick." This is very different from Bonaparte's task, which is to understand Poe's illness through his texts. Cf. essay by Shoshana Felman, cited later on.

6. Sigmund Freud, "Foreward," to Marie Bonaparte, *The Life and Works of Edgar Allan Poe: A Psycho-Analytic Interpretation*, trans. John Rodker (London: Imago Publishing Company, 1949), p. xi. Originally published as *Edgar Poe: Etude psychanalytique* (Paris: Denoël et Steele, 1933).

7. Cf. Edmund Wilson, "Dickens: The Two Scrooges," in *The Wound and the Bow: Seven Studies in Literature* (New York and London: Oxford University Press, 1941).

8. Cf. William Phillips, "General Introduction," in Kurzweil and Phillips, eds. *Literature and Psychoanalysis*, p. 4.

9. For reasons of space, I can only deal with the dominant traditions in this early work. Carl Jung and Otto Rank, in their different ways, both dissociated themselves from the neo-Freudian way of performing a psychoanalysis on a literary text and its author. Cf. essays in Kurzweil and Phillips, eds. *Literature and Psychoanalysis*.

10. Cf. Abram Kardiner, *The Individual and His Society: The Psychodynamics of Primitive Social Organization* (New York: Columbia University Press, 1939), p. 16. Page number refers to this edition.

11. Cf. Lionel Trilling's essays on "Freud and Literature" in *The Liberal Imagination* (New York: The Viking Press, 1950); and on "Freud Within and Beyond Culture," in *Beyond Culture: Essays on Literature and Learning* (New York: The Viking Press, 1955). Quotes are from the latter essays and this edition.

12. Steven Marcus, "Freud and Dora: Story, History, Case History," reprinted in Bernheimer and Kahane, eds., *In Dora's Case*, pp. 56–91.

13. Cf. Neil Hertz, "Dora's Secrets, Freud's Techniques," in Bernheimer and Kahane, eds., *In Dora's Case* pp. 221–242.

14. Readers may now find usefully gathered together in a single volume Poe's original story, Lacan's reading of it, and all the critiques and debates it spawned. Viz. *The Purloined Poe: Lacan, Derrida, and Psychoanalytic Reading*, eds. John P. Muller and William J. Richardson (Baltimore: The Johns Hopkins University Press, 1988).

15. Cf. *Yale French Studies*, nos. 55/56 (1977), volume on "Literature and Psychoanalysis" that has now become a classic statement of the relationship between literature and modern French psychoanalysis. (Later published as *Literature and Psychoanalysis: The Question of Reading Otherwise*, ed. Felman.)

16. Jacques Lacan, "Desire and the Interpretation of Desire in *Hamlet*," trans. James Hulbert, ed. Jacques-Alain Miller, and reprinted in Felman, ed., *Literature and Psychoanalysis: The Question of Reading Otherwise*, pp. 11–52.

17. Sigmund Freud, The *Interpretation of Dreams*, Standard Edition, Vols. 4 and 5 (London: The Hogarth Press, 1951).

18. Ernst Jones, *Hamlet and Oedipus* (New York: W. W. Norton, 1949) and his "The Death of Hamlet's Father," in *Psycho-Myth Psycho-History* (New York: Stonehill Publishing, 1974), pp. 323–328.

19. Morris Weitz, *Hamlet and the Philosophy of Literary Criticism* (Chicago and London: The University of Chicago Press, 1964).

20. Cf. Jacques Lacan, "Poe's Purloined Letter," in *Yale French Studies* 48, "French Freud" (1973), pp. 39–72. Partial translation from text in *Ecrits* (Paris: Seuil, 1966).

21. Cf. for example William Phillips's introduction already referred to in *Literature and Psychoanalysis*.

22. Cf. Felman, "To Open the Question," in Felman, ed., *Literature and Psychoanalysis: The Question of Reading Otherwise*, p. 6.

23. Shoshana Felman, "On Reading Poetry: Reflections on the Limits and Possibilities of Psychoanalytical Approaches," in Muller and Richardson, eds., *The Purloined Poe*, p. 153. Subsequent page numbers refer to this edition.

24. Cf. Peter Brooks, "The Idea of a Psychoanalytic Literary Criticism," in *Discourse in Psychoanalysis and Literature* ed. Rimmon-Kenan, pp. 1–18.

25. Cf. André Green, *The Tragic Effect* (Cambridge: Cambridge University Press, 1979). Translated from *Un oeil en trop* (Paris, 1969).

26. Meredith Anne Skura, *The Literary Use of Psychoanalytic Process* (New Haven and London: Yale University Press, 1981). Subsequent page numbers refer to this edition.

27. Reprinted in Felman, ed., *Literature and Psychoanalysis: The Question of Reading Otherwise*, p. 457–505.

28. For a detailed exploration of Barbara Johnson's essay, cf. Mary Jacobus, *Reading Woman: Essays in Feminist Criticism* (New York: Columbia University Press, 1986), pp. 286–292.

29. Viz., for example a new collection, *Images in Our Souls: Cavell, Psychoanalysis and Cinema*, ed. Joseph H. Smith and William Kerrigan (Baltimore and London: The Johns Hopkins University Press, 1988).

30. Cf. Donald Spoto, *The Dark Side of Genius: The Life of Alfred Hitchcock* (New York: Ballantine Books, 1983), and Raymond Durgnat, *Luis Buñuel*, revised ed. (Berkeley: University of California Press, 1977).

31. Cf. in particular work by Mary Gedo, e.g. "Art as Autobiography: Picasso's *Guernica*," *Art Quarterly*, 2 (1979): 191–210; John Gedo, e.g. "On the Methodology of Psychoanalytic Biography," *Journal of the American Psychoanalytic Association*, 20 (1972): 638–649; D. Posner, e.g. "Caravaggio's Homo-Erotic Early Works," *Art Quarterly*, 34 (1971): 301–324; Donald Kuspit, "Chaos in Expressionism," in Mary Gedo, ed., *Psychoanalytic Perspectives on Art*, Vol. I (Hillsdale, N.J.: The Analytic Press, 1985), pp. 61–71. In the late seventies, however, some artists became interested in Lacanian theory (e.g. Mary Kelly), and have begun to inspire a psychoanalytic method closer to that in film and literary studies. Meanwhile, in art history more than in literary and film studies, the whole new discourse of postmodernism has complicated methods even more. We thus find art history full of contradictory, even polarized methods, that are being brought to bear on texts all at the same historical moment.

32. Louis Althusser, "Ideology and Ideological State Apparatuses (Notes towards an Investigation)," in *Lenin and Philosophy and Other Essays*, trans. Ben Brewster (New York and London: Monthly Review Press, 1971), pp. 127–186.

33. Kate Millett's well-known *Sexual Politics* (New York: Doubleday, 1970) epitomizes the kind of position that was being developed at the time.

34. Juliet Mitchell's equally famous *Psychoanalysis and Feminism* (New York: Random House, 1974) was a forceful response to Millett's argument; and it prepared the way for the legitimation of psychoanalysis in several kinds of feminist work that followed—particularly in film studies. But cf. also the Julia Lesage-Ben Brewster/ Stephen Heath/Colin MacCabe exchange in *Screen* (Summer 1975), where Lesage expresses feminist rather than political concern with the Lacanian model.

35. For an excellent introduction to the British Psychoanalytical Society detailing the names of the people centrally involved, see *The British School of Psychoanalysis: The Independent Tradition*, ed. Gregorio Kohan (New Haven and London: Yale University Press, 1986). Kohan's useful introduction discusses the opposition to psychoanalysis in Britain from the start (cf. especially pp. 28 30).

36. Brooks, "The Idea of a Psychoanalytic Literary Criticism," in Rimmon-Kenan, ed.,

Discourse in Psychoanalysis and Literature, p. 2. Subsequent page numbers from this edition.

37. Lacan, "Desire and the Interpretation of Desire in *Hamlet*," in Felman, ed., *Literature and Psychoanalysis: The Question of Reading Otherwise*, p. 12.

38. Cf. Christian Metz, "The Fiction Film and Its Spectator: A Metapsychological Study," in *Apparatus*, ed. Theresa Hak Kyung Cha (New York: Tanam Press, 1980), pp. 373–414.

39. Cf., for example, Christine Gledhill, ed., *Home is Where the Heart Is: Studies in Melodrama and The Woman's Film* (London: The British Film Institute, 1987); and Deidre Pribram, ed., *Cinematic Pleasure and the Female Spectator* (London: Verso, 1988).

1. Afterthoughts on "Visual Pleasure and Narrative Cinema" inspired by *Duel in the Sun*

1. Sigmund Freud, *Analysis Terminable and Interminable*, vol. 23 of *The Complete Psychological Works, Standard Edition* (London: Hogarth Press, 1964), p. 251.

2. Sigmund Freud, *Femininity*, vol. 22 of *The Complete Psychological Works, Standard Edition* (London: Hogarth Press, 1951).

3. Freud, *Femininity*, Vol. 22 of *The Complete Psychological Works, Standard Edition* (London: Hogarth Press, 1951).

4. Sigmund Freud, *Creative Writers and Day-Dreaming*, vol. 9 of *The Complete Psychological Works, Standard Edition* (London: Hogarth Press, 1951).

2. A Denial of Difference: Theories of Cinematic Identification

1. This paper was originally written for a BFI Weekend School on "Film Stars" in January 1982 and titled: "Identification and The Star: A Refusal of Difference." In the last six years, work in feminist film theory has elaborated many of the questions posed here. Although the original paper was published in a BFI pamphlet called *Star Signs* (London: BFI Education, 1982) and portions of it have appeared in copyrighted course material for the Open University (Supplementary Material for U203 Popular Culture, *Stars: sexuality, representation, politics*, 1982, The Open University), the version that appears here has been revised for this volume. While I have retained the arch and polemical tone of this essay's general argument, it seems now to be a document of the mood of intervention in feminist theory *circa* 1981.

2. Sigmund Freud, *Interpretation of Dreams* (*Die Traumdeutung* [1900] G.W. [Frankfurt Am Maine: S. Fischer Verlag, 1968] II & II, p. 166. This quote is from the Brill translation (New York: Modern Library, Random House, Inc. 1938), p. 228. The James Strachey translation (S.E., Volume IV [London: Hogarth Press,] p. 150) varies slightly, and uses the word "resemblance" instead of "just like" as a translation of the German "gleichwie." The Strachey translation uses "common element" for "Gemeinsames," what Brill calls "common condition." These are subtle philological nuances, but the reason to turn toward the German here is to notice the relation between "Gemeinsames" as it appears in *Traumdeutung* and "Gemeinsamkeit" as it appears in *Massenpsychologie* in 1921 (G.W. Band IX, p. 100).

3. Sigmund Freud, "Hysterical Phantasies and their Relation to Bisexuality" (1908),

also recounted in "General Remarks on Hysterical Attacks" (1909), both in *Sigmund Freud: Collected Papers*, Volume 2 (New York: Basic Books, 1959).

4. Of course, the massive accumulation of literature on the Dora case has focused directly on Freud's counter-transferential blindness. See Jacques Lacan's "Intervention on Transference" (1952), translated by Jacqueline Rose and reprinted in *Feminine Sexuality: Jacques Lacan and the Ecole Freudienne*, Jacqueline Rose and Juliet Mitchell, eds. (New York: Norton, 1983); also see Charles Bernheimer and Claire Kahane, eds., *In Dora's Case: Freud-Hysteria-Feminism* (New York: Columbia University Press, 1985).

5. Sigmund Freud, "Psychopathic Characters on the Stage," S.E., Volume VII, p. 303–310.

6. The term was first used by Sandor Ferenczi in his essay, "Introjection and Transference" (1909).

7. Sigmund Freud, *Group Psychology and the Analysis of the Ego* (first published as *Massenpsychologie und Ich-analyse*, by Internationaler Psychoanlytischer Verlag, 1921), in S.E., Volume XVIII.

8. Freud, *Group Psychology and the Analysis of the Ego*, p. 108.

9. In *Fragment of an Analysis of a Case of Hysteria* (S.E., Volume VII, p. 3), Freud analyzes "the imaginary sexual situation which underlay" Dora's cough (*tussis nervosa*) as a phantasy in which "she must have been putting herself in Frau K.'s place"; part of Dora's double identification with her mother ("the woman her father once loved") and with Frau K. ("the woman he loved now"). But as Lacan will emphasize, Dora also identified with Herr K.

10. For a discussion of Lacan's theorizations of subject formation, see: Lacan, "Le stade du miroir comme formateur de la fonction du Je/The mirror stage as formative of the function of the I." The first version of this essay was delivered in 1936, and this version was published in 1949, republished in *Ecrits* (Paris: Editions du Seuil, 1966/ London: Tavistock Publications, 1977).

11. Otto Fenichel, "Identification" (first published in Int. A. Psa., Volume 12, pp. 309–325, 1926), republished in *Collected Papers of Otto Fenichel, First Series* (New York: W.W. Norton & Company, Inc., 1953), p. 97.

12. Otto Fenichel, "The Scoptophilic Instinct and Identification" (first published in Int. Z. Psa., Volume 21, 1935, pp. 561–583) republished in *Collected Papers of Otto Fenichel, First Series*, pp. 373–397.

13. Fenichel, "Scoptophilic Instinct and Identification," p. 373.

14. Jean Laplanche and J.B. Pontalis, *The Language of Psychoanalysis* (New York and London: W.W. Norton & Company, 1973), pp. 205–208.

15. "Probably no male human being is spared the fright of castration at the sight of the female genital." From Sigmund Freud, "Fetishism," *International Journal of Psychoanalysis*, Volume IX (1927).

16. The writings of Luce Irigaray take up this challenge. (See especially "The Blind Spot of an Old Dream of Symmetry" and "Any Theory of the 'Subject' Has Always Been Appropriated by the Masculine," in *Speculum of the Other Woman*, translated by Gillian C. Gill [Ithaca: Cornell University Press, 1985].) Irigaray problematizes the Freudian model for its maneuvers within implicit patriarchal ideology. In terms of the totalizing nature of the critique of identification which is put forth in this paper, consider Irigaray's description of identification as submission not mastery.

See *Speculum of the Other Woman*, and *Ce sexe qui n'en est pas un*, translated by Catherine Porter, *This Sex Which Is Not One* (Ithaca: Cornell University Press, 1985).

17. In film studies, Gaylyn Studlar's "Masochism and the Perverse Pleasures of the Cinema," reprinted in *Movies and Methods II* ed. Bill Nichols, (Berkeley: University of California Press, 1985) challenges the "Freudian-Lacanian-Metzian" model for its inadequacies in accounting for cinematic pleasure. Whereas her turn toward Gilles Deleuze's work on masochism does not offer a fully appealing alternative, her article does point to the possible pleasures of "gender mobility" in identification.

18. Christian Metz, "Le signifiant imaginaire," first published in *Communications*, no. 23 (1975). Translated by Ben Brewster and published in *Screen*, Volume 16, no. 2 (Summer 1975). This text as published with several other essays by Metz, under the title *Le Signifiant Imaginaire* (Paris: Union Generale D'Editions, 1977) and then translated into a volume, *The Imaginary Signifier* (Bloomington, Indiana: Indiana University Press, 1985).

19. Freud, *Group Psychology and the Analysis of the Ego*, p. 69.

20. Jean-Louis Baudry, "The Ideological Effects of the Basic Cinematic Apparatus," (first published in *Cinéthique* 7–8 [1970]), translated in *Film Quarterly*, Volume 28, no. 2, (Winter 1974–1975). Reprinted in *Movies and Methods II*. Baudry describes the mechanism of cinematic projection itself, its perceptual operation, as an apparatical technique where difference is denied (*la différence niée*); but in Baudry's account, the *différence* denied is between the piece of film as a series of framed images and the illusion of continuousness that is given in projection. Baudry also maintains that the spectator identifies more with the apparatus than with what is represented.

In "Woman, Desire and the Look," Sandy Flitterman extends this apparatical description in her precis of Raymond Bellour's "Hitchcock, The Enunciator" (*Camera Obscura*, no. 2 [Fall 1977]). In Bellour's discussion of Hitchcock's "enunciative" system, he describes the conflation of identification with the camera and identification with the object. While Flitterman points to the usefulness of this type of analysis for feminists, she halts short of gendering the entire cinematic apparatus as male. See "Woman, Desire and the Look," in *Theories of Authorship*, edited by John Caughie (London: Routledge & Kegan Paul, 1981), pp. 242–250.

21. Laura Mulvey, "Visual Pleasure and Narrative Cinema," *Screen*, Volume 16, no. 1 (Winter 1975).

22. Jean Baudrillard, *For a Critique of the Political Economy of the Sign*, translated by Charles Levin (St. Louis, Mo.: Telos Press, 1981). See particularly the chapter, "Fetishism and Ideology: The Semiological Reduction" (which first appeared as an article in *Nouvelle Revue de Psychoanalyse*, Volume II [Autumn 1970]).

23. See Karl Marx, *Capital* (Chapter 1, Part 4), "The Fetish of the Commodity and its Secret."

24. Tino Balio's account of the careers of Mary Pickford, Charles Chaplin, and Douglas Fairbanks, Jr., in *United Artists: The Company Built by the Stars* (Madison, Wisconsin: University of Wisconsin Press, 1976) exemplifies the negotiation of market power by early film stars.

25. This seems like an agreed-upon myth of origin for economic histories of the star system. One such succinct account is provided by Gorham Kindem in "Hollywood's Movie Star System: A Historical Overview," in *The American Film Industry*, edited by Gorham Kindem (Carbondale: Southern Illinois University Press, 1982). But the

same explanation is found in other histories: Benjamin B. Hampton, *History of the American Film Industry* (New York: Dover Publications, Inc., 1970); Tino Balio, ed., *The American Film Industry* (Madison, Wisconsin: University of Wisconsin Press, 1976).

26. Richard Dyer's *Stars* (London: BFI, 1979), remains the best succinct discussion of stars and their social signification. See also Edgar Morin's landmark study, *The Stars* (New York: Grove Press, 1960) for his discussion of identifications based on regional, age, and gender similarities.

27. How do we explain, for example, the commercial failure of George Cukor's *Sylvia Scarlett* (1936) and Rouben Mamoulian's *Queen Christina* (1933), while accounting for the·commercial success of Josef von Sternberg's *Blonde Venus* (1932) and *Morocco* (1930)? Each film has a female star in a "trouser-part" (Hepburn in *Sylvia Scarlett*, Garbo in *Queen Christina*; Dietrich in *Blonde Venus* and *Morocco*); is it Dietrich that "sells" in her two films? or is it that the disguise (and disavowal) of the female is treated differently in each of the films?

3. Remembering Women: Psychical and Historical Constructions in Film Theory

1. This paper was initially presented at a conference sponsored by the Australian Screen Studies Association, Sydney, December 1986. I would like to thank Liz Gross, Joan Copjec, Meaghan Morris, and Phil Rosen for their valuable comments on the manuscript.

2. *La Signora di tutti* is an extremely complex film and this brief analysis hardly exhausts its interest for the feminist critic. Indeed, there is a sense in which its delineation of the abstraction of Woman through the look and the voice is subjected to a critique within the same film. See my essay, "The Abstraction of a Lady: *La Signora di tutti*," in *The Critique of the Abstract: Language, Power, and the Senses*, ed. Julie Ellison, forthcoming.

3. See, for instance, Judith Mayne, "Feminist Film Theory and Criticism," *Signs: Journal of Women in Culture and Society*, vol. 11, no. 1 (1985), pp. 81–100; and Mary Ann Doane, Patricia Mellencamp, and Linda Williams, "Feminist Film Criticism: An Introduction," in *Re-vision: Essays in Feminist Film Criticism*, eds. Doane, Mellencamp, and Williams (Frederick, MD: University Publications of America and The American Film Institute, 1984), pp. 1–17.

4. Teresa de Lauretis, *Alice Doesn't: Feminism, Semiotics, Cinema* (Bloomington: Indiana University Press, 1984), p. 186.

5. See E. Ann Kaplan, "Feminist Film Criticism: Current Issues and Problems," *Studies in the Literary Imagination*, vol. xix, no. 1 (Spring 1986), pp. 7–20; and Annette Kuhn, *Women's Pictures: Feminism and Cinema* (London: Routledge & Kegan Paul, 1982).

6. These two essays by Baudry are anthologized in Philip Rosen, *Narrative, Apparatus, Ideology* (New York: Columbia University Press, 1986), pp. 286–318.

7. Jean Laplanche and J.-B. Pontalis, *The Language of Psychoanalysis*, trans. Donald Nicholson-Smith (New York: W.W. Norton & Company, Inc., 1973), p. 358.

8. *The Standard Edition of the Complete Psychological Works of Sigmund Freud*, vol. V, trans. and ed. James Strachey (London: The Hogarth Press and the Institute of Psycho-analysis, 1973), pp. 536–537. In the continuation of this quote Freud consid-

ers the possibility that the hypothesis of a *spatial* order is unnecessary (and could be replaced by that of a *temporal order*). But the appeal of the spatial ordering is evident in the analogies which he invokes.

9. Jean Laplanche, *Life and Death in Psycho-analysis*, trans. Jeffrey Mehlman (Baltimore and London: The Johns Hopkins University Press, 1976), p. 61.

10. Baudry, "The Apparatus," in Rosen, *Narrative, Apparatus, Ideology*, p. 300.

11. See Christian Metz, "The Imaginary Signifier," *Screen*, vol. 16, no. 2 (Summer 1975), pp. 14–76; Jean-Louis Comolli, "Technique and Ideology: Camera, Perspective, Depth of Field," (Parts 3 and 4) in Rosen, *Narrative, Apparatus, Ideology*, pp. 421–443.

12. Baudry, "Ideological Effects of the Basic Cinematographic Apparatus," in Rosen, *Narrative, Apparatus, Ideology*, p. 295.

13. Joan Copjec, "The Delirium of Clinical Perfection," *The Oxford Literary Review*, vol. 8, nos. 1–2 (1986), pp. 61 and 63. It is only fair to point out that Copjec develops this argument (whose substance I agree with) as a counterargument to a position presented in the introduction of a book I co-edited—*Re-vision: Essays in Feminist Film Criticism*. Copjec criticizes our invocation of Michel Foucault's panopticon as an analogy with the position of the woman (in relation to visibility and the gaze) in a patriarchal society. The reference in *Re-vision* is quite brief and not at all fully developed and I believe that Copjec's criticism is at some level quite justified. However, the paragraph she cites does not claim that the panopticon *perfectly* describes the woman's condition but, instead, *seems* to perfectly describe it. In the obsessive search for perfection, this is an important qualification. I find it much more difficult, as stated below in this essay, to see how Lacan's gaze can shed light on the analysis of sexual difference. In Foucault's description of the panopticon, it is not so important to claim that the gaze is fixed at a certain point, or that it *belongs* to someone who is in power, but that the inmate/woman incessantly feels herself to be the potential object of such a gaze.

14. Jacques Lacan, *The Four Fundamental Concepts of Psycho-analysis*, trans. Alan Sheridan (Harmondsworth: Penguin Books Ltd., 1979), p. 106.

15. Lacan, *Four Fundamental Concepts*, p. 103.

16. Lacan, *Four Fundamental Concepts*, p. 73.

17. Roger Caillois, "Mimicry and Legendary Psychasthenia," trans. John Shepley, *October* 31 (Winter 1984), p. 28.

18. Caillois, "Mimicry."

19. Lacan, *Four Fundamental Concepts*, p. 75.

20. Freud, *The Standard Edition*, vol. V, p. 511.

21. Samuel Weber, *The Legend of Freud* (Minneapolis: The University of Minnesota Press, 1982), p. xvi.

22. Weber, *The Legend of Freud*, pp. 13–14.

23. François Roustang, *Psychoanalysis Never Lets Go*, trans. Ned Lukacher (Baltimore and London: The Johns Hopkins University Press, 1980), p. 25.

24. Roustang, *Psychoanalysis Never Lets Go*, p. 17.

25. François Roustang, *Dire Mastery: Discipleship from Freud to Lacan*, trans. Ned Lukacher (Baltimore and London: The Johns Hopkins University Press, 1982), p. 70.

26. Roustang, *Dire Mastery*, p. 69.

27. Sigmund Freud, *The Origins of Psychoanalysis: Letters to Wilhelm Fliess*, trans. Eric Mosbacher and James Strachey (New York: Basic Books, Inc., 1954), p. 173.

28. Something of what Freud meant by the term "memory" can be gleaned from the way in which he used the term "forgetting." What is lost in forgetting is not an empirical event but a coherent discourse linking events. Freud frequently emphasizes the fact that forgetting involves the loss of connections *between* events. In this sense, it has similarities with Ramon Jakobson's "contiguity disorder" in aphasia. This is not necessarily to deny that there are events. Memory's relation to them is, however, tangential rather than direct, instigated rather than determined.

29. Sigmund Freud, "A Note upon the 'Mystic Writing-Pad,' " *The Standard Edition*, vol. XIX, p. 231.

30. For a discussion of the various ways of distinguishing between memory and history see David Lowenthal, *The Past is a Foreign Country* (Cambridge: Cambridge University Press, 1985), pp. 185–259.

31. Sigmund Freud, "Constructions in Analysis," *The Standard Edition*, vol. XXIII, pp. 258–259.

32. Freud, "Constructions in Analysis," pp. 265–266.

33. Roustang, *Psychoanalysis Never Lets Go*, pp. 36–37.

34. Sigmund Freud, "Further Recommendations in the Technique of Psychoanalysis: Observations on Transference-Love," *The Standard Edition*, vol. XII, pp. 166–167.

4. Femininity and the Masquerade: *Anne of the Indies*

1. This notion of woman as enigma also forms part of what Barthes calls the hermeneutic code (cf. *S/Z*, [trans. Richard Miller, New York: Hill and Wang, 1974]) where a succession of enigmas or the repetition of enigmas provide the basic impetus for the development of the narrative itself.

5. Cinematic Abreaction: Tourneur's *The Cat People*

1. The following is a plot summary: Irena Dubrovna, a fashion designer in New York City and a recent immigrant from Serbia in Yugoslavia, claims to be descended from a race of "cat people" the women of which, when sexually aroused or provoked, transform into great panthers and attack their lovers. Irena meets Oliver Reed in the Central Park Zoo; although she tells him the stories of her origins, he continues to court her and becomes her husband, but the marriage remains unconsummated due to her fears. As Irena's resistance to sexuality becomes more and more insistent, Oliver and his co-worker Alice, with the consent of Irena, call in a psychiatrist for her. As Irena begins consultation with this psychiatrist, Dr. Louis Judd, the liaison between Oliver and Alice tightens. Dr. Judd doesn't believe Irena's stories either, but whereas Oliver gradually withdraws from her, Dr. Judd tries to seduce her. Irena transforms into the panther of her "stories" four times in the narrative, thrice because of jealousy of Alice, and once because she is sexually provoked by Dr. Judd; whereas she does not directly attack either Alice or Oliver, she destroys Dr. Judd. Although a piece of the rapier with which he tries to fend her off is left stuck in her shoulder after the struggle, she dies from other causes: following her killing of Judd, she

releases a panther from its cage in the zoo, and it hits her, fatally, in its leap to freedom.

2. "Notes Towards the Construction of Readings of Tourneur," in Claire Johnston and Paul Willemen, eds., *Jacques Tourneur* (Edinburgh Film Festival 1975), pp. 16–35.

3. The first quatrain of the sonnet reads: "I am a little world made cunningly/ Of Elements, and an Angelike spright,/ But black sinne hath betraid to endlesse night/ My worlds both parts, and (oh) both parts must die." The "elements" thus comprise the one "part" and the angelic spirit the other; the quotation reinvokes the bad/ good binarism as a venerable and familiar matter/spirit one.

4. Melanie Klein, *Envy and Gratitude & Other Works 1946–63* (New York: Dell Publishing Co., Inc., 1977), p. 181. In normal resolutions of this extremely primitive dialectic between good and bad objects and introjects, hence between the life and death drives, the destructive impulses and the bad breast are split off, so that a good positive introject is built up and becomes the core of the personality. In pathogenic resolutions, for various reasons this primal division is inadequately maintained and the good introject is not built up; the subject accordingly experiences a preponderance of bad feelings of omnipotent destructiveness, and then intense guilt and anxiety. Mature envy reactivates the primitive splitting processes and the disavowed feelings of destructive power, with the persecutory anxiety that attends it (pp. 177–190).

5. This could be a shepherd: since the montage consists of unmatched shots and functions emblematically and allegorically, there is no necessity to naturalize it. Nevertheless, when Irena lets the panther out of its cage in the zoo, in the final sequence of the film, it jumps onto the spot above the wall where the bushes have been rustling, thence into the street below, that same street along which Irena and Alice have been walking. Thus it is possible to designate a specific *place* for the montage. Hence, a zookeeper.

6. Joel E. Siegel, *Val Lewton: The Reality of Terror* (London: Secker & Warburg, Ltd., 1972), p. 104.

7. Julia Kristeva, *Powers of Horror: An Essay on Abjection*, Leon Roudiez, trans. (New York: Columbia University Press, 1982), p. 36. Further citations will appear in the text.

8. His assumption would be that she is "ill" from excluded ideas and affects that have been blocked by splitting from any associative working-over or integration with the rest of her behavior, a symptomatology that would characterize a dual personality or an hysteric.

9. Kristeva distinguishes the semiotic from the symbolic, the former being a function of a binary logic which, "while being the precondition of language . . . is dependent upon meaning, but in a way that is not that of *linguistic* signs nor of the symbolic order they found" (p. 72). The semiotic is a set of codings that is diachronically anterior in the history of the subject to paternal laws, phallic organization, and the acquisition of language which together found the symbolic. The semiotic is thus tied to maternal authority and the "primal mapping of the body."

10. In terminating the analyst, then *The Cat People* deviates from an invariant coding in the "woman's film" and shifts toward another genre, namely the horror film. For as Mary Anne Doane points out in *The Desire to Desire* (Bloomington, Indiana University Press, 1987), the doctor typically appears in the woman's film as a figure who contains the feminine with a classifying gaze, entering her symptamotology as

a term in a medical discourse, and often eroticizing the clinical relationship (see pp. 38–69). In *The Cat People*, the inversion of these terms of containment, the asymptomaticity of the cat syndrome and its asymtotic relation to the medical discourse, as well as the evocation of the cat as a teratology to be repulsed, transpose the genre coding.

6. Believing in the Cinema: *Curse of the Demon*

1. Marc Vernet, "Clignotements du noir et blanc," in J. Aumont et al, eds., *Théorie du film* (Paris: Editions Albatros, 1980).

2. Here, for example, is an excerpt from an interview between Chris Wicking and Tourneur (from *Midi-Minuit Fantastique*, no. 12 [May 1965]): "It's a fascinating film. I'm thinking particularly of the use that is made of the spectator's identification: we see the demon, then Dana Andrews arrives and declares, 'There is no demon.' We no longer know what to believe: the hero or our own eyes."

   "The scenes where we really see the demon were shot without me. All except one. I shot the sequence in the woods where Dana Andrews is pursued by this sort of cloud. They should have used this technique for the other sequences. The public would not have been sure at all it had seen the demon. It should have been unveiled bit by bit without it ever really being shown." Tourneur here says two different things. In regard to the demon, he adds in another interview (with Joel Siegel in *Cinéfantastique*, 2, no. 4, [Summer 1973]) that he would like to have introduced four shots of the demon in the final scene in such a way that one wouldn't be sure if one had seen it or not.

3. There is nothing astonishing, moreover, in the fact that in this logic the very life of the characters is figured materially by books: Harrington's diary, Holden's appointment book, with the pages after the supposed date of their deaths torn out.

   One could also go into details: it seems that there are in fact two books even if everything is done to make us believe that they are one and the same. The first would primarily contain images of sorcery (it is connected to the demon) and the second would be written in runic characters (it is connected to the parchment).

   On film as book, see Thierry Kuntzel, "Volumen Codex" in "The Film Work 2," trans. Nancy Huston, *Camera Obscura*, no. 5 (1980), 11–12. Kuntzel has reworked this very image on his own tapes and video installations, "Nostos I" and "Nostos II."

4. Jacques Lacan, *The Four Fundamental Concepts of Psychoanalysis*, trans. Alan Sheridan-Smith (New York: W. W. Norton, 1977).

7. Historical Trauma and Male Subjectivity: *The Best Years of Our Lives*

1. For a discussion of cinema's relation to the imaginary register, see Christian Metz, *The Imaginary Signifier: Psychoanalysis and the Cinema*, trans. Celia Britton, Annwyl Williams, Ben Brewster, and Alfred Guzzetti (Bloomington: Indiana University Press, 1982), pp. 42–57; Jean-Louis Baudry, "The Apparatus," trans. Jean Andrews and Bertrand Augst, *Camera Obscura*, no. 1 (1976), 104–28; and Jacqueline Rose, "Paranoia and the Film System," *Screen* vol. 17, no. 4 (1976/77), 85–104.

2. Jacques Rancière, "Interview: The Image of Brotherhood," trans Kari Hanet, *Edinburgh Magazine*, no. 2 (1977), 28.

3. In "The Meaning of the Phallus," trans. Jacqueline Rose, in *Feminine Sexuality:*

Jacques Lacan and the Ecole Freudienne, eds. Juliet Mitchell and Jacqueline Rose (New York: Norton, 1982), p. 82, Lacan writes that "The phallus is the privileged signifier of that mark where the share of the logos is wedded to the advent of desire. One might easily say that this signifier is chosen as what stands out as most easily seized in the literal (typographical) sense of the term, since it is the equivalent in that relation of the (logical) copula. One might also say that by virtue of its turgidity, it is the image of the vital flow as it is transmitted in generation."

4. Jacques Lacan, *Seminaire XVIII*, p. 4 (quoted by Rose in *Feminine Sexuality*, p. 44).

5. Serge Leclaire, "Sexuality: A Fact of Discourse," trans. Hélène Klibbe, in *Homosexualities and French Literature: Cultural Contexts, Critical Texts*, ed. George Stambolian (Ithaca: Cornell University Press, 1979).

6. Martin Thom, "Verneinung, Verwerfung, Ausstossung: A Problem in the Interpretation of Freud," in *The Talking Cure*, ed. Colin MacCabe (New York: St. Martin's, 1981), p. 165.

7. Jacques Lacan, "The Signification of the Phallus," *Ecrits*, trans. Alan Sheridan (New York: Norton, 1976), p. 285.

8. See my "Lost Objects and Mistaken Subjects: Film Theory's Structuring Lack," *Wide Angle*, vol. 7, nos. 1 and 2 (1985), 14–29. A fuller version of that essay is included in Kaja Silverman, *The Acoustic Mirror: The Female Voice in Psychoanalysis and Cinema* (Bloomington: Indiana University Press, 1988).

9. Barbara Deming, *Running Away from Myself: A Dream Portrait of America Drawn from the Films of the 40's* (New York: Grossman, 1969), pp. 39–40. The first version of this book was completed in 1950, although it was not published in its entirety until nineteen years later.

10. As Nikolas Rose, Angie Solfield, Couze Venn, and Valerie Walkerdine go on to say in their summary of the recent ideology debate, "No region or level of the social formation is contemplated which stands *outside* the discursive practices in which the material activities of concrete human subjects consist. . . ." See "Psychology, Ideology and the Human Subject," *Ideology and Consciousness*, no. 1 (1977), 46.

11. Paul Hirst argues that because Althusser describes the ideological state apparatuses as apparatuses of the *state*, "They are unified, despite their apparent and necessary diversity, by this function and by the fact that they all represent ruling-class ideology. The unity of the ISAs is therefore the unity of their function and of the foundation of their function, ruling-class ideology and the ruling class. The state in Althusser's analysis can therefore be considered as unified by the function of maintenance of class society" (*On Law and Ideology* [London: Macmillan, 1979], p. 50).

12. Fredric Jameson, *The Political Unconscious: Narrative as a Socially Symbolic Act* (Ithaca: Cornell University Press, 1982), p. 30.

13. Ernesto Laclau, "The Impossibility of Society," *Canadian Journal of Political and Social Theory*, vol. 7, nos. 1/2 (1983), 24.

14. Jameson, *Political Unconscious*, p. 102.

15. Sigmund Freud, *Beyond the Pleasure Principle, The Standard Edition* Vol. 18, trans. James Strachey (London: Hogarth, 1951).

16. For a fuller discussion of binding, see Jean Laplanche, *Life and Death in Psycho-Analysis*, trans. Jeffrey Mehlman (Baltimore: Johns Hopkins University Press, 1976).

17. Jameson, *Political Unconscious*, p. 146.

18. Siegfried Kracauer, "Those Movies With a Message," *Harpers* (June 1948), 572.

19. André Bazin, *What Is Cinema?*, Vol. 2 (Berkeley: University of California Press, 1971), p. 60.

20. André Bazin, "William Wyler ou le janseniste de la mise-en-scene," *Qu'est-ce que le cinema?*, I (Paris: Editions du cerf, 1957), p. 156. English translation by Christopher Williams, *Realism and the Cinema: A Reader* (London: Routledge & Kegan Paul, 1980), pp. 40–41.

21. Bazin, "William Wyler ou le janseniste de la mise-en-scene," p. 155.

22. William Wyler, "No Magic Wand," in *Hollywood Directors 1941–1976*, ed. Richard Koszarski (New York: Oxford University Press, 1977), p. 104.

23. Wyler, "No Magic Wand," p. 116.

24. Jameson, *Political Unconscious*, p. 152.

25. This formulation of classic cinema was suggested by Andrew Tyndall in the context of a general discussion at the Cinema Histories/Cinema Practices Conference sponsored by the University of Wisconsin-Milwaukee in 1982.

26. For Freud's account of disavowal, see "Some Psychical Consequences of the Anatomical Distinction Between the Sexes," in *The Standard Edition*, Vol. 19, pp. 248–258, and "Fetishism," in *The Standard Edition*, Vol. 21, pp. 152–157.

27. Robert Warshow, "The Anatomy of Falsehood," in *The Immediate Experience: Movies, Comics, Theatre and Other Aspects of Popular Culture* (Garden City: Doubleday, 1962), p. 112.

28. Wyler, "No Magic Wand," p. 107.

29. Warshow, "Anatomy of Falsehood," p. 111.

30. Metz, *Imaginary Signifier*, p. 43.

31. Jean-Louis Comolli, "Machines of the Visible," in *The Cinematic Apparatus*, eds. Teresa de Lauretis and Stephen Heath (New York: St. Martin's Press, 1980), p. 133.

32. Julia Kristeva, *Powers of Horror: An Essay on Abjection*, trans. Leon S. Roudiez (New York: Columbia University Press, 1982), p. 65.

33. Kristeva speaks of "excrement and its equivalents (decay, infection, disease, corpse, etc.)" as "the danger to identity that comes from without: the ego threatened by the non-ego, society threatened by its outside, life by death" (p. 71).

34. Freud, "Some Psychical Consequences of the Anatomical Distinction Between the Sexes," *The Standard Edition*, Vol. 19, p. 252.

35. Roger Manvell, *Films and the Second World War* (New York: Dell, 1974), p. 248.

36. Michael Wood, *America in the Movies, or Santa Maria, It had Slipped My Mind* (New York: Basic Books, 1975), p. 119.

37. Kracauer, "Those Movies With a Message," p. 571.

38. Warshow, "Anatomy of Falsehood," p. 112.

39. Again, see my "Lost Objects and Mistaken Subjects."

40. A much lengthier version of the present essay, including discussions of *The Guilt of Janet Ames* and *It's A Wonderful Life*, will appear in my *Male Subjectivity at the Margins* (forthcoming).

8. Motherhood and Representation: From Postwar Freudian Figurations to Postmodernism—*Now Voyager* and *Marnie*

1. Cf. my forthcoming book, *Motherhood and Representation in Literature and Film, 1830–1960* (London and New York: Routledge, 1990) for bibliography and more discussion of these issues.

2. For details regarding psychiatrists in the Hollywood film, cf. Krin and Glen O. Gabbard, *Psychiatry and the Cinema* (Chicago and London: University of Chicago Press, 1987). While psychiatry entered the German film early on (viz. *The Cabinet of Dr. Caligari* (Robert Wiene, 1919); *The Secrets of a Soul* (G. W. Pabst, 1926), the first American film to figure the godlike psychiatrist was *Blind Alley* (Charles Vidor, 1939), according to the Gabbards. Earlier American treatments were largely comic.

3. Cf. Monique Plaza, "The Mother/The Same: The Hatred of the Mother in Psychoanalysis," *Feminist Issues*, Vol. 2, No. 1 (Spring, 1982), pp. 75–99.

4. Cf. Jeannie Allen, "Introduction" to her edition of the *Now Voyager* script (Madison: University of Wisconsin Press, 1986).

5. Phillip Wylie, *Generation of Vipers* (New York: Rinehart, 1942).

6. Karen Horney, "Maternal Conflicts" (1933), reprinted in *Feminine Psychology*, ed. Harold Kelman (New York: Norton, 1967), pp. 174–178.

7. Julia Kristeva, *Powers of Horror: An Essay on Abjection*, trans. Leon S. Roudiez (New York: Columbia University Press, 1982), p. 4. Subsequent page numbers refer to this edition.

8. Both films perhaps look back to the 19th-century novel that often combined melodrama and thriller. For discussion of one such text, cf. E. Ann Kaplan, "The Political Unconscious in the Maternal Melodrama: Ellen Wood's *East Lynne* (1861)," in Derek Longhurst, ed., *Genre, Gender and Narrative Pleasure* (Hemel Hempstead, UK: Unwin Hyman, 1988), pp. 31–50.

9. For a text that, by contrast, deals sensitively precisely with such "difficulties," cf. Maud Mannoni, *The Child, His "Illness" and the Others* (London: Tavistock Publications, 1970).

10. Critics like Raymond Durgnat have hypothesized a great deal about the mother's feelings and position from her scenes in the film (cf. Durgnat's *The Strange Case of Alfred Hitchcock: or The Plain Man's Hitchcock* [Cambridge, Mass.: MIT Press, 1974], pp. 357–358); but this material is read into the characters rather than being articulated in cinematic devices or dealt with as ideological.

11. Donald Spoto, *The Dark Side of Genius: The Life of Alfred Hitchcock* (New York: Ballantine Books, 1983), p. 17. Spoto quotes Hitchcock as follows:

    Fear? It has influenced my life and my career. I remember when I was five or six. It was a Sunday evening, the only time my parents did not have to work. They put me to bed and went to Hyde Park for a stroll . . . They were sure I would be asleep until their return. But I woke up, called out, and no one answered. Nothing but night all around me. Shaking, I got up, wandered around the empty, dark house, and finally arriving in the kitchen, found a piece of cold meat which I ate while drying my tears.

12. Cf. Jean Baudrillard, "The Ecstasy of Communication," in Hal Foster, ed. *The Anti-*

Aesthetic: Essays on Postmodern Culture (Townsend, Washington: The Bay Press, 1983), p. 127.

13. Cf. Arthur and Marilouise Kroker, "Body Digest: Theses on the Disappearing Body in the Hyper-Modern Condition," in *The Canadian Journal of Political and Social Theory*, Vol. XI, Nos. 1–2 (1987), p. xiii.

14. Interestingly, all three films are romantic comedies, suggesting a need to displace serious exploration into a comic terrain where issues evaporate in the laughter. In the case of the latest film, *Baby Boom* in particular, the mother-child relationship becomes merely a means for the heroine's life-change rather than being explored for its own sake. The contradictions in the heroine's life because of her becoming a mother are displaced into a comic play with Yuppie life rather than being central.

15. Cf. report on day-care center research in *The New York Times*, 5 November 1987, p. B9.

16. Cf. work by Meryl Kaplan on *Images of Mothers*, forthcoming from Columbia University Press.

17. Cf. Adrienne Harris, "Bringing Artemis to Life: The Role of Militance and Aggression in Women's Psychic Life and in Feminist Peace Politics," forthcoming in her co-edited volume.

9. Couching Resistance: Women, Film, and Postwar Psychoanalytic Psychiatry

I would like to thank Ellen Evans for her comments on an earlier version of this article, and Claudia Gorbman and Diane Waldman for their generous suggestions on the article in its present incarnation.

1. See, for example, B. Ruby Rich's article, "Cinefeminism and Its Discontents" (*American Film* [December 1983]) in which Rich criticizes E. Ann Kaplan's *Women and Film: Both Sides of the Camera* (Boston: South End Press, 1982) and Annette Kuhn's *Women's Pictures: Feminism and Cinema* (London: Routledge and Kegan Paul, 1982) for the books' concentration on psychoanalytic theory.

2. This article is extracted from my doctoral dissertation, "Couching Resistance: Women, Film, and Psychoanalytic Psychiatry from World War II through the mid-1960s" (University of California, Los Angeles, 1987). Also see my article, "Regulation and Contradiction: Hollywood, Freud, and Women" in *Home is Where the Heart Is: Studies in Melodrama and the Woman's Film*, Christine Gledhill, ed. (London: British Film Institute, 1987).

3. Psychiatry is that branch of medicine classified, like pediatrics or internal medicine, as a specialty with specific residency requirements and dealing with mental and emotional illness. Psychoanalysis is a theory and therapeutic methodology derived from the work of Sigmund Freud.

4. Betty Friedan, *The Feminine Mystique* (1963) (New York: Dell Publishing, 1974). Phyllis Chesler, *Women and Madness* (Garden City, New York: Doubleday & Co., 1972). Also see Diane Waldman's "Horror and Domesticity: The Modern Gothic Romance Film of the 1940s" (University of Wisconsin, Madison, Fall 1981) for an interesting and more recent account of the American popularization of Freudian psychoanalysis and its status as adjustment therapy.

5. Juliet Mitchell, *Psycho-Analysis and Feminism: Freud, Reich, Laing and Women* (New York: London: The Macmillan Press, 1982), p. 299.

6. Other films dealt with at greater length in my longer work include *Whirlpool, The Snake Pit, The Cobweb, Lilith, Spellbound* (Alfred Hitchcock, 1945), *Knock on Wood* (Norman Panama, 1954), and *3 on a Couch* (Jerry Lewis, 1966).

7. In "Clinical Eyes: The Medical Discourse," chapter two of *The Desire to Desire: The Woman's Film of the 1940s* (Bloomington and Indianapolis: Indiana University Press, 1987), Mary Ann Doane attributes this ideological weight to the textual function of the medical discourse in the woman's film. Diane Waldman in "The Modern Gothic Romance and Psychoanalysis," chapter five of the work cited above, draws similar conclusions about the function of psychoanalytic discourse in certain gothic romance films of the 1940s.

8. Michel Foucault, *The Archaeology of Knowledge and the Discourse on Language* (1971), translated by A. M. Sheridan Smith (New York: Vintage Books, 1975).

9. *A Psychiatric Glossary*, fifth edition, American Psychiatric Association (Boston: Little Brown & Co., 1980), p. 2.

10. William Menninger, *Psychiatry in a Troubled World: Yesterday's War and Today's Challenge* (New York: MacMillan, 1948), pp. 393–394.

11. Indeed, I would like to emphasize here that the rhetoric I am identifying does not preclude substantial variations among individual practitioners. I'm speaking of what happened when psychiatry was institutionalized and publicized—when it became a mass phenomenon.

12. Edward A. Strecker, A.M., M.D., Sc.D., Litt.D., LL.D., *Their Mothers' Sons: The Psychiatrist Examines an American Problem* (New York: J. B. Lippincott Co., 1947); Ferdinand Lundberg and Marynia F. Farnham, M.D., *Modern Woman: The Lost Sex* (New York: Harper & Brothers, 1947).

13. This derogatory identification of the neurotic mother was also the basis of Phillip Wylie's *Generation of Vipers* (New York: Rinehart & Co., Inc., 1942). But what Lundberg and Farnham and Strecker provided, which Wylie did not, was a psychiatric *antidote* to the problem they identify.

14. Robert P. Knight, M.D., "The Present Status of Organized Psychoanalysis in the United States," *Journal of the American Psychoanalytic Association*, Vol. I, No. 2 (April 1953). In 1938, the American Psychoanalytic Association broke with the International Psychoanalytic Association over the issue of "lay analysis," resolving that all members of the APA must be medical doctors (Reuben Fine, A History of Psychoanalysis [New York: Columbia University Press, 1979]).

15. Clarence Oberndor, *A History of Psychoanalysis in America* (New York: Harper and Row, 1953).

16. Franz Alexander, "Psychoanalysis and Psychotherapy," *JAPA*, Vol. II, No. 4 (October 1954), p. 726.

17. Phyllis Greenacre, M.D., "The Role of Transference: Practical Considerations in Relation to Psychoanalytic Therapy," *JAPA*, Vol. II, No. 4 (October 1954), p. 673. Greenacre did not *advocate* this form of the transference relationship, but rather a more "classical" form of transference in which non-intervention is crucial.

18. Leo Stone, "The Widening Scope of Indications for Psychoanalysis," *JAPA*, Vol. II, No. 4 (October 1954). "Borderline" designates "Those patients who present largely neurotic syndromes, sometimes quite conventional, who nevertheless induce in the clinician the conviction of strong suspicions of more grave illness" (p. 583).

19. According to Jean Laplanche and J.-B. Pontalis (*The Language of Psycho-Analysis*,

trans. Donald Michelson-Smith from the original French edition of 1967 [New York: W. W. Norton & Co., 1973], pp. 255–259), narcissism is that psychological phenomenon in which the subject takes himself, his own body, as a sexual or love object.

20. Stone, "Widening Scope," p. 585.

21. Laplanche and Pontalis, *Language of Psycho-Analysis*, p. 259.

22. Stone, "Widening Scope," p. 583.

23. Robert Lindner, *The Fifty-Minute Hour: A Collection of True Psychoanalytic Tales* (New York: Rinehart & Co., 1956).

24. Luli Barzman McCarroll, "Media/Bulimia, or The Politics of Cleanliness," *On Film*, No. 13 (Fall 1984).

25. Sigmund Freud, "Psycho-Analysis" (1922), *Collected Papers*, Vol. 5, ed. James Strachey (New York: Basic Books, 1959), pp. 107–135.

26. Merton Gill, M.D., "Psychoanalysis and Exploratory Psychotherapy," *Journal of the American Psychoanalytic Association*, Vol. II, No. 4, (October 1954).

27. Gill, "Psychoanalysis and Exploratory Psychotherapy," p. 776. Phyllis Greenacre is prominant among those whose view of transference as neutral non-intervention agrees with that of Gill.

28. Alexander Reid Martin, M.D., "Why Psychoanalysis?" in *Are You Considering Psychoanalysis?*, Karen Horney, ed. (New York: W. W. Norton, 1946).

29. Dorothy Ferman, "The Psychoanalytical Joy Ride," *The Nation* (August 26, 1950).

30. Gregory Zilboorg, M.D., "Ignorance—Amateur and Professional," *The Nation* (September 2, 1950).

31. Nancy Lynch, "A Walk in a Dark Room," *Mademoiselle* (October 1957).

32. Laplanche and Pontalis, *Language of Psycho-Analysis*, p. 92. In Freud's work the concept of transference developed from the original idea of transference as a mode of displacement in connection with dreams to the notion of the "transference-neurosis," the process of treatment where infantile conflicts are replayed in the doctor-patient relationship. According to Laplanche and Pontalis, Freud's definition of transference is: "For psychoanalysis, a process of actualization of unconscious wishes. . .its context *par excellence* is the analytic situation" (p. 455). Countertransference, in Freud's writing, then, is: "The whole of the analyst's unconscious reactions to the individual analysand—especially to the analysand's own transference" (p. 92).

    For overviews of the terms in American psychoanalytic literature see, Benjamin Wolstein, Ph.D., *Countertransference* (New York: Grune & Stratton, 1959); Douglas Orr, M.D., "Transference and Countertransference: A Historical Survey," *JAPA*, Vol. II, No. 4 (October 1954); Lucia Tower, M.D., "Countertransference," *JAPA*, Vol. IV (1956).

33. Quoted in Tower, "Countertransference," p. 226.

34. Rene Spitz, M.D., "Countertransference," *JAPA*, Vol. IV. No. 2 (April, 1956).

35. Sigmund Freud, "Observation of Transference-Love" (1915), S.E., Vol. 12.

36. Tower, "Countertransference," p. 225.

37. Juliet Mitchell and Jacqueline Rose (eds. *Feminine Sexuality: Jacques Lacan and the ecole freudienne*, trans. Jacqueline Rose [London: MacMillan Press, 1982]), among others, have questioned the radical potential of American psychoanalysis,

pointing to the desexualization of Freudian psychoanalysis in America. Yet, in Lucia Tower we have an example of an analyst publishing in the United States, who not only encounters the important area of infantile sexuality, but reflects on the centrality of the analyst's own Oedipal complex to the context of the analytic relationship.

38. Corbett Thigpen and Harvey M. Cleckley, *The Three Faces of Eve* (New York: Popular Library, 1957).

39. Morton Prince, *The Dissociation of a Personality: The Hunt for the Real Miss Beauchamp* (1905; Great Britain: Fletcher & Son Ltd., 1978). It is interesting to note that the *Journal of Abnormal and social Psychiatry* in which Thigpen's and Cleckley's study first appeared was founded by Morton Prince. Moreover, Prince's name is prominant in the short bibliography of *The Three Faces of Eve*.

40. Chris Costner Sizemore and Elen Sain Pittillo, *I'm Eve* (1977; New York: Jove Publications, 1983).

41. Clearly Sizemore's own version is produced through processes of mediation different from but every bit as complex as those which figure into the production of the book *The Three Faces of Eve*. I see *I'm Eve* as having emerged out of the socio-cultural currents of the late 1970s, crucially the feminist movement (which must have spurred Sizemore's desire to speak for herself) and out of the growing deemphasis on psychoanalytic therapy in the mental health professions in the late 1960s and 1970s. Thus, the point is not to take Sizemore's version as "the truth," but rather to read it against *The Three Faces of Eve* (book and film) to tease out some of the mediations or pressures which shaped the 1950s texts.

42. Sigmund Freud, "Femininity" (1933), *S.E.*, Vol. 22; "Feminine Sexuality" (1931), *S.E.*, Vol. 21; "Some Psychical Consequences of the Anatomical Distinctions Between the Sexes" (1925), *S.E.*, Vol. 19.

43. *The American Journal of Psychiatry*, Vol. 117, No. 1 (July 1960).

44. *AJP* (May 1956).

45. *AJP*, Vol. 109, No. 1 (July 1952).

46. *AJP*, Vol. 109, No. 1 (July 1952).

47. *AJP*, Vol. 112, No. 1 (January 1956).

48. *AJP*, Vol. 115, No. 4 (October 1958). Also see *AJP*, Vol. 114, No. 2 (May 1958).

49. Laura Mulvey, "Visual Pleasure and Narrative Cinema," in Karyn Kay and Gerald Peary, eds. *Women and the Cinema* (New York: E. P. Dutton, 1977). Also see E. Ann Kaplan's first chapter, "Is The Gaze Male?", pp. 23–35.

50. William H. Chafe, chapter nine, "The Debate on Woman's Place," *The American Woman: Her Changing Social, Economic, and Political Roles, 1920–1970* (New York: Oxford University Press, 1972).

10. Psychological Explanation in the Films of Lang and Pabst

1. This essay is part of a larger project attempting to show significantly different uses of available conventional systems within the same national cinema, Weimar cinema. See also my article "Sexuality at a Loss: The Films of F. W. Murnau," in *The Female Body in Western Culture*, ed. Susan Rubin Suleiman (Harvard University Press, 1986), pp. 243–261.

2. For a psychoanalytic reading of *Pandora's Box*, see Thomas Elsaesser's "Lulu and

the Meter Man: Louise Brooks, Pabst and 'Pandora's Box,' " *Screen* 24, no. 4–5 (July–October 1983), pp. 4–36.

3. I have considered this aspect of Lang's films in more detail in my manuscript *The Logic of Fascination: Fritz Lang and Cinematic Conventions*.

4. By contrast, after Schön has finally stated his intention to marry his fiancée, the large painting of Lulu as Pierrot is visible behind her, functioning as her double, as she appeals to Schön to approach her. She lies back on the divan, and the camera tilts up to the painting as Schön bends down to kiss her. This foreshadows Lulu's triumphant seduction drama backstage on the opening night of the show designed to make her a star, financed by Schön and produced by his son Alva, which results in Schön breaking off the engagement as has just now managed to announce.

5. See Thierry Kuntzel's excellent analysis of the movement of the entire first sequence in its elaborate repetition and variation of visual and aural patterns, "The Film-Work," *enclitic* 2, no. 1 (spring 1978).

6. Noël Burch analyzes the structure of *M* in "De *Mabuse* à *M*: Le travail de Fritz Lang" in *Cinéma: Théorie, Lectures*, numéro spécial de la *Revue d'Esthétique* (Paris: Klincksieck, 1973), pp. 227–248. A version of this article may be found in English in *Cinema: A Critical Dictionary*, (New York: Viking Press, 1980), ed. Richard Roud, as "Fritz Lang: German Period," trans. Tom Milne, pp. 583–599.

7. Siegfried Kracauer, *From Caligari to Hitler* (Princeton: Princeton University Press, 1947). Kracauer reiterates this theme throughout his study.

8. Kracauer, *From Caligari to Hitler*, p. 250.

9. An interesting alternative analysis may be found in "Dream and Photography in a Psychoanalytic Film: *Secrets of a Soul*" by Nick Browne and Bruce McPherson in *Dreamworks* 1, no. 1 (spring 1980).

10. For the history of the project and the reactions of the participants, see the account of Bernard Chodorkoff and Seymour Baxter in *American Imago* 31, no. 4 (Winter 1974), pp. 319–334.

11. See the booklet prepared by Hanns Sachs to accompany the film, *Psychoanalyse: Rätsel des Unbewussten* (Berlin: Lichtbild-Bühne, 1926), p. 31. The opening page lists the credits for *Secrets of a Soul*; three explanatory sections follow, on parapraxis, neurosis, and the interpretation of dreams. Stills from the film illustrate these sections. A brief conclusion connects Freud's work with the project of the film. The booklet, like the film, seems unnecessarily reductive in view of Freud's clarity of expression in his various introductory lectures prepared for a general public.

12. Several shots of the wife tossing and turning alone in bed, clearly unsatisfied sexually, provide an interesting exception that is unfortunately not sustained in the film.

13. Thomas Elsaesser's study of Lulu (and Louise Brooks—the two are frequently conflated in his essay) reduces her to an explanation while paradoxically maintaining that she eludes all such attempts. Although he flirts with concepts like indeterminacy, ambiguity, and androgyny, nonetheless "Lulu is forever image" (p. 29). Because of this reduction, she is ideally suited to (male) projection fantasies and is readily translated into a metaphor for the cinema itself, which is then characterized by the same terms used to describe Lulu. (See pp. 29–33). Patrice Petro addresses Elsaesser's equation of Lulu with the fascination of the cinema on the issue of female spectators in the Weimar period in "*The Joyless Street*: Censorship and the Female Spectator in Weimar," a paper delivered at the Society for Cinema Studies, Montreal, 1987.

14. Thomas Elsaesser offers a number of possible interpretations for the ending of the film, which have in common the fact that they suggest a resolution of the narrative by means of one or another form of doubling, and an implied recognition of a "sense of an ending." While many levels of interpretation are possible, what is important to me is that the narrative isn't directed toward a standard form of resolution; that is, it doesn't provide a conclusion at the most basic level of the plot, or in Roland Barthes's terms, at the level of the actions and enigmas constitutive of the classical text.

11. Not Speaking with Language/Speaking with No Language: Leslie Thornton's *Adynata*

1. Maurice Blanchot, *The Siren's Song*, ed. Gabriel Josipovici, trans. Sacha Rabinovitch (Bloomington: Indiana UP, 1982) 221.

2. Maurice Blanchot, *The Space of Literature*, trans. Ann Smock (Lincoln: U of Nebraska P, 1982) 263.

12. Some Ruminations around Cinematic Antidotes to the Oedipal Net(tles) while Playing with De Lauraedipus Mulvey, or, He May Be Off Screen, but . . .

1. 16mm, color, 125 min., 1985; distributed by First Run Features, 153 Waverly Place, New York, NY 10014.

2. Teresa de Lauretis, *Alice Doesn't: Feminism, Semiotics, Cinema* (Bloomington: Indiana University Press, 1984), p. 112.

3. Script of *Film About a Woman Who* . . . (16mm, black and white, 105 min., 1974), published in *October*, No. 2 (Summer 1976), p. 61.

4. Laura Mulvey, "Afterthoughts on 'Visual Pleasure and Narrative Cinema' inspired by *Duel in the Sun*," *Framework*, No. 15/16/17 (1981), pp. 14–15. Reprinted in this collection.

5. From Sigmund Freud, the standard edition of *The Complete Psychological Works of Sigmund Freud*, 13:213, quoted in Marie Balmary, *Psychoanalyzing Psychoanalysis: Freud and the Hidden Fault of the Father* (Baltimore: Johns Hopkins University Press, 1982), p. 80.

6. Meaghan Morris, "The Pirate's Fiancée," in *Michel Foucault: Power, Truth, Strategy*, ed. Meaghan Morris and Paul Patton, (Sydney: Feral Publications, 1979), p. 159.

7. "Power and Norm: Notes [taken at a lecture by Michel Foucault]," *Michel Foucault*, p. 62.

13. Dialogue: Remembering (this memory of) a film—translator's notes

1. The objectification of an hallucination in the specific sense given to this term by W. Bion in his study *Transformations: Change from Learning to Growth* (London: William Heinemann Medical Books, Ltd., 1965).

2. Raymond Bellour, "*The Birds*: Analysis of a Sequence," British Film Institute mimeograph. Originally published as "Les Diseaux: Analyse d'une séquence, "

Cahiers du cinéma, no. 219 (1969). A selected bibliography of Bellour's work can be found in *Camera Obscura* #3–4 (Summer 1979): 133–134.

3. Raymond Bellour. "Le blocage symbolique," *Communications* 23 (Paris: Seuil, 1975): 235–350; rpt. in Raymond Bellour, *L'Analyse du film* (Paris: Albatross, 1979): 131–246. Some of the major issues of this essay are discussed in an extended interview with Bellour conducted by Janet Bergstrom and entitled "Alternation, Segmentation, Hypnosis," *Camera Obscura* #3–4 (Summer 1979): 71–103.

4. Thierry Kuntzel, "The Film Work," trans. Lawrence Crawford, Kimball Lockhart, and Claudia Tysdal, *enclitic* 2:1 (1978): 39–62 ["Le travail du film, 1," *Communications* 19 (Paris: Seuil, 1972): 25–39]; and "The Film-Work, 2," trans. Nancy Huston, *Camera Obscura* 5 (1980): 7–68 ["Le travail du film, 2," *Communications* 23 (Paris: Seuil, 1975): 136–189]. Cf. also Thierry Kuntzel, "A Note upon the Filmic Apparatus," *Quarterly Review of Film Studies* 1:3 (August 1976): 266–271.

5. Guy Rosolato, "Paranoia et Scène Primitive" (1963), *Rivista sperimentale di freniatria* (1965, fasc. I): 99–137; rpt. in *Essais sur le symbolique* (Paris: Gallimard, 1966): 199–241; citation, p. 227.

6. Raymond Bellour, "Thierry Kuntzel and the Return of Writing," transl. Annwyl Williams, *Camera Obscura* 11 (Fall 1983): 29–59 ["Thierry Kuntzel et le retour de l'écriture," *Cahiers du Cinéma* 321 (March 1981): 40–50.

7. Guy Rosolato, "Souvenir-écran," in *La relation d'inconnu* (Paris: Gallimard, 1978): 199–210.

8. Donald Meltzer, *Explorations in Autism* (Strath Tay, Scotland: Clunie Press, 1978).

9. David Rodowick, "Le circuit du désire," trans. Michèle-Irène Brudny, *Le Cinema américain: Analyses de films*, ed. Raymond Bellour and Patrick Brion, Volume II (Paris: Flammarion, 1980): 163–190. An expanded version of this essay appeared as "Vision, Desire and the Film Text" in *Camera Obscura* 6 (Fall 1980): 55–89.

Bibliography

Alexander, Franz. "Psychoanalysis and Psychotherapy," in *Journal of the American Psychoanalytic Association*, Vol. 2, no. 4 (October 1954).

Allen, Jeannie, ed. *Now, Voyager*. Madison, Wisconsin: The University of Wisconsin Press, 1986.

Althusser, Louis. "Ideology and Ideological State Apparatuses (notes toward an investigation)," in *Lenin and Philosophy and Other Essays*. New York and London: Monthly Review Press, 1971.

Baudrillard, Jean. "The Ecstasy of Communication," in Hal Foster, ed. *The Anti-Aesthetic: Essays on Postmodern Culture*. Townsend, Washington: The Bay Press, 1983.

Baudry, Jean-Louis. "The Apparatus." Trans. Jean Andrews and Bertrand Augst, *Camera Obscura*, no. 1 (1976).

Bergstrom, Janet, ed. *The Logic of Fascination: Fritz Lang and Cinematic Conventions*. Unpublished.

Bernheimer, Charles and Claire Kahane, eds. *In Dora's Case: Freud-Hysteria-Feminism*. New York: Columbia University Press, 1985.

Brooks, Peter. "The Idea of Psychoanalytic Literary Criticism," in Shlomith Rimmon-Kenan, ed., *Discourse in Psychoanalysis and Literature*, London and New York: Methuen, 1987.

Browne, Nick and Bruce McPherson. "Dream and Photography in a Psychoanalytic Film: *Secrets of a Soul*", *Dreamworks*, Vol. 1, no. 1 (Spring 1980).

Burch, Noel. "De *Mabuse* à *M*: Le Travail de Fritz Lang", in *Cinema: Théorie, Lectures*, numéro special de la *Revue d'Esthetique*. Paris: Klincksieck, 1973.

Comolli, Jean-Louis. "Machines of the Visible," in Teresa de Lauretis and Stephen Heath, eds., *The Cinematic Apparatus*. New York: St. Martin's Press, 1980.

Deming, Barbara. *Running Away From Myself: A Dream Portrait of America Drawn from the Films of the 40s*. New York: Grossman, 1969.

Durngat, Raymond. *Luis Buñuel*. New rev. ed. Berkeley: University of California Press, 1977.

Elsaesser, Thomas. "Lulu and the Meter Man: Louise Brooks, Pabst and 'Pandora's Box' ", *Screen*, Vol. 24, no. 4–5 (July-October 1983).

Felman, Shoshana, ed. *Literature and Psychoanalysis: The Question of Reading: Otherwise*. Baltimore and London: The Johns Hopkins Press, 1982.

Freud, Sigmund. "Psycho-Analysis" (1922), *Collected Papers*, Vol. 5. London: Hogarth Press, 1950.

———. "Fragment of an analysis of a case of hysteria." in *The Standard Edition of the Complete Psychological Works*. London: Hogarth Press, 1905.

————. "The dynamics of transference." *The Standard Edition of the Complete Psychological Works*. London: Hogarth Press, 1912.

————. "Remembering, repeating and working-through." *The Standard Edition of the
Complete Psychological Works*. London: Hogarth Press, 1914.

————. "Observation of Transference-Love" (1915), *The Standard Edition of the Complete Psychological Works of Sigmund Freud*. James Strachey, ed. and trans. London:
The Hogarth Press, 1955. Vol. 12.

————. "Some Psychical Consequences of the Anatomical Distinctions Between the
Sexes" (1925), *S.E.*, Vol. 19.

————. "Fetishism", *S.E.*, Vol. 21.

————. "Feminine Sexuality" (1931), *S.E.*, Vol. 21.

————. "Femininity" (1933), *S.E.*, Vol. 22.

————. "Constructions in analysis." *The Standard Edition of the Complete Psychological
Works*. London: Hogarth Press, 1937.

————. "Forward," *The Life and Works of Edgar Allen Poe: A Psycho-Analytic Interpretation*. Trans. John Rodker. London: Imago Publishing Co, 1949.

Friedan, Betty. *The Feminine Mystique*. 1963. Reissued by Dell Publishing in 1974.

Gabbard, Glen O. *Psychiatry and the Cinema*. Chicago and London: The University of
Chicago Press, 1987.

Gedo, John. "On the Methodology of Psychoanalytic Biography," Journal of the American
Psychoanalytic Association (1972).

Gedo, Mary. "Art as Autobiography: Picasso's *Guernica*." Art Quarterly (1979).

Gill, Merton, M.D. "Psychoanalysis and Exploratory Psychotherapy", in *Journal of the
American Psychoanalytic Association*, Vol. 2, no. 4 (October 1954).

Green, Andre. *The Tragic Effect*. Cambridge: Cambridge University Press, 1979.

Greenacre, Phyllis, M.D. "The Role of Transference: Practical Considerations in Relation
to Psychoanalytic Therapy", *Journal of the American Psychoanalytic Association*, Vol.
2, no. 4 (October 1954).

Horney, Karen. "Maternal Conflicts" in Harold Kelman, ed., *Feminine Psychology*, New
York: Norton, 1967.

Jacobus, Mary. *Reading Woman: Essays in Feminist Criticism*. New York: Columbia
University Press, 1986.

Jameson, Frederic. *The Political Unconscious: Narrative as a Socially Symbolic Act*.
Ithaca: Cornell University Press, 1982.

Kaplan, E. Ann. *Women and Film: Both Sides of the Camera*. Boston: South End Press,
1982.

————. *Motherhood and Representation in Literature and Film, 1830-1960*. London and
New York: Routledge, 1988.

————. "The Political Unconscious in the Maternal Melodrama: Ellen Wood's *East Lynne*
(1861)", in Derek Longhurst, ed., *Popular Fictions: Genre, Gender and Narrative
Pleasure*. Hemel Hempstead, UK: Unwin Hyman, 1988.

Kaplan, Meryl. *Images of Mothers*. Forthcoming from Columbia University Press.

Kardiner, Abram. *The Individual and His Society: The Psychodynamics of Primitive Social
Organization*. New York: Columbia University Press, 1939.

Knight, Robert P., M.D. "The Present Status of Organized Psychoanalysis in the United

States", in *Journal of the American Psychoanalytic Association,* Vol. 1, no. 2 (April 1953).

Kohan, Gregorio, ed. *The British School of Psychoanalysis: The Independent Tradition.* New Haven and London: Yale University Press, 1986.

Kracauer, Siegfried. *From Caligari to Hitler.* Princeton: Princeton University Press, 1947.

Kris, Ernst. *Psychoanalytic Exploration in Art,* New York: International Universities Press, 1952.

Kristeva, Julia. *Powers of Horror: An Essay on Abjection,* trans. Leon S. Roudiez. New York: Columbia University Press, 1982.

Kroker, Arthur and Marilouise. "Body Digest: Theses on the Disappearing Body in the Hyper-Modern Condition," in *The Canadian Journal of Political and Social Theory,* Vol. 11, nos. 1–2 (1987).

Kuhn, Annette. *Women's Pictures: Feminism and Cinema.* London: Routledge and Kegan Paul, 1982.

Kuntzel, Thierry. "The Film-Work", *Enclitic,* Vol. 2, no. 1 (Spring 1978).

Kurzweil, Edith and William Phillips, eds., *Literature and Psychoanalysis.* New York: Columbia University Press, 1983.

Lacan, Jacques. "Poe's Purloined Letter," in *Yale French Studies* 48, *French Freud,* 1973. Partial translation from text in *Ecrits.* Paris: Seuil, 1966.

———. "The Signification of the Phallus", in *Ecrits,* trans. Alan Sheridan. New York: Norton, 1976.

———. "Desire, and the Interpretation of Desire in *Hamlet,"* trans. James Hulbert, ed. by Jacques-Alain Miller and reprinted in Shoshana Felman, ed. *Literature and Psychoanalysis: The Question of Reading: Otherwise.* Baltimore and London: The Johns Hopkins University Press, 1982.

LaPlanche, J. and J.-B. Pontalis. *The Language of Psycho-Analysis,* trans. Donald Michelson-Smith from the original French edition of 1967, New York: W.W. Norton and Co., 1973.

———. *Life and Death in Psycho-Analysis.* Baltimore: Johns Hopkins University Press, 1976.

Lindner, Robert. *The Fifty-Minute Hour: A Collection of True Psychoanalytic Tales.* New York: Rinehart and Co., 1956.

Lundberg, Ferdinand and Marynia F. Farnham, M.D. *Modern Woman: The Lost Sex.* New York: Harper and Brothers, 1947.

MacCabe, Colin. *The Talking Cure.* New York: St. Martin's Press, 1981.

Manoni, Maud. *The Child, His "Illness" and the Others.* London: Tavistock Publications, 1970.

Marcus, Steven. "Freud and Dora: Story, History, Case History," reprinted in Charles Bernheimer and Claire Kahane, eds. *In Dora's Case: Freud-Hysteria-Feminism.* New York: Columbia University Press, 1985.

Martin, Alexander Reid, M.D. "Why Psychoanalysis?", in *Are You Considering Psychoanalysis?.* Karen Horney, ed. New York: W.W. Norton, 1946.

McCarroll, Luli Barzman, in "Media/Bulimia, or The Politics of Cleanliness", in *On Film,* no. 13 (Fall 1984).

Menninger, William. *Psychiatry in a Troubled World: Yesterday's War and Today's Challenge.* New York: Macmillan Press, 1948.

Metz, Christian. "The Fiction Film and Its Spectator: A Metapsychological Study," in Theresa Hak Kyung Chai, ed., *Apparatus,* (New York: Tanam Press, 1980).

————. *The Imaginary Signifier: Psychoanalysis and the Cinema.* Trans. Celia Britton, Annwyl Williams, Ben Brewster and Alfred Guzzetti. Bloomington: Indiana University Press, 1982.

Millett, Kate. *Sexual Politics,* New York: Doubleday, 1970.

Mitchell, Juliet. *Psycho-Analysis and Feminism: Freud, Reich, Laing and Women.* New York, London: the Macmillan Press, 1982.

Mitchell, Juliet, and Jacqueline Rose, eds. *Feminine Sexuality: Jacques Lacan and the ecole freudienne,* trans. Jacqueline Rose. London: Macmillan Press, 1982.

Muller, John P. and William J. Richardson, eds., *The Purloined Poe: Lacan, Derrida, and Psychoanalytic Reading.* Baltimore: The Johns Hopkins University Press, 1988.

Oberndor, Clarence. *A History of Psychoanalysis in America.* New York: Harper and Row, 1953.

Phillips, William, "General Introduction," in Edith Kurzweil and William Phillips, eds. *Literature and Psychoanalysis.* New York: Columbia University Press, 1976.

Plaza, Monique. "The Mother/The Same: The Hatred of the Mother in Psychoanalysis", in *Feminist Issues,* vol. 2, no. 1 (Spring 1982).

Posner, D. "Caravaggio's Homo-Erotic Early Works." Art Quarterly (1971).

Rimmon-Kenan, Shlomith, ed., *Discourse in Psychoanalysis and Literature.* London and New York: Methuen, 1987.

Rose, Jacqueline. "Paranoia and the Film System", *Screen,* Vol. 17, no. 4 (1976/77).

Rose, Nikolas; Solfield, Angie; Venn, Couze; Walkerdine, Valerie; "Psychology, Ideology and the Human Subject", *Ideology and Consciousness,* no. 1 (1977).

Sachs, Hanns. *Psychoanalyse: Rätsel des Unbewussten.* Berlin: Lichtbild-Buhne, 1926.

Silverman, Kaja. "Lost Objects and Mistaken Subjects: Film Theory's Structuring Lack", *Wide Angle,* Vol. 7, no. 1 and 2. A fuller version of this essay is included in Kaja Silverman, *The Acoustic Mirror: The Female Voice in Psychoanalysis and Cinema.* Bloomington: Indiana University Press. 1988.

Skura, Meredith Anne. *The Literary Use of the Psychoanalytic Process.* New Haven and London: Yale University Press, 1981.

Smith, Joseph H. and William Kerrigan, eds. *Images in Our Souls: Cavell, Psychoanalysis and Cinema.* Baltimore: The Johns Hopkins University Press, 1988.

Snitow, Ann, Christine Stansell and Sharon Thompson, eds., *Powers of Desire: The Politics of Sexuality.* New York: Monthly Review Press, 1983.

Spector, Jack. *The Aesthetics of Freud.* New York: Praeger, 1973.

Spitz, Rene, M.D. "Countertransference", in *Journal of the American Psychoanalytic Association,* Vol. 4, no. 2, (April 1956).

Spoto, Donald. *The Dark Side of Genius: The Life of Alfred Hitchcock.* New York: Ballantine Books, 1983.

Stambolian, George. *Homosexualities and French Literature: Cultural Contexts, Critical Texts.* Ithaca: Cornell University Press, 1979.

Stone, Leo. "The Widening Scope of Indications for Psychoanalysis", in *Journal of the American Psychoanalytic Association,* Vol. 2, no. 4 (October 1954).

Strecker, Edward A. *Their Mother's Sons: The Psychiatrist Examines an American Problem.* New York: J.B. Lippincott Co., 1947.

Suleiman, Susan R., ed. *The Female Body in Western Culture: Contemporary Perspectives.* Cambridge, Mass.: Harvard University Press, 1986.

Walker, Janet. "The Representation of Hollywood, Freud, and Women: Regulation and Contradiction", in Christine Gledhill, ed. *Home is Where the Heart Is: Studies in Melodrama and the Woman's Film,* London: British Film Institute, 1987.

Wilson, Edmund. "Dickens: The Two Scrooges," in *The Wound and the Bow: Seven Studies in Literature.* New York and London: Oxford University Press, 1941.

Wylie, Phillip. *Generation of Vipers.* New York: Rinehart and Co., Inc., 1942.

Subject Index

244

Name Index

Abraham, Karl, 146
Adynata, 22, 181, 183–187
Alexander, Franz, 145–46
Aliens, 141
Althusser, 9, 20
Ambassadors, The, 53
American Journal of Psychiatry, The, 154, 156
Andrews, Dana, 101
Ann of the Indes, 18
Anti-Oedipus, 81
"The Apparatus: Metaphysical Approaches to the Impression of Reality in the Cinema," 49, 54
"Are You Considering Psychoanalysis?", 149

Baby Boom, 139
Balmary, Marie, 192–193
Barrie, J. M., 66
Barthes, Roland, 64–65, 213
Baudrillard, Jean, 43, 138, 142
Baudry, Jean-Louis, 41, 49, 50–51, 52, 54, 55, 57
Bazin, André, 51, 118–119
Benton, Robert, 139
Bergstrom, Janet, 21–22
Best Years of Our Lives, The, 20, 114–120, 122, 125–127
Beyond the Pleasure Principle, 116
Bicycle Thief, The, 118
Birds, The, 200, 203,
Blanchot, Maurice, 185–186
Blue Gardenia, The, 134
Bonaparte, Marie, 2
Bowlby, 10
Brahm, John, 129
Brooks, James, 139
Brooks, Peter, 6, 7, 11, 12, 14, 15
Brewster, Ben, 18, 70–71
Bunuel, Luis, 8

Cabinet of Dr. Caligari, The, 163, 165,
Cahiers du Cinéma, 65

Caillois, Roger, 53–54
Camera Obscura, 11
Cameron, James, 141
Capra, Frank, 127
Cat People, The, 19, 70, 73
Chesler, Phyllis, 143, 149
Chodorow, Nancy, 16
Charcot, J. M., 72
Cixous, Hélène, 16
Clifford, Graeme, 139
Cobweb, The, 152
Coleridge, Samuel Taylor, 3
Comencini, Luigi, 212
Comolli, 51, 122
"Constructed in Analysis," 59
Cook, Alistair, 152
Cook, David, 138
Cook, Pam, 65
Copjec, Joan, 51–52
"Creative Writing and Day Dreaming," 4
Cukor, George, 65, 66
Curse of the Demon, a.k.a. *Night of the Demon*, 19, 98
Curtiz, Michael, 134

Dark Mirror, The, 152
"The Death of Hamlet's Father," 4
de Lauretis, Teresa, 48, 189, 190, 191, 192, 194, 195
Deleuze, Gilles, 81
Derrida, Jacques, 7, 8
Der Schatz, 163
De Sica, Vittorio, 118
"Desire in Narrative," 189
Deutsch, Helene, 128, 134
da Vinci, Leonardo, 2
Diary of a Lost Girl, 166
Diderot, 53
Dissociation of a Personality, 153
Donne, John, *The Holy Sonnets*, 75
Dostoevsky, Fyodor, 2

246